The
Great
Verses

The
Great
Verses

365 Verses to Learn,
to Love, to Live

Jeff Wells

BROWN
CHRISTIAN
PRESS
A DIVISION OF
BROWN BOOKS PUBLISHING

The Great Verses
365 Verses to Learn, to Love, to Live

Brown Christian Press
16250 Knoll Trail Drive, Suite 205
Dallas, Texas 75248
www.BrownBooks.com
(972) 381-0009

A New Era in Publishing™

ISBN 978-1-61254-173-0
LCCN 2014955696

Printed in the United States
10 9 8 7 6 5 4 3 2 1

For more information or to contact the author, please go to www.WoodsEdge.org

For my parents, Harold and Pat Wells, who have loved me since before I was born.

For our three adult children and their three spouses, Mike and Sarah Grenz, Paul and Callie Thomas, John Paul and Michelle Wells, each one an all-out lover of Jesus. And our three grandkids (so far!), Ryanne, Rhett, and Evie Grenz, precious beyond words and learning to love Jesus.

But mostly for Gayle. Where would I be without you? It's been thirty-four years, and I love you more and more.

Preface

These may not be the 365 greatest verses in the Bible, for only God could make that list. But these are 365 *of* the greatest verses in the Bible.

I chose these 365 verses because they are especially meaningful, important, inspiring, or comforting. There is something special about each one of them.

I realize that *every* verse in the Bible is inspired by God and therefore important. But some verses are more crucial than others.

Of course, many more verses could have been included, some of which I feel are more important than verses that I included. But again, this is not a book *on* the 365 greatest verses but on 365 *of* the greatest verses in the Bible.

These are verses to learn, to love, to live. First, they are verses to learn. These are passages that believers should know, study, be familiar with, perhaps memorize.

But they are also verses to love. They are not just for the head, but also for the heart, just as all the Bible is. These are verses to love, to value, to cherish, to treasure.

But they're still more than that. These are verses to live by, verses to stand upon, verses to lay hold of and claim for your own life. We want to be active practitioners of the Bible and not merely passive listeners.

My prayer, dear reader, is that God himself will take these verses to speak to your soul, transform your life, and cause you to fall ever deeper in love with him.

Acknowledgments

I serve Jesus with the wonderful congregation at WoodsEdge Community Church, people I love dearly.

The elders team and the staff team at WoodsEdge are gifted, godly Christ-followers. It's a privilege to journey together.

My long-time assistant, Glena Siebert, spent tons of hours on the various drafts of these devotionals. I cannot imagine a better assistant for a pastor.

John Townsend and Lauren Platt gave me important nudges to write at just the right time.

It has been a pleasure to work with the team at Brown Books, especially Jason McBride, Derek Royal, Kathy Penny, and Omar Mediano.

Genesis 1:1

*In the beginning, God created the heavens
and the earth.*

The Bible begins with this simple, sublime statement: "In the beginning, God created the heavens and the earth."

In the beginning, there is God. Before anything else, there is God. Above everything else, there is God. Behind everything else, there is God. He is the uncreated Creator of all creation.

The Bible begins with God. Above all else, the Bible is a book about God. This is God's story, God's revelation, God's book.

The Bible never argues for God's existence. It assumes God's existence. Down deep, every human knows that God exists, that God is Creator.

To say that God created the heavens and the earth is to say that God created the vast universe that is staggering in size. Yet God created it without any effort whatsoever.

When we look at creation all around us, we see God's glory. We see God's thumbprint. We see his power, his beauty, his majesty, and his vastness. How great is our God!

The poet Gerard Manley Hopkins wrote, "The world is charged with the grandeur of God."

Elizabeth Barrett Browning penned the words:

> Earth's crammed with heaven,
> And every common bush aflame with God:
> But only he who sees, takes off his shoes,
> The rest sit round it and pluck blackberries.

Jonathan Edwards put it simply: "Nature is God's greatest evangelist."

That God is Creator means that God made us. You belong to him because he made you. You are accountable to worship him, to serve him, to obey him. He is your God.

Everything begins right here with the truth of creation. That God is Creator is essential to God's nature. No wonder Satan opposes this truth in any way possible. No wonder the Bible begins with, "In the beginning, God created the heavens and the earth."

1

Genesis 1:3

And God said, "Let there be light," and
there was light.

It is only fitting that God's first act following the creation of heaven and earth is the creation of light. Light is a symbol of truth and life, of grace and goodness.

The creation of light in Genesis 1:3 represents the Bible's first faint reference to God's redemption of us through Jesus Christ. Just as light shines in the darkness, Jesus is the light of the world and will shine into the darkness of our hearts.

Paul uses this very image when he quotes Genesis 1:3 in 2 Corinthians: "For God, who said, 'Let light shine out of darkness,' has shone in our hearts to give the light of the knowledge of the glory of God in the face of Jesus Christ" (2 Cor. 4:6).

God is not only Creator, he is also Redeemer. The great Creator of the universe is also the God who saves. Where would we be if God were only great and not also good?

From the outset of the Bible, we see that God is both great and good.

And we see it throughout the Bible, up to the great crescendo of Revelation 4-5, where God is worshiped as Creator (Rev. 4) and as Redeemer (Rev. 5).

This is our God. This is your God. He is Creator and Redeemer. He is great and good.

Genesis 1:27

*So God created man in his own image, in the image
of God he created him; male and female
he created them.*

Set apart from all of God's creatures, we alone bear his image. This tells us our identity and who we are as humans. We are image bearers with a basic likeness to God. We are relational beings, we are rational, emotional persons with volition. We are God's representatives on earth.

This is the central truth about us. We are image bearers of the eternal God. This gives us worth, dignity, and value. We matter. We matter not because of our achievements, money, or looks, but simply because we bear God's image.

If you are a human being, then this is the truth about you: you matter. No matter what you have achieved. No matter what you look like or how much money you have. No matter how you have failed or how much you have struggled, you have worth, dignity, and value simply because you bear the image of the immortal God. Nothing can change that.

If the first two lines emphasize our identity as image bearers, the third line reveals our sexuality. We are sexual beings. God did not create neutered human beings. He made us male or female, man or woman.

Sexuality goes far deeper than our physical aspects. It's far more than plumbing. Males and females not only have differently shaped bodies, we have differently shaped souls.

Indeed, gender is the only fundamental distinction among humans. Other distinctions, such as ethnicity, language, race, economic status, or nationality don't really matter. They are superficial distinctions. But gender, this matters.

We see this when a baby is born. Our first question is, "Is it a boy or a girl?" For some reason, gender matters to us in so many ways.

This is who you are. You are an image bearer of God, either male or female. You matter. To the God of the universe, the God who made you, the God who cares about you, you matter incredibly.

Genesis 1:28

And God blessed them. And God said to them, "Be fruitful and multiply and fill the earth and subdue it, and have dominion over the fish of the sea and over the birds of the heavens and over every living thing that moves on the earth."

In Genesis 1:28, we come to the very first command that God gives the human race. It is two-fold: First, be fruitful. Second, have dominion over the earth.

It is noteworthy that both commands express the image of God that was stated in Genesis 1:27. Because we are image bearers of God, we get to share in God's work of creating human life and ruling over creation. Both commands reflect our identity as image bearers of God.

It is striking that God's very first command involves sex. The point of the command is not the act of sex itself, but creating children. God tells us to be fruitful and multiply. However, the command inherently involves the sex act. When it comes to sex, God is no Scrooge. He created it. Sex is God's idea, God's creation, God's gift. Within the context of marriage, sex is wholly good.

The second command is the charge to rule over the earth and everything in it. This is often referred to as the "cultural mandate." We have the privilege of ruling over creation, but our rule is not the rule of an owner, it is the rule of a steward. We rule as God's representatives.

This is our calling as humans: to be fruitful and rule over creation.

Genesis 2:3

So God blessed the seventh day and made it holy,
because on it God rested from all his work
that he had done in creation.

God did not rest on the seventh day because he was tired or weary. Omnipotence does not get weary.

Rather, God rested because he was finished. His work of creation was completed, but God also rested for our sakes. We needed to see the rhythm of work and rest. He rested for our sakes, not for his.

The Bible says God blessed the Sabbath and made it holy. In what sense is the Sabbath holy? Well, it is special. It is God's gift to us. A day of rest and worship, a day to pray and play. A day to stop working.

God designed you for a regular day of rest, one day in seven. Your body needs it. Your mind needs it. Your soul needs it.

But the Sabbath is more than an absence of work; it is also the presence of worship. It is a day to live in God's presence, a day of drawing close to God. The reason why the weekend doesn't refresh some people, who are just as weary on Monday morning as on Friday afternoon, is because they don't honor the Sabbath. They may abstain from work but not participate in worship. We need our souls restored, and that only comes when we touch God and let God breathe life into our weary souls. This comes with worship.

This is the Sabbath. Rest and worship, pray and play. This is God's gift to you.

Genesis 2:15

The LORD God took the man and put him in the Garden of Eden to work it and keep it.

At the outset of the Bible, God gives man work. This means work is inherently good, not bad. Work is not the result of sin. It is not a consequence of the fall, nor a necessary evil. Work was created before the fall. In fact, God himself works. When the Bible opens, God is at work. Work in itself is completely good.

Moreover, we are designed for work. We are image bearers of the God who works. Work is part of our design, part of our humanness, and part of the image of God in us. We need work. We are not fully alive without work.

This is not to say that we need a job. We do not need a paying job to be fully alive, but we do need work, whether it is housework, schoolwork, volunteer work, or a paying job. We are designed for work.

Our work matters to God. Just as God cared about Adam's work, he cares about our work. He wants this work to be fulfilling and not frustrating.

How does this happen? How does our work become a source of fulfillment? It happens when we turn our work into worship. If we do our work for God, to please him and to honor him, then that work becomes an act of worship. It is when we work for God that we find our deliverance from drudgery.

A classic tale that represents this idea is that of the medieval construction supervisor who asked three of his workers about their tasks. The first worker replied, "I am laying bricks." He went a little farther along and asked the second worker, who replied, "I am building a wall." He went farther along and asked the third worker, who replied, "I am building a great cathedral for the glory of God." The third worker had it right. He found deliverance from drudgery because his work became worship.

In all things, work for the Lord.

Genesis 2:18

Then the LORD God said, "It is not good that the man should be alone; I will make a helper fit for him."

Marriage is God's idea, God's creation, and God's gift to man. The foundational passage about marriage in the Bible appears in Genesis 2:18-25.

Adam is in a kind of paradise unlike any we can imagine. He has God above him and the animals below him. But he has no one alongside him, nobody to share his life with.

God says this is not good. We immediately see the goodness of God in his response. God says that he will provide what Adam needs. He will provide a helper.

The Hebrew term "helper" carries no notion of inferiority. The term refers to someone who has resources and capacities that we lack. In fact, the term is used of God himself, who is the Great Helper of Israel.

God is telling us that women have capacities and gifts that men lack, implying that men have capacities and gifts that women lack.

Here is God's ideal partnership in marriage: a man and woman, gloriously different, helping each other be all they can be for God. As Allen P. Ross once pointed out in the theological magazine *Kindred Spirit*, marriage was not given to accumulate possessions but to develop persons. Two equals, two life partners, each supporting the other and working for God.

Perhaps pair figure skating demonstrates this idea best. The man and the woman are equal partners but serve different roles. One is strong and the other is graceful. One lifts and the other jumps. Each member of the partnership is essential. When they work together, something beautiful happens.

This is God's ideal for every marriage.

Genesis 2:24

*Therefore a man shall leave his father and his mother
and hold fast to his wife, and they shall
become one flesh.*

This is the essence of biblical marriage: leave, cleave, and become one flesh.

First, leave. If a couple does not adequately separate themselves from their parents, then the marriage is torpedoed from the start. Honor your parents, love your parents, but look to each other for primary support and direction. You are a new family; live like it. Beware of undue dependence on your parents.

Second, cleave. The idea behind this term is permanence. God's ideal is marriage for life, "till death do us part." At the beginning of your marriage, decide that divorce is not an option. If marriage is to be permanent, if you know that you are sticking together no matter what happens, it will make all the difference in how you tackle problems as a couple.

Third, become one flesh. One flesh means oneness at every level: emotionally, spiritually, socially, intellectually, and physically. The concept behind the phrase "one flesh" is intimacy, a sense of closeness. You are soul mates, lovers, and best friends. You live life together. You pursue a shared life. You are alert to any signs of creeping separation. And over time, despite many challenges and hardships, you become close, so close that you can scarcely believe it.

This is God's dream for every marriage: a one-flesh marriage. This is the beauty and glory of marriage as God intended it.

Make God's dream yours and pursue it with all your heart.

Genesis 2:25

*And the man and his wife were both naked and
were not ashamed.*

This verse, early in the Bible, surprises us. It is so stark, so unusual, and yet it has such power and poignancy. "They were both naked and they were not ashamed." What is God telling us about marriage?

There are naked bodies and yet no shame, no embarrassment, no fear, no masks, no walls. What intimacy, closeness, freedom, trust. What transparency.

They trusted one another. And because they trusted one another, they felt safe, accepted, and secure in their relationship. No threats, no fears, no shame. They could trust each other with their bodies because they trusted each other with their hearts. They were open and honest, transparent, and secure.

Sounds pretty good, doesn't it? Can you imagine this kind of marriage, feeling so understood, so accepted, so safe?

How does this happen? It starts with trust. Trust comes when you are always truthful and honest, when you are dependable, when you do what you say, when you are loyal and faithful no matter what.

When you tell the truth and do what you say day by day, week by week, year by year, you build trust. As trust builds, you feel safe. You open your heart. You let her or him know what's really going on inside. You connect at the heart level.

You listen deeply, with all your heart, because you long to understand your spouse. And over time, you feel incredibly close. You begin to experience the magic and mystery of one-flesh marriage.

Genesis 3:1

*Now the serpent was more crafty than any other beast
of the field that the LORD God had made. He said to
the woman, "Did God actually say, 'You shall
not eat of any tree in the garden'?"*

Genesis 1-2 gives no word of the upcoming battle. We see God's creation. It was good. God creates Adam, then he creates Eve. The Creation narrative ends with Adam and Eve naked and unashamed. There is trust and transparency in paradise. Things are very good.

But wait! Genesis 3 opens with a crafty snake that subtly suggests that God is not good and he cannot be trusted. There is an enemy in paradise, an opponent of God, who turns out to be Satan.

Satan comes to deceive and devour. What is his strategy? Listen to his words to Eve: "Did God actually say, 'You shall not eat of any tree in the garden'?"

Can you hear the incredulity in his tone? "I can't believe it," he seems to be saying. "Has God really said that you can't eat of any tree in the garden? How unfair."

What is Satan doing? He is suggesting that God is not good. He is questioning God's love for Eve. He is casting doubt on God's goodness to Adam and Eve. He is insinuating that God is holding something back from Eve that she really needs.

This is still the satanic strategy. Satan wants to devour you. Expect to hear the same voice in your head.

You will hear a voice suggesting that God is not good, that God does not really love you, that God is unfair to you, that God is hard to please, that God is in fact a cosmic Scrooge.

Have you heard that voice? Sure you have. When you do, recognize its source. Don't be naïve about the unseen spiritual war.

Behind all sin is the suspicion that God isn't very good and therefore he cannot be trusted. This is Satan's main ploy in his quest to ruin your life and devour your soul.

You will hear things like:

· God is being so unfair in what he says about divorce (or adultery, or honesty in your business, or generous giving, or forgiving your father, or Christians marrying only Christians, or pornography).
· God is holding back something I need to be happy.
· What applies to others doesn't apply to me. My situation is different.

Don't listen! Shut your ears to the voice of the deceiver. Stand firm in Christ's strength.

Genesis 3:7

*Then the eyes of both were opened, and they knew
that they were naked. And they sewed fig leaves
together and made themselves loincloths.*

In Genesis 2:25, Adam and Eve were naked and felt no shame. They felt no shame because there was no sin. But by 3:7 they have sinned, and now they feel shame in their nakedness.

Satan had suggested to Eve that she was missing out, that God was holding back something she needed, that God could not be trusted. Satan lied.

What does sin bring Adam and Eve? Exactly what sin brings us: guilt, shame, fear, mistrust, alienation from God, rupture of relationships, the end of all joy and peace. In a word, sin brings death.

So much for Satan's promise.

Sin may look good, but it hurts us. It always hurts us. Remember: sin will always hurt you sooner or later. It often hurts others too.

How did Adam and Eve respond to their shame? Fig leaves. They tried to hide behind fig leaves. Trust and transparency had vanished and barriers went up. And ever since Adam and Eve, we have all been wearing masks, hiding, posing, pretending, running from God, and blaming others.

Our only escape is the grace of God. God alone can tear the walls down and set us free. How does God set us free? It takes blood because someone has to die for sin. So God threw away the fig leaves and clothed Adam and Eve with animal skins. To get these animal skins required death, bloodshed, and sacrifice. This is the first faint echo of a savior, the first faint echo of a future day when God himself would shed his blood for you and for me.

Genesis 3:8-9

And they heard the sound of the LORD God walking
in the garden in the cool of the day, and the man and
his wife hid themselves from the presence of the LORD
God among the trees of the garden. But the LORD God
called to the man and said to him, "Where are you?"

The first thing Adam and Eve do after they sin is hide. They feel guilt and shame, unworthy of being with God. So they hide.

How does God respond to this hiding? Does he turn his back on them? Fold his arms in disgust? Give them a disapproving scowl?

Hardly! He does the opposite. He pursues them, seeks them, chases after them. It's the first game of hide and seek. They hide and God seeks.

When God asks Adam, "Where are you?" it's not a request for information. Omniscience does not need to request information. God doesn't need to ask, but Adam needs to be asked. God is drawing Adam out of hiding ever so gently. God is wooing, drawing, and pursuing, just like he woos you.

Adam and Eve were hiding because of their sin. We do the same thing. When we sin, we run from God because we feel guilt and shame. We are uncomfortable with ourselves, uncomfortable with others, and uncomfortable with God. So we hide.

How do we hide? We hide with busyness, with shopping, with overwork. We hide with TV, with Facebook (ironically), with travel. We hide with humor, with sarcasm, with shyness. We hide in a thousand ways.

Me? I hide by being in control (or trying to be in control). I hide by reading, by running, by asking questions. I hide in all kinds of ways, some of which I'm unaware. I hide so well that sometimes I hide from myself that I'm hiding.

How about you? How are you hiding these days?

Here's the good news: you can stop hiding. Hiding is the fundamental human strategy of dealing with sin. God's strategy is better. Confess your sin and receive God's overwhelming grace.

Genesis 3:15

I will put enmity between you and the woman, and between your offspring and her offspring; he shall bruise your head, and you shall bruise his heel.

Genesis 3:15 is so important because it is the first direct reference to the coming Messiah, Jesus.

In the aftermath of sin, God pronounces judgment on Satan, the power behind the serpent. The judgment is enmity and hostility between Eve's offspring and Satan's offspring. The woman's offspring refers to all people, including Jesus Christ. Satan's offspring includes people who reject God and demonic beings.

God also announces the outcome of this enmity. Satan will deliver a glancing blow against Jesus, a blow to the heel, which is a reference to the cross. But Jesus, by that very death on the cross, will deliver a fatal blow, a blow to the head, against the devil.

The outcome of the battle was never in doubt.

Be ever mindful: the battle is real. We ignore the battle and the enemy at our own peril.

Dr. Haddon Robinson describes this attack:

> When Satan comes to you, he does not come in the form of a coiled snake. He does not approach with the roar of a lion. He does not come with the wail of a siren. He does not come waving a red flag. Satan simply slides into your life. When he appears, he seems almost like a comfortable companion. There's nothing about him that you would dread. The New Testament warns that he dresses as an angel of light…One point seems quite clear: when the enemy attacks you, he wears a disguise. As Mephistopheles says in Faust, "The people do not know the devil is there even when he has them by the throat"…He does not whisper to Eve, "I am here to tempt you"…He doesn't come and knock on the door of your soul and say, "Pardon me buddy, allow me a half hour of your life. I'd like to damn and destroy you."

Satan slides in. He slithers. He comes to deceive, accuse, tempt, and condemn.

Don't listen! Recognize his schemes. Resist his attack. Fight the battle in Christ's strength.

Genesis 11:4

Then they said, "Come, let us build ourselves a city and a tower with its top in the heavens, and let us make a name for ourselves, lest we be dispersed over the face of the whole earth."

The Tower of Babel stands forever in our memory as a tragic monument to pride and fear.

People band together to build a vast tower reaching into the heavens so that they can make a name for themselves. Their pride is seen in their independence from God, their self-reliance, and their desire for fame. Their fear is seen in their building a tower lest they be scattered over the earth. Rather than trust a loving God to protect them, they give way to fear and trust in their own efforts alone for security.

God's response is decisive. He confuses their speech and scatters them over the earth. Their potential for rebellion and wickedness is simply too great if they stay together. The tone of God's response is not that of a rival's jealousy, but of a father's concern. For their sake, God takes radical measures. He does the same for you, too.

At Babel, people set out to make a name for themselves. But God is easily able to humble those who exalt themselves. Our calling is never to make a name, but to exalt a name. That name is Jesus.

That is your mission: exalt Jesus. Lie low and exalt Jesus.

Genesis 12:1

*Now the LORD said to Abram, "Go from your country
and your kindred and your father's house to the
land that I will show you."*

Genesis 12 is one of the great dividing points in the Bible. In Genesis 1-11, God deals with humanity and people in general. But in Genesis 12, everything changes. God chooses a man, Abram, later to be called Abraham, to create a special people, the people of Israel. Using this people, God will reveal the Scriptures, bring the Messiah, and show the world what it means to be the people of God.

Genesis 12 is the turning point. Throughout the rest of the Old Testament and the Gospels, God's plan focuses on Israel. Only in Acts 2, with Pentecost and the birth of the church, does God's focus shift from the nation of Israel to the international church of Jesus Christ.

Genesis 12 is not only a huge dividing line in salvation history, it is also a remarkable example of faith. In the ancient world, asking someone to leave their ancestral home and all they knew was asking the impossible. People stayed within their city walls, with their family, with their people. But Abraham obeys God and leaves his home. He leaves Ur, in modern Iraq, travels 650 miles to Haran, in modern Turkey, and then travels 450 miles to Canaan, in modern Israel.

Why did Abraham obey God? Because he trusted God. He believed that God was the true God, that God knew best, and that God could be trusted, so Abraham obeyed.

God is still looking for people who dare to trust him. He is still looking for people who will obey him regardless of the circumstances. He is still looking for people who will live by faith.

Will you be one of these people? Will you be a man or woman who trusts God, no matter what?

Genesis 12:2

*And I will make of you a great nation, and I will bless
you and make your name great, so that you
will be a blessing.*

Genesis 12:1-3 is one of the most important passages in the Bible.
This passage marks a new beginning in God's dealings with man.
God chooses a man, Abraham, to begin a people that God will use
to bless all people.

In verse 1, addressed in the previous entry, God commands
Abraham to leave everything. In the next two verses, God gives him
seven promises, each promise pregnant with implications.

Let's look at the promises. There are four in verse 2, which will
be examined here, and three more in verse 3, which I will cover in
the next entry.

"I will make of you a great nation": This is quite a promise,
considering that Abraham was seventy-five years old with no
children and a barren wife. But this is just like God, who delights in
doing the impossible.

And against all odds, it happened. In fact, the nation of Israel
still exists today, some four thousand years later, with a power and
influence far beyond its size.

"I will bless you": God richly blessed Abraham for the rest of
his life. In fact, he becomes the most important man in the Old
Testament and appears in the New Testament more than any other
Old Testament figure. Abraham is the father of the Jews and the
greatest example of faith in the entire Bible. Yes, God blessed him.

"And make your name great": Did this happen? Yes. This
unknown man, a childless nomad, is known and revered throughout
the world today, four millennia later, by Christians, Jews, and
Muslims.

When we exalt ourselves, like the people of Babel in Genesis 11
who cried, "Let us make a name for ourselves," then God humbles us.
When we humble ourselves, then God exalts us. Every time.

"You will be a blessing": God blessed Abraham so that he could
be a blessing to others. That's why he blesses you and me, so we too
can be a blessing to others. You are a river, not a reservoir. Each day,
seek out people to bless. Look to bring God's love and hope to the
people you encounter.

Genesis 12:3

I will bless those who bless you, and him who dishonors you I will curse, and in you all the families of the earth shall be blessed.

Genesis 12:1-3 is one of the defining passages in the Bible, for God takes one man and begins a new nation. From this point until Acts 2, with the birth of the church, God's plan revolves around the nation of Israel.

First, God commands Abraham to leave his homeland, then God gives him seven epic promises. The final three promises come in verse 3.

"I will bless those who bless you": God so identifies with his friend Abraham that to bless Abraham and his descendants is to bless Abraham's God.

"Him who dishonors you I will curse": To oppose God's people is to oppose God. Throughout history, Satan has fostered an anti-Semitic attack on God's people. This is an attack waged by Egyptians, Assyrians, Babylonians, Persians, Romans, numerous European peoples in the Middle Ages, the Nazis of twentieth-century Germany, and more. All of these governments have been toppled, not because Israel or the Jews are always right, but because the Jews have a special place in God's plan and in God's heart. God will curse those who curse Israel.

"In you all the families of the earth shall be blessed": God's ultimate plan was never to focus on Israel alone, but rather to use Israel to bring blessings to all the peoples on earth. Israel was created to be a light to the nations and an instrument of God's grace for the entire world. God's heart has always been for all the nations and peoples. "In you all the families of the earth shall be blessed" (Gen.12:3).

When Jesus was about to return to heaven after the Resurrection, he gathers his disciples together and charges them, "Go therefore and make disciples of all nations" (Matt. 28:19). It is no longer the time to focus on one nation. Now the focus is on all nations, so that people "from every nation, from all tribes and peoples and languages" (Rev. 7:9) can be reached with the Gospel and declare God's glory over all the earth, for the living God is a missionary God.

17

God's heart for all the nations of the earth means that we cannot just focus on our own country or our own people. Genesis 12:1-3 condemns narrow nationalism, racial pride, and ethnocentricity. God's heart must become our heart, and we must become globally focused, mission-minded Christians.

Genesis 15:1

*After these things the word of the LORD came to
Abram in a vision: "Fear not, Abram, I am your
shield; your reward shall be very great."*

In the Bible, God repeatedly says to us, "Do not fear," or "Do not
be afraid." It is commonly said that God makes this type of statement 365 times in the Bible. It's almost like God wants us to have
a reminder for each day of the year.

We need the continual reminder because fear is so pervasive
and so deadly. Fear can sap all joy and ruin all peace. Fear can
grip us by the throat and toss us back and forth like a rag doll.
Fear is lethal. So over and over in the Bible, God urges: fear not,
fear not, fear not.

The first time we hear these words is here in Genesis 15:1.
Every time God says to someone, "Fear not," you can be sure that
person is scared to death.

So why is Abraham so afraid in Genesis 15? What exactly is
Abraham afraid of?

The previous passage in Genesis 14 tells us the story. A band
of marauding kings combined their armies and attacked the Jordan Valley. They took much spoil and many captives, including
Lot, Abraham's nephew. Abraham responded with a courageous
act of faith. He gathered his men, set off in pursuit of the ma-
rauders, and rescued Lot and the other captives. What a bold act
of faith.

However, Abraham realizes that these kings will likely attack
again. And when they do, they will be looking for one man in
particular: Abraham. The thought is terrifying, and Abraham,
like us, succumbs to fear.

What does God say to Abraham? "Abraham, do not be afraid.
Do not give way to fear. I will protect you. I will be your shield. I
will be your protector. Abraham, I will take care of you, for I am
your God."

That's exactly what God wants you to know. Is there a fear
that has been plaguing you, attacking you, depleting you? Then
hear God's words to you: "Do not be afraid. I will take care of you.
I will protect you. I will see you through. Do not be afraid."

Give your fear to God. Receive God's peace. Trust God's love.

19

Genesis 15:6

*And he believed the L*ORD*, and he counted it to him
as righteousness.*

For the first time in the Bible, Genesis 15:6 clearly states how we are saved. We are saved by believing God, by trusting God, by putting our faith in God.

In Genesis 15:1, Abraham attacked a marauding army and rescued his nephew Lot. In the aftermath, his fears grew quickly. Will they counterattack? So God comes to Abraham, assures him he is protected, and repeats his promise to make Abraham a great nation.

Abraham hears God's promise, an astounding promise for an elderly, childless couple, and Abraham believes him. Abraham believes that God is faithful and that God can be trusted. In response, God declares Abraham righteous (right with God). "And he believed the LORD, and he counted it to him as righteousness."

That's exactly the way you and I are saved. We believe God, we trust God's promise, we place our faith in God's Son, and God credits it to us as righteousness.

Salvation by faith: it is so humbling. We admit that we cannot save ourselves or earn salvation. We cannot trust ourselves to be good enough or religious enough. Our only hope is to abandon self-trust and place our trust in the Savior.

Faith is the same as trust or belief. Faith is the humble trust by which we receive the grace of God. Faith is the empty hand of a beggar receiving a gift. It is not doing something but receiving something.

This is God's way, the only way. Salvation is given by God's grace through faith in Jesus Christ. If you have never done so, call out to Jesus, even now, to save you.

He will hear that prayer.

Genesis 18:14a

Is anything too hard for the LORD?

Abraham sits under the shade of his Bedouin tents in the stifling desert heat. That's when he notices them: three men, just standing there. Moved by the Bedouin hospitality of the Middle East, Abraham scurries to serve them.

At some point, it becomes clear to Abraham that one of these men is none other than God in human form (most likely the preincarnate Christ). God promises Abraham that in one year, his wife, the ninety-year-old Sarah, will give birth to a son. Sarah, meanwhile, is eavesdropping from inside the tent. When she hears this incredible promise, she laughs to herself in disbelief. "No way."

God, knowing all things, knows that Sarah laughed and why Sarah laughed. He responds, interestingly, to Abraham: "The Lord said to Abraham, "Why did Sarah laugh and say, 'Shall I indeed bear a child, now that I am old?' Is anything too hard for the Lord? At the appointed time I will return to you, about this time next year, and Sarah shall have a son" (Gen.18:13-14).

The question "Is anything too hard for the Lord?" is etched in my mind and it echoes in my heart. I can't get away from it. "Is anything too hard for the Lord?"

God says to me and to you, "Is anything too hard for the Lord?" Is anything too hard for the God who spoke the sun and the stars into existence? Is anything too hard for the God who raises the dead?

What are you facing today that seems impossible? Do you need healing? Do you have a teenager headed for disaster? Do you have a marriage that needs a miracle? Would you love to have a baby? Do you have a hopeless addiction? Is there a non-Christian loved one who is hardened against God? Does your problem seem impossible?

God's word to Sarah is God's word to you. Never forget God's question: "Is anything too hard for the Lord?"

Genesis 22:2

He said, "Take your son, your only son Isaac, whom
you love, and go to the land of Moriah, and offer him
there as a burnt offering on one of the mountains
of which I shall tell you."

Abraham is the greatest example of faith in the Old Testament, and the greatest example of his life of faith is found in Genesis 22.

Can you imagine what Abraham felt when God told him to sacrifice his son? Can you imagine the heartache, the pain, the anguish?

And yet, in the very next verse we read, "So Abraham rose early in the morning, saddled his donkey, and took two of his young men with him, and his son Isaac" (Gen. 22:3). He doesn't object, argue, negotiate, filibuster, or delay. Abraham obeys immediately. Abraham obeys because he has learned that God is God and he should not question God's will. He knew that God would take care of him no matter what happened. Understanding can wait, but obedience cannot.

When Abraham and Isaac arrive at the mountain, can you see Abraham as he slowly, somberly gathers stones for the altar, taking all the time he can, hoping against hope that God will change his mind? After gathering stones, he arranges the wood for the fire. Finally, the moment has arrived. He must tell Isaac what God had commanded.

With broken sobs and tear-brimmed eyes, Abraham tells him. He hugs him as if he will never let go. Tears flow freely and unashamedly for both father and son. There's a final "I love you, Son," and "I love you, Father."

Finally, he can delay no longer. Isaac, too big to be forced, climbs onto the altar. All heaven watches as Abraham grabs the knife and lifts it overhead, fully intending to kill his deeply loved son. But at the last moment, at the very last moment, God stops him. "He said, 'Do not lay your hand on the boy or do anything to him, for now I know that you fear God, seeing you have not withheld your son, your only son, from me'" (Gen. 22:12).

Can you see Abraham now? Sobbing openly. Embracing Isaac. His chest heaving with relief, joy, and deep gratitude.

Did ever a man show such childlike faith in God? Did ever a man show such fierce loyalty by obeying God no matter what? He had such a strong belief that God was God and that God could be trusted.

Abraham, over a lifetime, had learned to trust God.

Two thousand years later, perhaps on the very same spot, which was then named Calvary, another son would be sacrificed. Except this time, the son was God's son, and the father would not spare the knife.

Genesis 32:26

I will not let you go unless you bless me.

This is Jacob's prayer: "I will not let you go unless you bless me." It has to rank as one of the most unique prayers in the Bible, as well as one of the more bizarre episodes in the Bible.

This is the story: Jacob has lived his life relying upon himself. He has lived by scheming and manipulating. He has accumulated wealth, and now he is returning to his homeland with the prospect of meeting his brother, Esau. Esau, who had been wronged by Jacob, could wipe out Jacob and everything he has, and Jacob is terrified. Finally, the self-dependent and scheming Jacob recognizes his need for God.

On the night before Jacob meets Esau, a stranger assails Jacob in the darkness. They begin to wrestle; in fact, they wrestle through the night. Over time, it becomes clear to Jacob that this stranger is none other than God himself in human form.

And when God is about to leave, Jacob holds on for dear life. He won't let go. Clinging to God, Jacob blurts out, "I will not let you go unless you bless me."

What is it about this prayer? It sounds selfish, but God loved it and answered it. God blessed Jacob.

God loved this prayer because Jacob, a self-reliant schemer, is calling out to him in dependence. "Lord, I need you. Lord, I need your blessing. Lord, I need your grace. Without your blessing, there is no hope. Lord, I won't let you go unless you bless me."

Dependence. Desperation. Trust.

For proud, self-reliant people like Jacob, like me, and perhaps like you, that's a prayer God loves. At times, God will wrestle with us and perhaps even give us a limp, like the one he will eventually give Jacob, in order to show us how much we need him and teach us to call out, "Lord, we need you. I need you. I need your blessing, your rescue, and your protection. Without you, I have no hope."

That's a prayer God loves.

Genesis 50:20

As for you, you meant evil against me, but God
meant it for good, to bring it about that many people
should be kept alive, as they are today.

This is a classic passage about forgiveness. Joseph had been wronged so deeply by his jealous brothers—sold into slavery, transported to a strange land, and made a slave in the household of an Egyptian. He would spend thirteen years in prison before being rescued and elevated to prime minister of all Egypt.

Years later, in the midst of a great famine, Joseph rescues his brothers, forgives them, and brings them to Egypt. However, when their father dies, they are terrified that their powerful brother will take his vengeance. They are scared to death, so they throw themselves at Joseph's feet and shout, "We are your servants!" (Gen. 50:18).

Joseph's reply is classic. "But Joseph said to them, 'Do not fear, for am I in the place of God?'" (Gen. 50:19).

Forgiveness won't come if we try to play God. When we are wronged, we subconsciously feel we have the right to try, convict, sentence, retaliate, and hold others under judgment.

But God, not us, is the judge of all the earth. Only God has the right to judge and execute justice. Refuse to retaliate. Refuse to play God. Joseph continues, "As for you, you meant evil against me, but God meant it for good, to bring it about that many people should be kept alive, as they are today" (Gen. 50:20).

Notice that Joseph doesn't deny the wrongdoing. He doesn't excuse it or whitewash it. "You meant evil against me."

But he doesn't stop there. He trusts God to redeem their wrongdoing, to take the harm that was caused and bring good out of it.

When we are wronged, we have a choice. We can focus on the wrong, the hurt, and the evil. Or, we can believe in God to bring good out of evil, to redeem the wrongdoing.

Joseph made the choice to forgive, the healing choice. So can you. By God's grace, so can you.

Exodus 3:7

Then the LORD said, "I have surely seen the affliction
of my people who are in Egypt and have heard
their cry because of their taskmasters.
I know their sufferings."

The Israelites were enslaved and mistreated by the Egyptians for four hundred years. Four hundred bitter years of pain, anguish, and shame. Four hundred years of wondering: Where is God? Why does God ignore us? Why has God abandoned us?

And then God speaks to Moses from a burning bush. "I have surely seen the affliction of my people who are in Egypt and have heard their cry because of their taskmasters. I know their sufferings." Despite all their doubts and fears, God had been there the whole time. He had *seen* their misery. He had heard their crying out. He cared about their suffering.

We must know this about God. He is the God who sees, the God who hears, and the God who cares.

We can identify with the suffering of the Israelites. In our lives, there are periods of pain, fear, and anguish. At times, we too wonder: Does God care? Does God see? Has God abandoned me?

We must turn to Exodus 3 and read again that God is the God who sees our pain, the God who hears our crying out, and the God who cares about our suffering.

So don't give up. Never give up. God is right there with you. We don't understand his delays, but he's the sovereign God, and we don't understand all of his ways. We may not understand, but we must know he is right there with us. He sees, he hears, and he cares.

Moreover, in the very next verse, we see that God rescues. "And I have come down to deliver them" (Exod. 3:8).

That's my God. That's your God. The God who sees, the God who hears, the God who cares, and the God who rescues.

Exodus 3:14

God said to Moses, "I AM WHO I AM."
And he said, "Say this to the people of Israel,
'I AM has sent me to you.'"

It was a pivotal moment in biblical history. God appears to Moses in the burning bush to call him to lead his people out of slavery. In the poignant exchange, Moses asks about God's name. Keep in mind that in the Israelite culture, your name was not a label but a disclosure of who you were. Names mattered.

So God replies, "I AM WHO I AM…Say this to the people of Israel, 'I AM has sent me to you.'"

That reply is not so clear, is it? What is God saying about himself? "I AM WHO I AM?" At the very least, this name is rather enigmatic and mysterious. But that fits, doesn't it? There is mystery with God. He's incomprehensible. Who else but God would have a name like this: "I AM WHO I AM?"

But we can say more about this name. It suggests that God has life in himself. He is completely free, self-existent, and sovereign. He is eternal and unchanging. He is not dependent on anything else, and because he is not dependent on anything else, he is invincible. He does as he chooses. His Word cannot be stopped. This all means that God is trustworthy. He has sovereign power to come through for us.

This is who God is: sovereign, unchanging, eternal, self-existent, free. The source of all life everywhere. Not dependent on anything else. Mysterious. Incomprehensible in his greatness. Completely trustworthy.

God gives Moses a shortened version of his name when he says, "Tell them that 'I AM' has sent me to you." This is where things get interesting. Because when Jesus shows up on the scene in the book of John, he uses seven "I am" statements to describe who he is, such as "I am the door," "I am the vine," and "I am the bread of life." These seven "I ams" echo the burning bush passage of Exodus 3.

But there's more. In one discussion, Jesus tells the Jews that he was alive during Abraham's lifetime. At this, the Jews become apoplectic. They are furious at what Jesus is suggesting, but Jesus doesn't back down an inch. "Truly, truly, I say to you, before Abraham was, I am" (John 8:58).

Jesus does not say, "Before Abraham was born, I already existed," or "I was already alive." No, in a pointed reference to Exodus 3, Jesus proclaims, "Before Abraham was, I am."

The Jews understood exactly what Jesus was saying. So they picked up stones to kill him, for he was claiming to be God.

This is Jesus, the same one who spoke to Moses in the burning bush. The great 'I am,' sovereign and eternal and unchanging, here to rescue his people from bondage.

Exodus 14:13-14

And Moses said to the people, "Fear not, stand firm,
and see the salvation of the LORD, which he will work
for you today. For the Egyptians whom you see today,
you shall never see again. The LORD will fight for
you, and you have only to be silent."

There is one event that the Old Testament keeps going back to time after time. In fact, the Old Testament refers to this event one hundred times. This episode is not only the central example of God's power to rescue his people, but it is also the main Old Testament picture of what God does for us in Christ.

This central event is the Exodus, the deliverance of the Israelites out of slavery with the ten plagues and the parting of the Red Sea.

But the Exodus is not just of paramount theological importance; it is also of greatest practical encouragement to spiritual life.

Moses and the Israelites have reached the shore of the sea when they see the Egyptian army bearing down on them. The people are terrified. After all they have been through, will they be massacred when they have almost made it? They complain bitterly to Moses.

Moses's response is classic. This is his finest hour of leadership. "Fear not, stand firm, and see the salvation of the Lord, which he will work for you today. For the Egyptians whom you see today, you shall never see again. The Lord will fight for you, and you have only to be silent" (Exod. 14:13-14).

These words are life-giving words. They speak to our overwhelming problems and needs. They speak to the biggest challenges in our lives. They speak to the problems we are wrestling with right now.

Consider your biggest burden as you prayerfully hear God's voice to you: "Fear not. Stand firm and see the salvation of the Lord. The Lord will fight for you. You need only be silent."

The Israelites were in an impossible situation that day. Maybe you feel you are in an impossible situation right now. It's not impossible for God. Nothing is too hard for God. He can do it.

Trust the Lord. Trust the Lord with all your heart. Cry out to him. Refuse to give way to fear, for the Lord will fight for you.

Why don't you call out to him right now?

Exodus 20:3

You shall have no other gods before me.

This is the first of the Ten Commandments—not just first in order, but first in importance.

Whatever is first in our lives, whatever is most important to us, that's our god. Whether it is money, work, family, a hobby, sports, your house, your car, or a host of other things, whatever is most important to us, that's our god. And if it is anything other than the true living God of the universe, then the Bible calls that idolatry.

Put God first.

God has supremacy in the universe. After all, he's the Creator. He's the Almighty. He's the sovereign, holy, infinite God. He is King of kings and Lord of lords. In every way, God has supremacy in the universe. He must have supremacy in our lives and hearts.

If we put God first, what does that mean? It means wholehearted devotion, total obedience, and absolute loyalty. It means we will love him, serve him, obey him, trust him, worship him, seek him, please him, fear him, and follow him. It means we will stop playing God in our lives and let God be God. It means surrender. Unconditional surrender, glad surrender, surrender of all that we have and all that we are.

Nothing must come before God in our lives. He alone is God and King. He calls us to loyalty and fidelity because he alone is God.

We must ask ourselves, what is the most important thing in my life?

Exodus 20:4

*You shall not make for yourself a carved image, or
any likeness of anything that is in heaven above, or
that is in the earth beneath, or that is in
the water under the earth.*

The first commandment warns us to not worship false gods. The second commandment warns us to not worship the true God in a false way. Don't worship God with idols or images.

The problem with images is simple. Any image of God inevitably reduces God to less than he really is. Any idol inevitably obscures the glory of God.

It is vital that we see God as he is, as the great, loving, infinite, sovereign, and merciful God that he is. Because if we do not see God as he is, in all his glory, then we will not worship him or love him or trust him or enjoy him as we ought.

That's why, in the opening sentence of his book *The Knowledge of the Holy*, A.W. Tozer wrote, "What comes into our minds when we think about God is the most important thing about us."

For years I struggled with my view of God. I tended to see God as great, big, holy, and sovereign. But in my heart of hearts, I did not see him as kind, loving, forgiving, or gentle, and this distorted view of God hurt me. How it hurt me! It strangled the life and joy out of my relationship with God. I still haven't arrived at what my view of God is, but I am well on the journey, and today I see God more and more as he is, full of relentless affection and overflowing grace.

The second commandment, like all ten of the commandments, is for our good. It tells us that God has not given us tangible images to reveal who he is. Rather, he has given us his Word.

To see God as he really is, read God's Word. Every day, open God's Word and meet him there in the pages of Scripture.

See God as he really is, in all of his resplendent glory and grace.

Exodus 20:7

*You shall not take the name of the LORD your God
in vain, for the LORD will not hold him guiltless who
takes his name in vain.*

Why did God give us the Ten Commandments?
God did not give us the Ten Commandments for our salvation, as in "Keep these commandments in order to be saved." That would be futile, for no one would be saved. Thankfully, salvation has always been by the grace of God. It has always been God's work for man, not man's work for God.

So why did God give us the Ten Commandments? Three reasons. First, the Ten Commandments (and all 613 commandments in the Mosaic Law) reveal the nature and character of God. Implicitly, by the nature of these commandments, we see that God is holy, that God is good, that God is wise, that God is just, and that God is sovereign. The Ten Commandments reveal God's character.

Second, the Ten Commandments reveal to us how to live our lives well. These commandments are God's gift to us, given for our good to guide and protect us.

Third, the Ten Commandments reveal our sin. They show us that we fall short of God's perfection, that we could never be good enough to please a holy God and save ourselves, and that we need him as Savior. The law leads us to Christ.

The third commandment concerns the name of God. Do not misuse God's name. Do not profane God's name. Do not take God's name in vain.

This commandment carries several implications. First of all, don't use God's name as profanity. Don't take God's holy name and use it to give voice to your unholy feelings. Honor God's name, because to honor God's name is to honor God.

There's a second part to it: Don't swear falsely in God's name. Don't use God's name in an oath to make a false statement.

Then there is a third part: Do not treat God as if he is unreal, as if he did not exist, as if he were not present with you. Never live your life as if God didn't exist, for God does exist. He is right here with you. Live your life in the presence of God. Live your life in the awareness of the presence of God.

If we do, I imagine that it would change how we live.

God is real. God is here. Practice the presence of God.

Exodus 20:8

Remember the Sabbath day, to keep it holy.

On the seventh day of creation, God rested. He rested and blessed the seventh day. In the Ten Commandments, he calls us to remember the Sabbath and keep it holy.

God has designed us for Sabbath rest. We need it. We need one day in seven to stop working and rest.

The point of the Sabbath is not a bunch of man-made rules about what you can and cannot do. The Pharisees made that mistake. The point is simple: Sabbath rest is God's gift to you. Receive the gift. Enjoy it. Take a break from work routines. Relax. Rest.

God has designed you for a true Sabbath rest.

But what is a true Sabbath rest? First, it is the absence of work. Second, it is the presence of worship.

The absence of work means you cease from whatever activities constitute work for you—your job, housework, bills, or errands.

The presence of worship means a day lived in God's presence, a non-hectic, non-harried day to pray and play.

People live for the weekend, but the weekend doesn't refresh. People are just as soul-weary on Monday mornings as they were on Friday afternoons. Why is this? The problem is that there is no true Sabbath. They have the absence of work without the presence of worship. If you fill the weekend with entertainment, sports, recreation, and work on the house, then your spirit is never refreshed. Your soul is never restored. You need to let God breathe life into your soul.

Sabbath rest, regular Sabbath rest, true Sabbath rest, is God's gift to us. It is God's antidote to keep us from ruining our lives with hurry and busyness and overcommitment. It is a gift that is absolutely essential for our physical, emotional, and spiritual health.

Exodus 20:12

*Honor your father and your mother, that your days
may be long in the land that the LORD your
God is giving you.*

There are innumerable books on marriage and just as many
on parenting. But how many books have you seen on the
responsibility of children to their parents? Yet when God chooses
one aspect of the family to include in the Ten Commandments,
he does not choose marriage or parenting. Instead, God speaks
to children about their parents, saying, "Honor your father and
your mother."

Why is this so important to God? There are at least three
reasons:

> First, a stable society needs stable families, and there
> are no stable families unless children honor their
> parents.
>
> Second, children must learn respect for authority or
> they will not make it in life, and respect for authority
> begins in the home, with their parents.
>
> Third, it is only right that children honor their
> parents, for all normal parents sacrifice endlessly for
> their kids. Most parents would die for their kids in a
> heartbeat.

But how do we practically obey the fifth commandment and
honor our parents? When we are young, it's pretty simple: we
obey. We obey right away, preferably with a good attitude.

As we grow older and leave the home, we no longer obey our
parents, but we do honor them. We express respect, appreciation,
and love. We call or write. We help them if they need it. We care
for them if they need to be cared for. We treasure them and affirm
them.

In all these ways, we honor our parents. In doing so, we honor
God as well.

Exodus 20:13

You shall not murder.

No human being has the right to take the life of another human being because human life is sacred. Only God has authority over life and death.

The sixth commandment may seem as dry as dust, but behind this commandment is the unfathomable love God has for each one of us. Every human being on the planet matters to God. He sent his Son to die for us. We have inestimable worth to him. He loves us. That's why murder is so serious to our God.

This commandment not only prohibits murder, but it also prohibits suicide (self-murder), infanticide (murder of the newborn), abortion (murder of the unborn), and euthanasia (murder of the aged and ill). In every way, God calls us to have a profound respect for human life.

In the Sermon on the Mount, Jesus takes this commandment to a deeper level. "You have heard that it was said to those of old, 'You shall not murder; and whoever murders will be liable to judgment.' But I say to you that everyone who is angry with his brother will be liable to judgment; whoever insults his brother will be liable to the council; and whoever says, 'You fool!' will be liable to the hell of fire" (Matt. 5:21-22).

It's not enough just to avoid the act of murder. God is also concerned about angry attitudes and words because they come from the same hate-filled heart and can lead to murder. Jesus tells you and me, "These are wrong too. These are unacceptable for my followers. Bring these to me and let me fill your heart with my love and forgiveness."

Human life is sacred.

Exodus 20:14

You shall not commit adultery.

Sex within marriage is wholly good. It is God's gift to every married couple. But sex is powerful. It is not just the merger of two bodies, but the merger of two souls. When sex is treated casually and promiscuously, then great damage is done. People are hurt. Marriages are wrecked. Families are destroyed.

Our culture may minimize adultery, and Hollywood may even glamorize it, but deep down every person knows instinctively that adultery is wrong. It is a terrible betrayal of the love, commitment, and loyalty of marriage.

So God gives us the seventh commandment for our good. He gives us the commandment for our protection, to protect us from the pain, hurt, and destruction of adultery.

In the Sermon on the Mount, Jesus quotes this commandment and gives the true spirit of it. "You have heard that it was said, 'You shall not commit adultery.' But I say to you that everyone who looks at a woman with lustful intent has already committed adultery with her in his heart" (Matt. 5:27-28).

Jesus is teaching us that the seventh commandment includes not just physical adultery, but also adultery of the heart. Don't look at other people as objects to be used, but as persons to be loved.

This does not mean it is wrong to notice attractive members of the opposite sex. That's not lust, but the normal response of a human being. Lust comes when we go beyond that and begin to fantasize about having sex. Then it becomes a violation of the seventh commandment.

One more issue: How can we avoid adultery and stay faithful to God and, if married, stay faithful to our spouse? Three brief suggestions:

> First, give constant priority to your marriage. Work on your marriage and never take it for granted.
>
> Second, guard friendships with the opposite sex. Don't be reckless. Decide in advance on appropriate boundaries and guidelines.
>
> Third, draw close to Jesus. Fall in love with Jesus. Find all your satisfaction in the one who alone can fill the human heart.

Exodus 20:15

You shall not steal.

Because God wants us to respect the property of others, because God wants us to treat others in the way we want to be treated, because God wants us to love our neighbor as ourselves, he tells us plainly to not steal.

Stealing is more nuanced than we might think.

One way to steal is seizure—old-fashioned theft. This includes burglaries, shoplifting, car theft, muggings, and store robberies. It includes pilfering items from your workplace. Moreover, we can steal productivity from our employer if we consistently come in late, take too long for lunch, or work on personal things. Unless we make this time up, we are stealing time from our employer.

Another form of seizure could be called long-term borrowing. We borrow something from a friend, such as a ladder, book, or CD. We intend to return it, but the days go by, perhaps the months go by, and we just don't return it.

Besides seizure, there's deception. We are not honest about the house or the car we are selling. A businessman is not honest about a product or a service. A mechanic is not honest with a customer about the brakes. A physician is not honest with a patient about a surgery. We lie on our income tax return. Will Rogers once said that "the income tax has made more liars of the American people than the game of golf has."

In addition to seizure and deception, there's fraud—withholding something that belongs to someone else. If we hit a car in a parking lot and don't leave a note, if a husband does not make child support payments, if a landlord does not return a deposit that is due, if we do not pay a bill we owe (assuming we are not unemployed and make some provision to repay), we violate the eighth commandment.

There are a lot of ways to steal besides robbing a store. God tells us, "Do not steal. Treat your neighbor the way you want to be treated. In obeying my commands, you are liberated to enjoy life and to enjoy me."

Exodus 20:16

*You shall not bear false witness against
your neighbor.*

Though God uses the vocabulary of the law courts in the ninth commandment, he is calling us to tell the truth in every way.

The truth matters to God. He is a truth teller and a lover of truth. Lying is a failure at loving because lying ruins relationships and destroys the threads of trust that bind people together.

We can lie in all sorts of ways. When we inflate stories or résumés, we lie to impress people. If we are afraid to be honest and disagree with a strong person, then we lie to please people. We can also lie to make a profit if we lie to a customer or make false advertising claims. When we slander, we lie to discredit someone. A big reason we lie is just to avoid trouble or punishment. At other times, people lie for convenience. For example, if we call in sick at work when we are not sick, or if we say we've shipped a package when we haven't. There are also the small lies of exaggeration.

But no matter the form of our dishonesty and duplicity, God calls us to stop lying and tell the truth. He knows that every lie poisons human relationships and erodes our character.

God hates lying and he delights in truth telling. Even though dishonesty may be extremely common, we must obey God, declare an all-out spiritual war on lying, and decide we will follow in the footsteps of our truth-telling God rather than in the footsteps of Satan, who is the arch deceiver and the father of lies.

Tell the truth!

Exodus 20:17

*You shall not covet your neighbor's house; you shall
not covet your neighbor's wife, or his male servant, or
his female servant, or his ox, or his donkey,
or anything that is your neighbor's.*

In the tenth commandment, God tells us to not lust for things
that don't belong to you. Don't become obsessed with things
that belong to others. Don't let something become an idol to you
because it has become too important.

The tenth commandment takes us from actions to attitudes.
It concerns the desires of our heart. To be clear, the problem is
not with desire itself, but with desiring the wrong things, desiring
things that don't belong to us, and giving free rein to our desires.

The problem with coveting things that don't belong to us is
that we believe a lie. We believe the lie that if I had *that thing* I
would be happy. But life doesn't work that way, does it? We get
that thing and then we want something else. Our desires and
longings are satisfied only in Jesus.

Bruce Marshall, in his book *The World, the Flesh, and Father
Smith,* sagely observed, "The young man who rings the bell at the
brothel is unconsciously looking for God."

The opposite of coveting is contentment. God had blessed
King David in so many ways, and yet when he saw Bathsheba
on the roof, he violated the tenth commandment by coveting.
That in turn led to the violation of the eighth commandment by
stealing, then the seventh commandment by adultery, and finally,
the sixth commandment by murder. God's way is always best.
Whenever we break God's commandments, we hurt ourselves—
and so often, we hurt others.

In contrast to David, Paul could say, "Not that I am speaking
of being in need, for I have learned in whatever situation I am
to be content. I know how to be brought low, and I know how
to abound. In any and every circumstance, I have learned the
secret of facing plenty and hunger, abundance and need" (Phil.
4:11-12). That's contentment, and that's where joy and peace are
found. God's way is always best.

Exodus 33:18-19a

Moses said, "Please show me your glory." And he said,
"I will make all my goodness pass before you and will
proclaim before you my name 'The LORD.'"

All throughout the book of Exodus, we see the greatness of God. We see God's greatness and glory in the burning bush, the ten plagues on Egypt, the parting of the Red Sea, the destruction of Pharaoh's army, and more. Perhaps more than any book in the Old Testament, we see the power, the glory, the majesty, the grandeur, the sovereignty, and the holiness of our great God.

Then, after all of these incredible events, Moses makes this bold request of God, "Please show me your glory."

The request reveals Moses's passion for God. Not a passion for what God can do for Moses, but a passion for God himself. This is a passion not for God's power, but for God's face. For God himself.

Augustine once wrote: "Give me a man in love; he knows what I mean. Give me one who yearns; give me one who is hungry; give me one far away in this desert, who is thirsty and sighs for the spring of the Eternal Country. Give me that sort of man; he knows what I mean. But if I speak to a cold man, he just doesn't know what I am talking about." This describes Moses in Exodus 33.

God loved Moses's request and he replied affirmatively. But note what God says when he answers, "I will make all my goodness pass before you." Not his greatness, but his goodness. When God reveals the essence of his glory to Moses, he will reveal his goodness. Yes, God's greatness is vital, but God's glory is seen primarily in his goodness.

The next morning, God does what he promised and reveals his glory to Moses. "The LORD descended in the cloud and stood with him there, and proclaimed the name of the LORD. The LORD passed before him and proclaimed, 'The LORD, the LORD, a God merciful and gracious, slow to anger, and abounding in steadfast love and faithfulness, keeping steadfast love for thousands, forgiving iniquity and transgression and sin'" (Exod. 34:5-7a).

When he reveals his glory to Moses, he proclaims his goodness, that he is merciful and gracious, slow to anger and loving, faithful, and forgiving.

The glory of our God.

Exodus 34:6-7a

The LORD passed before him and proclaimed, "The LORD, the LORD, a God merciful and gracious, slow to anger, and abounding in steadfast love and faithfulness, keeping steadfast love for thousands, forgiving iniquity and transgression and sin."

In Exodus 33, Moses made an audacious request of God: "Show me your glory." God loves the request, a request born of hunger to know God, and he replies, "Yes."

Early the next morning, Moses chisels two stone tablets and climbs Mt. Sinai. God comes down to earth in a cloud and reveals his glory to Moses. "The LORD passed before him and proclaimed, 'The LORD, the LORD, a God merciful and gracious, slow to anger, and abounding in steadfast love and faithfulness, keeping steadfast love for thousands, forgiving iniquity and transgression and sin'" (Exod. 34:6-7a).

God is revealing to Moses his glory, his attributes, and his essence. "Moses, this is my glory."

God is saying for all time:

> This is who I am. This is my essence. I am the compassionate God, bursting with relentless tenderness and affection for you. I am the gracious God, the God who extends grace to those who don't deserve it. I am abounding in love. I don't have just a little love for you. No! I am crazy about you. I am overflowing with love for you. I am abounding in faithfulness. I am worthy of your complete trust because I am faithful and true. I will do what I say. I am forgiving. I am the God who can remove your sin as far as the east is from the west.

Is this the way you see God? I hope so, because this is who God is. And how you see God will shape everything in your life. See God the way he is, in his resplendent glory.

Leviticus 11:44a

For I am the LORD *your God. Consecrate yourselves*
therefore, and be holy, for I am holy.

To say that God is holy is to say that God is not only separate
from sin, but that God is separate from everything. God is
different from everything else in the universe. God is far above
everything else and everyone else in the universe. Nothing can
even be compared to God. God is the holy God. As the exalted
seraphim call out in Isaiah 6:3, "Holy, holy, holy is the LORD of
hosts; the whole earth is full of his glory!"

The book of Leviticus proclaims that God is the holy God.
Every sacrifice, every law, every command declares that God is
holy. In fact, the word *holy* appears in Leviticus more than in any
other book of the Bible.

Moreover, several times in Leviticus God commands his
people that they also must be holy, separate from all sin, and
dedicated wholly to God:

> For I am the LORD your God. Consecrate yourselves
> therefore, and be holy, for I am holy. (Lev. 11:44a)
> For I am the LORD who brought you up out of the
> land of Egypt to be your God. You shall therefore be
> holy, for I am holy. (Lev. 11:45)
> You shall be holy, for I the LORD your God am holy.
> (Lev. 19:2b)
> Consecrate yourselves, therefore, and be holy, for I
> am the LORD your God. (Lev. 20:7)
> You shall be holy to me, for I the LORD am holy and
> have separated you from the peoples, that you should
> be mine. (Lev. 20:26)

The people of Israel were to be different because they belonged
to God. They were a chosen people, a special people.

That is also our calling as followers of Jesus. We are a special
people, a chosen people, a holy people, the people of God, set
apart from sin and dedicated wholly to God. "But as he who
called you is holy, you also be holy in all your conduct, since it is
written, 'You shall be holy, for I am holy'" (1 Pet. 1:15-16).

This is our identity. This is our calling. This is our destiny as
God's holy people.

Leviticus 17:11

For the life of the flesh is in the blood, and I have given it for you on the altar to make atonement for your souls, for it is the blood that makes atonement by the life.

So much blood is shed in the Bible. So many sacrifices, so many bulls and rams and goats and lambs are sacrificed. Blood runs freely.

What is God saying to us?

God is teaching us about sin. God is teaching us that sin is serious before a holy God and that sin must be paid for with our lives. Our only hope is if a substitute dies in our place, if the blood of a substitute is shed instead of our blood.

This truth begins in the Garden of Eden after Adam and Eve sin. Fig leaves won't do, and God covers Adam and Eve with animal skins. Blood is shed.

It continues all through the Old Testament. So many sacrifices. So much blood. All of it as a covering for sin.

And then Jesus shows up. His messenger, John the Baptist, calls out, "Behold, the Lamb of God, who takes away the sin of the world" (John 1:29). Then his life culminates on a cross. His blood is shed. Sin is paid for. Your sin. My sin.

> Without the shedding of blood there is no forgiveness of sins. (Heb. 9:22b)
>
> To him who loves us and has freed us from our sins by his blood. (Rev. 1:5b)
>
> Knowing that you were ransomed from the futile ways inherited from your forefathers, not with perishable things such as silver or gold, but with the precious blood of Christ, like that of a lamb without blemish or spot. (1 Pet. 1:18-19)

The precious blood of Christ. The Lamb of God.

Deuteronomy 6:4

Hear, O Israel: The Lord our God, the Lord is one.

Deuteronomy 6:4-9 ranks as one of the pivotal passages in the Old Testament. It is the basic Jewish confession of faith, recited twice daily by devout Jews. To this day, the synagogue service begins with this passage, known as the *Shema* after the first Hebrew word, which means "hear."

Moreover, when Jesus was asked about the greatest commandment in the law, he quotes verse 5 from this passage. Furthermore, this passage may be the single most important passage on parenting in the Bible.

For all these reasons, Deuteronomy 6:4-9 is an extremely significant passage. It begins with a simple, succinct statement about God. "Hear, O Israel: The Lord our God, the Lord is one." The Lord, the God of the Scriptures, the God who revealed himself to Moses, the God who would reveal himself in Jesus: he is God and he alone is God.

This is a statement of monotheism. It is a confession of God's uniqueness. The Israelites had to be crystal clear on this because they were immersed in a pagan, polytheistic world, with all kinds of fears about appeasing various gods. The Israelites had to grasp the basic truth. These gods are not real. There is only one God. Yahweh alone is God.

This foundational confession carries immense connotations. To confess that the Lord is God is to confess that he is Creator, King, Judge, Ruler, Savior, and Shepherd. It means that he is our God and we are his people. It means that we are accountable to him, to love him and obey him, to worship him, and to serve him.

We join in the historic confession: "Hear, O Israel: The Lord our God, the Lord is one." The God of the Scriptures is the one and only real God.

Deuteronomy 6:5

*You shall love the LORD your God with all your heart
and with all your soul and with all your might.*

Remarkable, isn't it? The main thing God wants from us is our love. He's the God of the universe and he longs for us to love him back.

What does this tell us about God? At heart, he is a lover. He is the God who loves. In fact, 1 John 4:8 declares, "God is love."

What does this verse tell us about the Christian life? It's a love affair. If you thought the Christian life was about religious rules or church rituals or being good enough, you have God all wrong. It's all about love; receiving God's love for you and then loving him back. As Brennan Manning notes in his book *The Ragamuffin Gospel:*

> Over a hundred years ago in the Deep South, a phrase so common in our Christian culture today, "born again," was seldom or never used. Rather, the phrase used to describe the breakthrough into a personal relationship with Jesus Christ was, "I was seized by the power of a great affection."

These words describe both the initiative of God and the explosion within the heart when Jesus, instead of being a face on a holy card with long hair and a robe with many folds: becomes real, alive, and Lord of one's personal and professional life. Seized by the power of a great affection was a visceral description of the phenomenon of Pentecost, authentic conversion, and the release of the Holy Spirit. The phrase lent new meaning to the old Russian proverb "those who have the disease called Jesus will never be cured."

What does it mean to love God? It includes affection, devotion, tenderness, and gratitude. It includes loyalty, obedience, and surrender. You want to know him, be close to him, and please him.

Furthermore, this love relationship is not tepid and lukewarm, but passionate and wholehearted. Love the Lord with all your heart, all your soul, and all your might. Go all out. Give yourself in love and obedience to the God who made you.

Jesus was once asked, "What is the greatest commandment in the Law?" He didn't hesitate. He went right to Deuteronomy 6 and quoted this verse. "The greatest commandment is to love God with all your heart, with all your soul, with all your might" (Matt. 22:34-40).

Dear friend, this is your purpose in life. This is your top priority. This is your mission. Love him with all you've got. Love him with all you are.

Deuteronomy 6:6

And these words that I command you today shall
be on your heart.

Deuteronomy 6:4-9 is full of God's most important guidelines for our lives. Verse 4 contains the theological foundation of our faith, and verse 5 is the most important command in the law. Verses 6-9 are the crucial passages on parenting in the Bible.

When God turns to parenting, he begins with the hearts of parents, not the hearts of children. God is saying to us:

> First, focus on your own heart. These commands must be on your heart. Before they will be on the hearts of your kids, they must be on your heart. Model what you want to see in your children. If you want your kids to love God and obey God, let it begin with you. The first task of parenting is right here: love and obey your God.

The word is authenticity. Parents don't have to be perfect, but they do need to be authentic. Be the kind of person you want your child to become. The essence of parenting is not what we do but who we are. The focus is not changing your children but changing you. Or, more accurately, letting God change you.

Albert Schweitzer, a brilliant philosopher, mathematician, and medical doctor, who spent much of his life as a missionary to Africa, once remarked, "There are only three ways to teach a child. The first is by example, the second is by example, the third is by example."

In some ways, parenting is an overwhelming task. There are so many principles to know and follow. You need more wisdom than you've got.

However, in some ways, the task is simple: Be the person God wants you to be. Be a man or woman who loves God and obeys God with all your heart. Be the kind of person you want your kids to become.

Deuteronomy 6:7-9

*You shall teach them diligently to your children, and
shall talk of them when you sit in your house, and
when you walk by the way, and when you lie down,
and when you rise. You shall bind them as a sign
on your hand, and they shall be as frontlets
between your eyes. You shall write them on the
doorposts of your house and on your gates.*

When it comes to parenting, the first task is to be the kind of person you want your children to become. Be a model of loving and obeying Jesus.

Then you will be ready to teach your children God's Word, the "words that I command" (Deut. 6:6). When God tells parents to talk to their children "when you sit in your house, and when you walk by the way, when you lie down, and when you rise," he is not calling us to give our kids a non-stop theological lecture. The burst-dam approach doesn't work very well with children. Rather, God's point is for parents to always be alert to the teachable moment, at all places and at all times. Bring God's Word to bear on the situation, both in private (home) and in public (along the road), both in the evening (lie down) and in the morning (get up).

He goes on to make a similar point in verses 8-9: "You shall bind them as a sign on your hand, and they shall be as frontlets between your eyes. You shall write them on the doorposts of your house and on your gates."

God's Word must govern all we do (our hands) and all we think (our foreheads). It must govern all we do privately (houses) and publicly (city gates).

God is telling parents to teach your children God's Word in every situation all though the day. When your child lies, when your child has fears, when your child is nervous about a test, when your child is hurt by a friend, when you lose your temper, when your child doesn't want to go to church, when you buy a new car, or when your child gives part of his or her allowance to God. In all these situations, bring God's Word to bear. Seize the teachable moment.

But remember, your first focus is not teaching, but doing. Love and obey Jesus yourself, for when it comes to parenting, the aphorism is true: more is caught than taught.

Joshua 1:8

*This Book of the Law shall not depart from your
mouth, but you shall meditate on it day and night,
so that you may be careful to do according to all that
is written in it. For then you will make your way
prosperous, and then you will have good success.*

Joshua faced the biggest challenge of his life.
Moses had just died. Joshua was now the leader of God's people.
The Israelites were ready to cross the Jordan River and begin
the conquest of their long-promised land. This conquest would
not be quick or easy, and Joshua suddenly had to lead them.
Undoubtedly, Joshua felt intimidated and alone. Could he do it?

God comes to Joshua and bestows him with the crucial
ingredient that he would need above all others.

> Joshua, I have given you a Book, the Book of the Law.
> Treasure this Book. Study this Book. Follow this Book.
> Fill your heart with this Book so that you think about
> it all the time and speak of it in every situation. Above
> all, Joshua, obey my Book. The point is not to know
> my commands but to obey my commands. Joshua, if
> you do this, then no matter what else happens, you
> will succeed. I will put my hand upon you and you
> will have success in life.

God's message to Joshua is God's message to you. If you want
your life to prosper, if you want true success in life, if you want
success in the eyes of God, then the path is simple: Treasure God's
Word. Fill your heart with God's Word. Live your life by God's
Word.

If you do that, your life may not be easy, but you will have
God's hand on your life and you will know true success.

There is no other way.

Joshua 1:9

*Have I not commanded you? Be strong and
courageous. Do not be frightened, and do not
be dismayed, for the LORD your God is with you
wherever you go.*

Apparently, Joshua was terrified by the challenges. And who could blame him? Moses's recent death had thrust him into the leadership role of a great nation. He was no longer the lieutenant to the leader. He *was* the leader.

Moreover, Joshua was assuming leadership at the critical moment, just as Israel would cross the Jordan River and begin the conquest of the land.

Who was adequate for this challenge? Who could follow a Moses? Would the people follow him as they had followed Moses? What kind of opposition would the Israelites face? And most importantly, would God be with Joshua as he had been with Moses?

It was all most intimidating, and anyone who has ever led can empathize.

God empathized. Three times in the first nine verses, God encourages Joshua, "Be strong and courageous" (Josh. 1:6, Josh. 1:7, Josh. 1:9).

God addresses Joshua's fear:

> Do not be frightened; do not be dismayed. Yes, the challenges are enormous. But Joshua, do not give way to fear and discouragement (two of Satan's sharpest arrows). Do not give way to fear and discouragement for one basic reason: I will be with you. I will be with you, Joshua. Wherever you are, I will be with you. Wherever you go, I will be with you. Joshua, you will be fine, no matter what happens, no matter what you go through. Because the Lord, your God, will be with you wherever you go.

Is this not the Golden Promise? Is this not God's message to us? When we are overwhelmed by fear and discouragement, when we lose our job, when a teenager rebels, when the diagnosis is cancer, when we lose a loved one, when we battle depression, or when we are not sure we will make it, God says to us: "I will be with you."

Remember God's word to you in Psalm 23: "Even though I walk through the valley of the shadow of death, I will fear no evil, for you are with me."

Remember Jesus's word to you before he returned to heaven: "And behold, I am with you always, to the end of the age" (Matt. 28:20).

Remember that God is with you. Right now. Right beside you. Remember!

Ruth 1:16b-17a

For where you go I will go, and where you lodge I will
lodge. Your people shall be my people, and your
God my God. Where you die I will die,
and there will I be buried.

This is a classic statement of love and loyalty. Remarkably, these words were not spoken by a husband to his wife or a wife to her husband. They were not spoken by a parent to a child or a child to a parent. They were not spoken by close friends like David and Jonathan.

No, they were spoken by a bereaved daughter-in-law to her bereaved mother-in-law, both of whom had lost their husbands. Moreover, Ruth was a Moabitess and Naomi was a Jewess returning to her Jewish homeland. Naomi was urging Ruth to return to her home and find a husband there.

Naomi did not have wealth, privilege, or position. Ruth would be in a vulnerable position if she went with the widowed Naomi. Furthermore, she would likely never again see her parents, her siblings, or her homeland. Ruth's loyalty to Naomi would cost her enormously.

Yet Ruth knew it was the right thing to do. And so, despite the cost, with loyalty born of faith, she proclaimed her unwavering commitment to go with Naomi.

> But Ruth said, "Do not urge me to leave you or to return from following you. For where you go I will go, and where you lodge I will lodge. Your people shall be my people, and your God my God. Where you die I will die, and there will I be buried. May the LORD do so to me and more also if anything but death parts me from you." And when Naomi saw that she was determined to go with her, she said no more. (Ruth 1:16-18)

God honored Ruth's faith. God honored Ruth's loyalty. For God would give Ruth a wonderful husband, Boaz, a kind and generous man. God would also give Ruth a child, Obed, and this child would have a son, Jesse, and a grandson, David. Ruth, not even Jewish, was chosen by God to be the great-grandmother of Israel's greatest king, King David.

Even more importantly, Ruth would be in the royal line of the Messiah, the Son of David. And when God had the ancestors of Jesus recorded in Matthew 1, you find Ruth's name right in the middle of all the male ancestors.

Yes, God honored Ruth, the woman of faith, the woman who exemplified love and loyalty, no matter what it might cost her.

1 Samuel 15:22

And Samuel said, "Has the Lord as great delight in burnt offerings and sacrifices as in obeying the voice of the Lord? Behold, to obey is better than sacrifice, and to listen than the fat of rams."

Saul disobeyed God's command to kill all the animals, rationalizing that he could use the animals for sacrifice. God's response, declared through the prophet Samuel, was unequivocal.

God wants obedience, not sacrifice. God wants obedience, not religious ceremony. Never, ever choose religious ritual over obedience.

We still need this message. How many people attend church, thinking they have done their religious duty, and yet their lives are filled with self-centered thoughts and disobedience to God's holy commands?

How many Christians show up at church, put their time in, hear God's Word, and think they have earned God's favor?

But our all-holy, sovereign God expects us to do the Word of God, not just hear it. The Lord God Almighty expects obedience, not mere ceremony or ritual. God expects us to come, hear His Word, and then obey it.

This lesson to Saul is a lesson to us: there is no substitute for obedience. Unreserved, wholehearted, immediate obedience.

In his book *Authentic Christianity*, John Stott said, "Greatness in the kingdom of God is measured in terms of obedience."

Or, as Oswald Chambers put it, "The best measure of a spiritual life is not its ecstasies, but its obedience."

In the kingdom of God, there is simply no substitute for obedience. God wants us to obey him, no matter what it costs us.

And in that obedience, we will find our joy.

1 Samuel 16:7

But the LORD said to Samuel, "Do not look on his appearance or on the height of his stature, because I have rejected him. For the LORD sees not as man sees: man looks on the outward appearance, but the LORD looks on the heart."

God had rejected Saul as king because of his disobedience and rebellion. Now, God has sent the prophet Samuel to the house of Jesse, for one of Jesse's eight sons will be the next king.

When Samuel arrived and saw Eliab, the oldest, he assumed that Eliab must be God's choice. Apparently, Eliab was physically impressive. But Eliab was not God's choice, and God admonishes Samuel for a serious flaw in the way he viewed people, a flaw that we still have today. "Do not look on his appearance or on the height of his stature, because I have rejected him. For the LORD sees not as man sees: man looks on the outward appearance, but the LORD looks on the heart" (1 Sam. 16:7).

We look at outward appearance. God looks at inward character. We look at external traits. God looks at internal traits. We look at the body. God looks at the heart. We look at superficial things. God looks at substantial things, things that matter.

We can be so enamored by the body. By beauty and muscles, by fitness and thinness. By hair and tans, by athletic prowess and physical gifts. We give adulation to sports celebrities while largely ignoring the unsung heroes around the world who delight the heart of God.

We are so shallow. We, who are followers of Jesus Christ, who claim to live for the next world and not for this world, who serve the one who was nailed naked to a bloody cross, should know better. It is high time that we start seeing people as God sees them. Our perspective can be worldly (like the world) or godly (like God). It is time for God's people to be godly.

God chose David, the runt of the family. Why? Not because of David's appearance, but because David had a heart for God. As Samuel had earlier said to Saul, "But now your kingdom shall not continue. The LORD has sought out a man after his own heart, and the LORD has commanded him to be prince over his people, because you have not kept what the LORD commanded you" (1 Sam. 13:14).

That's what God is looking for: men and women whose hearts beat for God.

1 Samuel 17:47

*And that all this assembly may know that the LORD
saves not with sword and spear. For the battle is the
LORD's, and he will give you into our hand.*

Few stories in the Bible have captured our imagination like the
story of David and Goliath. Goliath was a giant of a man, over
nine feet tall, who taunted the Israelite soldiers and arrogantly
challenged Israel's God. David? A mere teenager, a shepherd, but
full of faith, courage, and heart for his God.

When David arrived at the front lines and heard this man defy
the armies of the living God, he could not stand it. In contrast to
the Israelite soldiers who were terrified by Goliath, David was
not intimidated and unimpressed. Who was Goliath, a mere man,
compared to God? David was impressed with the size of God, not
the size of Goliath.

So David, the teenager, volunteers to fight Goliath. Two
things characterize his attitude: his burning zeal for the glory of
God and his childlike trust in the faithfulness of God.

Firstly, there is his burning zeal for God's glory:

> Your servant has struck down both lions and bears,
> and this uncircumcised Philistine shall be like one of
> them, for he has defied the armies of the living God.
> (1 Sam. 17:36)
>
> This day the LORD will deliver you into my hand,
> and I will strike you down and cut off your head. And
> I will give the dead bodies of the host of the Philistines
> this day to the birds of the air and to the wild beasts
> of the earth, that all the earth may know that there is
> a God in Israel. (1 Sam. 17:46)
>
> And that all this assembly may know that the LORD
> saves not with sword and spear. For the battle is the
> LORD's, and he will give you into our hand. (1 Sam.
> 17:47)

When a man is more concerned about God's reputation than
his own reputation, watch out. This is a dangerous man. A man
who will impact the kingdom of God.

Secondly, his childlike trust in the faithfulness of God:

The LORD who delivered me from the paw of the lion and from the paw of the bear will deliver me from the hand of this Philistine. (1 Sam. 17:37)

Then David said to the Philistine, "You come to me with a sword and with a spear and with a javelin, but I come to you in the name of the LORD of hosts, the God of the armies of Israel, whom you have defied." (1 Sam. 17:45)

This day the LORD will deliver you into my hand, and I will strike you down and cut off your head. (1 Sam. 17:46)

And that all this assembly may know that the LORD saves not with sword and spear. For the battle is the LORD's, and he will give you into our hand. (1 Sam. 17:47)

God loves it when his people dare to trust him, no matter if the problem seems impossible. Which is bigger? Your problem or your God? What is God calling you to trust him for today?

Put your trust in God to deliver you, for the living God dwarfs the giants in your life.

2 Samuel 6:14-15

And David danced before the LORD *with all his
might. And David was wearing a linen ephod.
So David and all the house of Israel brought
up the ark of the* LORD *with shouting and
with the sound of the horn.*

Imagine this scene: the Ark of the Covenant, so sacred to the
Israelites, is being brought back to Jerusalem in a holy, festive
procession. People are everywhere, and King David is right there
among them. Music and shouts of joy fill the air. There is dancing
and celebration before the Lord. Every six steps, an animal is
sacrificed to atone for people's sins. What an unforgettable scene.

But what captures my attention is David. I cannot quite get
over David. Thinly clad in a linen ephod, right there among the
people, dancing to the Lord with all he has. Seemingly, he forgets
his dignity and who he is because he is focused completely on God.
David epitomizes self-forgetfulness and God intoxication. That's
what worshippers do. Worshippers are caught up in preoccupation
with God.

Moreover, David is so passionate. He is unrestrained, even
reckless, in his worship. He dances before the Lord "with all his
might." He doesn't hold back a bit from what he's feeling inside.
That's what worshippers do. Worshippers are passionate in
expressing worship to God.

Furthermore, David is filled with joy and exuberance. This is
no grim, sour-faced duty. He celebrates the goodness and greatness
of God with dancing, and no doubt with singing, laughter, and a
big smile. That's what worshippers do. Worshippers celebrate God's
goodness with exuberant joy.

But above all else, David is performing for a one-person
audience. He is dancing "before the Lord." Not before the people.
Not before God and the people. No, he is dancing to please the
Lord, to express joy before the Lord. He was not attired in a king's
wardrobe. He was not dignified and proper. He may have even
looked silly, but he didn't care. He didn't care how it looked to the
people, because it wasn't for them—it was for God. For God alone.
That's what worshippers do. Worshippers focus all their attention
on a one-person audience.

David teaches us what true worship is all about. The Father is
seeking these kinds of worshippers.

1 Kings 18:38

Then the fire of the LORD fell and consumed the burnt offering and the wood and the stones and the dust, and licked up the water that was in the trench.

Elijah is one of the most storied prophets in the history of Israel. He served God in a time of great sin and rebellion, and God did tremendous miracles through him. He never died; instead, he was transported directly to heaven. In the Bible, Enoch and Elijah are the only people who never die. In so many ways, he, fearless and faithful, epitomized the life of the rugged Old Testament prophet.

The high point in his life comes with a battle of the prophets in 1 Kings 18. This was a battle between the 450 prophets of Baal and 400 prophets of Asherah against Elijah, the prophet of God. Elijah laid down the challenge: each side would sacrifice a bull and place it on the wood, then ask their god to send fire.

Everyone was assembled on Mount Carmel near the sea. All heaven was watching. The prophets of Baal and Asherah called and called, but they called in vain. There was no fire for them.

Then Elijah called on the Lord:

> O LORD, God of Abraham, Isaac, and Israel, let it be known this day that you are God in Israel, and that I am your servant, and that I have done all these things at your word. Answer me, O LORD, answer me, that this people may know that you, O LORD, are God, and that you have turned their hearts back. (1 Kings 18:36-37)

The moment of truth. Everyone waits with bated breath.

> Then the fire of the LORD fell and consumed the burnt offering and the wood and the stones and the dust, and licked up the water that was in the trench. (1 Kings 18:38)

Can you imagine what it must have been like that day on Mount Carmel when fire fell from heaven?

> And when all the people saw it, they fell on their faces and said, "The LORD, he is God; the LORD, he is God." (1 Kings 18:39)

The message to Israel in the time of Elijah is the message to us today. The Lord is God. The Lord alone is God. He is all you need. Serve him only. Worship him only. Trust him only, for he is your God.

1 Kings 19:11-12

And he said, "Go out and stand on the mount before the LORD." And behold the LORD passed by, and a great and strong wind tore the mountains and broke in pieces the rocks before the LORD, but the LORD was not in the wind. And after the wind an earthquake, but the LORD was not in the earthquake. And after the earthquake a fire, but the LORD was not in the fire. And after the fire the sound of a low whisper.

In the aftermath of the titanic battle at Carmel, when God sent fire on the sacrifice to demonstrate that he alone is God, Elijah goes from his highest high to his lowest low. Discouraged by Jezebel's opposition and afraid for his life, he flees into the wilderness. He journeys forty days to Horeb, also known as Sinai, the mountain of God.

God meets Elijah there. God sends a fierce wind, but he is not in the wind. God sends an earthquake, but he is not in the earthquake. God sends a fire, but he is not in the fire. Finally, God speaks to Elijah with a whisper.

God certainly could have spoken to Elijah in the powerful wind, or in the fearsome earthquake, or in the consuming fire. But he chose to speak to Elijah with a whisper. A gentle and soft whisper.

It's hard to hear a whisper, especially if you're talking, busy, or hurrying. It's hard to hear a whisper if you spend the entire day with no silence in your life, if there is always a radio, a TV, a CD, or a person right there with you.

Solitude. Silence. Stillness. Quiet. We in the West aren't so good at these. We don't tend to value these so much. We are active go-getters, can-do folks, people on the move. We live our lives immersed in an atmosphere of noise, music, and talking.

But the whisper is God talking to our hearts and giving us advice, guidance, and assurance.

Some of us, myself included, aren't so good at listening to God. We think prayer is all about talking to God, but talking to God is just part of prayer. There's also a time to be quiet and still before God, and hear the whisper.

1 Chronicles 29:11

*Yours, O LORD, is the greatness and the power and
the glory and the victory and the majesty, for all that
is in the heavens and in the earth is yours. Yours
is the kingdom, O LORD, and you are
exalted as head above all.*

David has come to the end of his forty-year reign as king. In fact, he is at the end of his life. He gathers the people together in a final convocation. He tells them that he has generously donated his personal fortune for the Temple of God, a temple that his son Solomon will build. The people then give generously and joyfully. Everyone is excited and rejoicing.

At this point of high emotional fervor, David lifts his voice in prayer. He praises God for his unspeakable greatness, power, glory, majesty, and splendor. Reading this prayer, you get the impression that David is overwhelmed by the greatness of God, that his heart is bursting with love and gratitude, that he lacks the words to adequately express praise for his God.

If David was anything, he was a worshipper. David exuded this exalted view of God. David had this burning heart that was lost in love, wonder, and praise of his God.

And here at this solemn moment, he cannot hold back his heart. He cannot not worship. He erupts in a burst of heartfelt praise. Listen to his heart:

> Blessed are you, O LORD, the God of Israel our father, forever and ever. Yours, O LORD, is the greatness and the power and the glory and the victory and the majesty, for all that is in the heavens and in the earth is yours. Yours is the kingdom, O LORD, and you are exalted as head above all. Both riches and honor come from you, and you rule over all. In your hand are power and might, and in your hand it is to make great and to give strength to all. And now we thank you, our God, and praise your glorious name. (1 Chron. 29:10-13)

This is what worshippers do. They have seen the glory of God. They have tasted the goodness of God. They have felt the love of God, and they worship.

With all their hearts, they worship.

God is seeking these kinds of worshippers: worshippers who cannot not worship, people with burning hearts.

1 Chronicles 29:14

But who am I, and what is my people, that we should be able thus to offer willingly? For all things come from you, and of your own have we given you.

Other than God himself, is there a better example of a giving heart in the entire Bible?

David has given his personal fortune for the future temple. The people have responded with their own generosity. Everyone has given with a sense of deep gladness.

With a heart brimming with joy, David can only praise his God:

> Lord, it is our privilege to give to you. Who am I, and who are my people, that we have this privilege of giving like this?
>
> For Lord, it all belongs to you. It all comes from you. When we give, we are only giving back to you. We are only giving what you gave to us. We are only giving what belongs to you still.
>
> For Lord, you own it all. It all belongs to you. You are the owner, and we are only the messengers.

David teaches us what giving is all about. Giving is a privilege. We are privileged to give back to God, to give back to God what came from his hand.

Sometimes when I give (I hate to admit it), I feel virtuous or noble, not privileged. But David, through Holy Scripture, thrashes this haughty attitude. When it comes to giving, the act is a privilege.

To the God who has freely given us everything—life, breath, heaven, forgiveness, eternity, and his own dear son—to this God, we have the privilege of giving in glad gratitude.

When it comes to giving, giving back to our gracious God, remember that it is a privilege.

2 Chronicles 7:14

If my people who are called by my name humble themselves, and pray and seek my face and turn from their wicked ways, then I will hear from heaven and will forgive their sin and heal their land.

2 Chronicles 7:14 is addressed specifically to the people of Israel, but surely the passage shows God's heart for any people and any land.

What does God want from us?

> First, we must humble ourselves. We must admit that God is God and we are not. We must submit to God and come to him in brokenness and repentance.
>
> Second, we must pray and seek God's face. No revival or awakening comes without prayer. Extensive, fervent, corporate, continual, and united prayer.
>
> It is worth noting that the prayer here is focused on seeking God's face and not God's hand. We are seeking God for himself, not for what he gives us. We are locked in on God's glory, not on our need.
>
> Third, we must turn from our wicked ways. God wants obedience, not religious ceremony. We cannot just say the words and pray the prayers of repentance. We must also do the deeds of repentance and obey God in every part of life.

If we do these three things, then God promises to respond in three ways. First, he will hear us. He will hear those prayers. Second, he will forgive our sin. He will remove our sin as far as the east is from the west. And third, God will heal our land. He will pour out his favor and blessing upon us.

In 1861, Abraham Lincoln had just been elected president and the nation was teetering on the brink of war. There was cruel slavery in the land. The president faced widespread opposition and hostility. He issued a proclamation for our country, a proclamation that expressed the spirit of the Chronicles passage above:

> Whereas a joint committee of both houses of Congress has waited on the President of the United States

and requested him to recommend a day of public humiliation, prayer and fasting to be observed by the people of the United States with religious solemnities, and the offering of fervent supplications to Almighty God for the safety and welfare of these states, his blessing on their arms, and a speedy restoration of peace. And whereas it is fit and becoming in all people at all times to acknowledge and revere the supreme government of God, to bow in humble submission to his chastisement, to confess and deplore their sins and transgression, in the full conviction that the fear of the Lord is the beginning of wisdom, and to pray with all fervency and contrition for the pardon of their offenses and for a blessing upon their present and prospective action. Therefore I, Abraham Lincoln, President of the United States, do appoint the last Thursday in September next as a day of humiliation, prayer and fasting, for all the people of the nation. And I do earnestly recommend to all the people, and especially to all ministers and teachers of religion of all denominations, and to all heads of families, to observe and keep that day, according to their several creeds and modes of worship, in all humility, and with all religious solemnity, to the end that the united prayer of the nation may ascend to the Throne of Grace, and bring down plentiful blessings upon our country.

May that be our prayer today, and may God grant it.

2 Chronicles 20:12b

For we are powerless against this great horde that is coming against us. We do not know what to do, but our eyes are on you.

The vast enemy army was bearing down. Things looked bleak. Annihilation loomed dark and heavy.

King Jehoshaphat and the people gather to fast, pray, and cry out to God. The prayer they pray is one of the classics in the Bible.

Why? Why do they fast, pray, and call out to God? They are desperate. Their situation is hopeless–unless God intervenes.

They pour their hearts out to God, then King Jehoshaphat concludes the prayer by saying, "For we are powerless against this great horde that is coming against us. We do not know what to do, but our eyes are on you."

The king is expressing their desperate situation and their utter dependence upon God. Specifically, they lack power ("For we are powerless against this great horde that is coming against us") and they lack wisdom ("We do not know what to do") (2 Chron. 20:12b).

King Jehoshaphat is teaching us how to pray when we face overwhelming problems:

> Lord, we have no power in ourselves to take care of this problem. Lord, we don't know what to do. But Father, our eyes are on you. Lord, we're looking to you. Lord, you do what we cannot do.

That's how to pray. That's dependence. That's desperation. That's humility. That's trust.

Do you have an overwhelming problem in your marriage? With parenting? At work? With in-laws? With finances? With health? With mental illness? With addiction? Trying to reach a lost friend? A stubborn habit?

> O Lord, I have no power to solve this. I don't know what to do. But my eyes are upon you.

This is how to pray. This is the prayer that God loves.

Esther 4:16

If I perish, I perish.

Courage is not the absence of fear. Courage is doing the right thing in the presence of fear.

In the book of Esther, we see the courage of a young Jewish queen who faces a desperate crisis. The evil official, Haman, has obtained King Xerxes's approval to annihilate all the Jews in the kingdom. Imagine! An entire people! The times are desperate. Jews throughout the empire weep, fast, and cry out to God.

Mordecai, who raised Queen Esther, gets word to her of the looming genocide and asks her to go to the king and beg for mercy, but there is a gigantic obstacle. No one can approach the king unless summoned or they will be executed. Moreover, the king is volatile and hotheaded, as the last queen learned the hard way.

What would you do? You are in your early twenties, you find yourself the queen of the vast Persian Empire, and you face a crisis that could cost you your life.

Mordecai challenges her:

> For if you keep silent at this time, relief and deliverance will rise for the Jews from another place, but you and your father's house will perish. And who knows whether you have not come to the kingdom for such a time as this? (Est. 4:14)

Esther's reply is a classic in the annals of courage:

> Go, gather all the Jews to be found in Susa, and hold a fast on my behalf, and do not eat or drink for three days, night or day. I and my young women will also fast as you do. Then I will go to the king, though it is against the law, and if I perish, I perish. (Est. 4:16)

There was a real possibility that Esther could die, but Esther decides to take the risk.

Courage is not the absence of fear. Courage is doing the right thing despite the presence of fear.

Perhaps you are in a fearful situation right now. Maybe God is calling you to trust him for your job, your wayward teenager, or for a health crisis. Perhaps God is calling you to obey him with sexual purity, with faithfulness to your marriage vows, with your giving, or with confronting an addiction. Maybe God is calling you to share your faith with a coworker, start a ministry, challenge someone, get help for an addiction, or join a small group at your church.

Like Esther, will you decide to act courageously, despite your fears? Will you say with Esther, "If I perish, I perish?"

Job 1:1

There was a man in the land of Uz whose name was Job, and that man was blameless and upright, one who feared God and turned away from evil.

Never assume that your suffering is due to sin in your life. Sometimes when we undergo trials and adversity, we wonder, "What did I do to deserve this?" Quite possibly, we did nothing to deserve it.

We live in a fallen world. This is earth, not heaven. The world is broken. Bad things happen to good people, and some of the worst things happen to some of the best people.

Suffering and pain have multiple causes. Sometimes our suffering is primarily due to sin. If so, it will usually be pretty obvious. If you get drunk and fall down a flight of stairs, yes, your pain is caused by your sin.

The book of Job decisively refutes the idea that all of our suffering is due to our sins. Job suffered more than most people have ever suffered. I cannot fathom losing ten children. Plus, he lost his health and most of his wealth. Job's pain was excruciating.

Was all of his pain due to his sin? His friends assumed it was. At the end of the book, God rebukes Job's friends. "My anger burns against you and against your two friends, for you have not spoken of me what is right, as my servant Job has" (Job 42:7).

In fact, Job was far from being an egregious sinner. He was the single godliest man in all the earth. As God says to Satan, "Have you considered my servant Job, that there is none like him on the earth, a blameless and upright man, who fears God and turns away from evil?" (Job 1:8).

The next time you assume that your suffering is always due to your sins or that the suffering of someone else is due to theirs, think of Job. Better yet, think of Jesus. Jesus endured agonizing pain, and yet he was the sinless and holy Son of God.

Job 1:21

*And he said, "Naked I came from my mother's womb,
and naked shall I return. The LORD gave, and the
LORD has taken away; blessed be the
name of the LORD."*

Despite his immense pain, despite his disappointments and complaints, Job refused to stop trusting God. Job refused to renounce God, turn away from God, or ignore God.

Near the beginning of the book of Job, we read Job's remarkable response:

> Then Job arose and tore his robe and shaved his head and fell on the ground and worshiped. And he said, 'Naked I came from my mother's womb, and naked shall I return. The LORD gave, and the LORD has taken away; blessed be the name of the LORD.' In all this, Job did not sin or charge God with wrong. (Job 1:20-22)

Much later, he exclaims:

> For I know that my Redeemer lives, and at the last he will stand upon the earth.
> And after my skin has been thus destroyed, yet in my flesh I shall see God. (Job 19:25-26)

Suffering is always a test of faith for the believer. That was the reason Job suffered—to test his faith. Satan had said to God, "But stretch out your hand and touch all that he has, and he will curse you to your face" (Job 1:11).

It is the same for you and me. Will we trust God despite our suffering and pain, or will we not?

If you choose to trust God, what will that look like? You too will refuse to renounce God, turn away from God, or ignore God. You will keep praying, even if your prayers are full of pain and questions. At least you're talking.

Moreover, you will not insist on answers. As it says in Proverbs 3:5-6, you can ask for them, but you probably won't get them until heaven. Ultimately, you need faith, not answers. You need trust, not understanding.

Finally, you will cling to God, no matter how dark it gets. You will stand on the promises of God's Word: that God is right there with you, that God cares, that God is still good, that God will have the final word, and that it will be good.

Will you trust God in your time of suffering, or will you not?

I can only imagine that Job, throughout eternity, is so glad that he chose to trust his God. And so will you.

Psalm 1:2

But his delight is in the law of the LORD,
and on his law he meditates day and night.

My favorite dessert would have to be blackberry cobbler with Blue Bell ice cream on top—plenty of ice cream. I take great delight in that dessert.

God calls us to delight in his Word. To savor it, to enjoy it, to revel in it. But perhaps you are thinking to yourself, "If I am honest with myself, I don't really delight in God's Word." Reading God's Word is more duty than delight.

Let me encourage you by letting you know that you are not alone. The Bible is not an easy book. Reading the Bible is an acquired taste, but you can develop a delight in God's Word. I have two simple suggestions to help.

First, read the Bible every day. Don't wait until you delight in it. If you wait to read the Bible when you delight in it, then you won't ever get started. Read it daily and ask God to speak to you. Ask God to meet you there in the pages. Don't decide each day whether or not you will read the Bible that day. Decide right now before God that, by his strength, you will read the Bible every day.

Second—and this is big—engage fully when you read it. Engage with God. Pray about what you're reading. Talk with God about it. Confess, give thanks, and call out. Be active. Be alert. Be praying. Be all there.

The more engaged you are, the better you will like it. If you just read to get through the passage or to check a box in your mind, then it's boring. But if you fully engage with God as you read, then it becomes delightful.

The second line of this passage calls us to meditate on God's Word. The term "meditate" is used elsewhere to mean to mutter, to talk lowly, or to chat with yourself. That's the idea. Be vocal as you read and pray. Talk to yourself. Engage with God. Meditate on God's Word.

If you do this, day in and day out over a long period of time, what will happen? You will thrive and flourish. The next verse gives the glad result of delighting in God's Word.

> He is like a tree
> planted by streams of water,
> that yields its fruit in its season
> and its leaf does not wither.
> In all that he does, he prospers. (Ps. 1:3)

71

Psalm 8:3-4

When I look at your heavens, the work of your
fingers, the moon and the stars, which you have set in
place, what is man that you are mindful of him,
and the son of man that you care for him?

It must have been a clear night in Palestine when David looked up at the sky full of stars and wondered. Humbled by what he saw above (nothing in creation is as humbling as the stars), he wondered at God's handiwork. He wondered at the glory and the greatness of God reflected in the night sky. But mostly, he wondered how a God so big could care about us.

If David only knew the half of it! If David had a true grasp of the size of the universe, if he had some notion that there are billions of galaxies, each containing billions of stars, how much more amazed he would be?

If you grabbed a handful of sand, you would pick up around 10,000 grains of sand. That's a lot of grains of sand. Then think about all the sand on all the beaches around the world, and all the sand in all the deserts of our planet. That is one big number! Now think about how there are more stars in the sky than grains of sand on our planet. In fact, there are ten times more stars than grains of sand.

When we contemplate the size of our universe, our minds reel. The God who created all of that, with his mere command, is so big. He is, indeed, without any limits whatsoever to his greatness and power. He is the infinite God.

But how can a God so great care for mere humans? How could a God so big even notice those odd creatures living on one tiny planet in one medium-sized galaxy?

God, do you really take notice of me? Are you mindful of me? Do you care about me? The entire Bible shouts, "Yes! A thousand times, yes!" In fact, David goes on to say:

> Yet you have made him a little lower than the heavenly
> beings and crowned him with glory and honor.
> You have given him dominion over the works of
> your hands; you have put all things under his feet.
> (Ps. 8:5-6)

God has bestowed upon us dignity, majesty, glory, and honor.

God has given us authority over the earth, the animals, the birds, and the fish. We bear God's image. We reflect his glory. He has placed eternity in our hearts. We will live forever.

We mean so much to the infinite God that he sent his own eternal son to become one of us, so that he could die on a cross and win our salvation. So great is God's love for us. So great is God's love for you.

Stand back and wonder.

Psalm 16:11

You have made known to me the path of life; in your presence there is fullness of joy; at your right hand are pleasures forevermore.

Life. Joy. Pleasures.
That's what God wants for you. That's the kind of God he is. Not in small measure, mind you. No, God wants you to experience life in all its richness, joy in all its fullness, and pleasures in all their abundance.

The God of the Bible, the God of all creation, the God revealed in Jesus Christ is the happiest person in the universe, and he wants happiness for you as well. A deep, abiding, and lasting happiness, no matter the circumstances of life or the storms that assail you.

He is the life-giving, joy-exuding, pleasure-delighting God. He is indeed the ultimate hedonist. God is all about joy, both his and yours.

Pastor and writer John Ortberg commented, "Joy is at the heart of God's plan for human beings. The reason for this is worth pondering awhile. Joy is at the heart of God himself. We will never understand the significance of joy in human life until we understand its importance to God. I suspect that most of us seriously underestimate God's capacity for joy."

Do you see God this way? Or have you bought into Satan's lie that God is a cosmic Scrooge and out to get you? Be careful of that lie. It can ruin your life and your eternity.

God aims to fill you with joy. He does not seek to drip a little joy in your life or sprinkle some joy upon you. No, he aims to flood your soul with as much joy as you can hold.

The closer you get to God, the more you experience joy, and the farther you go from God, the less you experience joy. For joy, true joy, deep and lasting joy, is found only in God himself.

It has been well stated that "Joy is the surest sign of the presence of God." The presence of God is the presence of joy. The absence of God is the absence of joy.

What does this tell us about our vain pursuit of happiness in other things, in houses or cars, in money or investments, in careers or retirement, in marriage or kids, in sports or hobbies, or in beauty or fitness? Can joy be found there? It cannot. Only if we first find our delight in God himself can we find any real delight in the gifts of God.

C.S. Lewis taught us, "God cannot give us a happiness and peace apart from himself, because it is not there. There is no such thing."

I ask you again, do you see your God this way? Do you see him as the joy-delighting, joy-giving, joy-bursting God, as the one who longs to fill you with joy? As the only source of real happiness in the universe?

See your God.

Psalm 18:1

I love you, O LORD, my strength.

What is prayer all about? What is the essence of prayer?
Is the essence of prayer talking to God? Asking things of God? Praising God? Giving thanks to God? Listening to God? Confessing our sin to God?

All of these things are important, but I could not say that any of them is the essence of prayer.

Prayer, at its core, is all about loving God. Prayer is connecting with God, drawing close to God, communing with God.

Prayer is all about a love relationship, a love relationship between you and—get this—the God of the universe. He already loves you perfectly, infinitely, and outlandishly. And you, ideally, are falling in love with him more and more. You have fallen for him.

Prayer is the overflow of this love. And right here we come to the essence of prayer: the overflow of a loving relationship between you and your God.

Lovers talk. Lovers hang out together. Lovers enjoy each other's presence.

David felt this love. Oh, did he ever. "I love you, O LORD, my strength" (Ps. 18:1).

What about you? Do you feel this love? Deep within your heart, do you sense the stirrings of love? This thirst for God, this hunger for God, this spontaneous outburst of your soul that says, "I love you, O LORD, my strength" (Ps. 18:1).

This is prayer. Not religious duty. Not checking a box. Not clocking in. Not ritual or liturgy. Not talking God into something.

Prayer is the overflow of love.

"I love you, O LORD, my strength" (Ps. 18:1).

Psalm 18:2

*The LORD is my rock and my fortress and my
deliverer, my God, my rock, in whom I take refuge, my
shield, and the horn of my salvation, my stronghold.*

David faced some fearful situations. He fought the lion and the
bear when he was a shepherd. He faced the giant Goliath, who
wanted to crush him. King Saul wanted him dead. His own son
plotted against him. David faced foes of all sorts.

We too face fearful situations at times. The giants in our
life may be different than David's, but our giants are fearsome
too. Unemployment, debt, divorce, discouragement, depression,
despair, cancer, a rebellious teenager, addiction, cancer, back
pain, loneliness, and more.

Life can be so hard, so difficult; at times, it can be
overwhelming. Do what David did and depend upon the Lord.
Run to the Lord. Call out to the Lord.

Look again at this remarkable testimony of trust and see God
the way David saw him:

> The LORD is my rock and my fortress and my deliverer,
> my God, my rock, in whom I take refuge,
> my shield, and the horn of my salvation, my
> stronghold. (Ps. 18:2)

It is amazing how many expressions David uses to make his
point about the faithfulness of God to deliver us. Seven times in
one verse: my rock, my fortress, my deliverer, my rock (maybe
he needed to hear it again), my refuge, my shield, the horn of my
salvation, and my stronghold.

David exclaims for the entire world to hear, "That's God.
That's *my* God. That's what my God has been to me." And that's
what God can be for you. Run to him. Call to him. Depend upon
him:

> When troubled, cry out: the Lord is my rock.
> When discouraged, cry out: the Lord is my stronghold.
> When weary, cry out: the Lord is my strength.
> When fearful, cry out: the Lord is my deliverer.
> When overwhelmed, cry out: the Lord is my fortress.

When worried, cry out: the Lord is my refuge.
When alone, cry out: the Lord is the horn of my salvation.
When tempted, cry out: the Lord is my rock.

For every need, on every occasion, cry out to God, who is your rock and your refuge.

Psalm 19:1

The heavens declare the glory of God,
and the sky above proclaims his handiwork.

The Creator calls to us through his creation. When we gaze up at the wide blue sky, when we feel the warmth of the morning sun, when we see the crescent moon on a clear night, when ominous thunderclouds roll in, when streaks of lightning flash across the night, when we are out in the wild and endless stars crowd the night sky: it is in these moments that we see the thumbprint of God, hear his voice, sense his glory, and feel his power.

What do the heavens tell us about God? They tell us that God exists, that there is a Creator behind the creation. Deep down, we know that there is an unseen Creator.

Moreover, they tell us that God is big, so big. And as we learn more and more about the size of the universe, our appreciation of God's power and greatness grows ever deeper. This God, this Creator, is immense beyond words.

The heavens also tell us that God is good. He is the God who "makes his sun rise on the evil and the good, and sends rain on the just and on the unjust" (Matt. 5:45). He is good and gracious to all that he has made.

The heavens tell us much more: that God is faithful, that God is wise, that God is unpredictable, that God is consistent, that God is majestic, that God is kind. He is the sovereign and infinite God. He is the God of overwhelming beauty and majesty. As Simone Weil put it, "The beauty of the world is Christ's tender smile for us coming through matter."

How great is our God.

When we see the glory of God in the heavens, we are humbled, undone, and thunderstruck. This is God and he must be worshiped. This is God and he must be obeyed. This is God and he must be loved.

Psalm 19:7a

The law of the LORD is perfect,
reviving the soul.

At times, we grow weary. We are confused and lonely. We struggle with doubts and fears. We battle disappointment and anger, guilt, and shame. We are so human.

In any and all of these dark times, flee to God and his Word. Meet God in the pages of Scripture. Let the Word of God wash over you, cleanse you, and heal you. The Spirit of God will take the Word of God and revive your soul.

How does this happen? Why does this happen? Simple—this book is alive. It pulsates with life, God's life. A dead, dry book of theology? Hardly. Rather, it is aflame with life-giving power.

When we read this book, we breathe the breath of God. Our soul is renewed, restored, rejuvenated.

John White was a psychiatrist, counselor, missionary, pastor, and writer. He penned eloquent words on the power of Scripture to revive his soul, and below is an excerpt from his book *The Fight*:

> In the darkest periods of my life when everything seemed hopeless, I would struggle in the grey dawns of many faraway countries to grasp the basic truths of Scripture passages. I looked for no immediate answers to my problems. Only did I sense intuitively that I was drinking drafts from a fountain that gave life to my soul.
>
> Slowly as I grappled with textual and theological problems, a strength grew deep within me. Foundations cemented themselves to an other-worldly rock beyond the reach of time and space, and I became strong and more alive. If I could write poetry about it I would. If I could sing through paper, I would flood your soul with the glorious melodies that express what I have found. I cannot exaggerate for there are no expressions majestic enough to tell of the glory I have seen or of the wonder of finding that I, a neurotic, unstable, middle-aged man have my feet firmly planted in eternity and breathe the air of

heaven. And all this has come to me through a careful study of Scripture.

That's exactly how I feel about God's Word. Without it, I would not have made it. "The law of the LORD is perfect, reviving the soul" (Ps. 19:7a).

Psalm 20:7

Some trust in chariots and some in horses,
but we trust in the name of the LORD our God.

Lurking within us is the persistent tendency to trust in other things besides God.

We all encounter a steady stream of challenges and burdens, and sometimes these problems feel overwhelming. Unemployment, financial pressure, depression, a rebellious teenager, the death of a loved one, a difficult decision, a feeling of failure, debilitating back pain, trouble in a marriage, a big project at work, and so much more. In John 16:33, Jesus taught us that we would face tribulations in this world.

When we face these challenges, do we trust in God, or do we trust in other things? Do we trust our own efforts, our own resources, and our own thinking? Do we first look to other people to guide us, rescue us, or protect us? Do we rely on our careful research, our diligent efforts, our network, and our abilities? Is our reliance on the best doctors and wisest counselors?

God can use any of these things, of course, and he frequently does. But in our heart of hearts, where is our trust? Where is our confidence? Is our trust in God to guide us and deliver us, or is our trust in ourselves or other people? Do we feel a deep sense of dependence on the Lord? Do we recognize that God may use some of these resources, but our ultimate trust is in God alone? Do we feel deeply that we need the Lord?

God delights in the man or woman who chooses to trust in him. God loves it.

It would have been easy for a powerful king like David to trust in his chariots and his horses. It would be expected for a brilliant general like David to trust in his strategy and cunning. It would be easy for a mighty ruler like David to look to his officers and his army.

But that was not the way David lived. Others might trust in their own resources, but not David. Not the man after God's own heart. As for David, he would trust his God. "Some trust in chariots and some in horses, but we trust in the name of the LORD our God" (Ps. 20:7).

May it be the same for you and me.

Psalm 22:1

My God, my God, why have you forsaken me?

Psalm 22 describes a time of intense suffering in David's life. He is on the run. Perhaps Saul is pursuing him. David is desperate and cries out to God.

Little does David know that these words the Holy Spirit puts on his tongue describe the crucifixion of God's own son a thousand years in the future. What's even more remarkable is that David describes crucifixion, which he had never seen, which had not even been invented, as a form of execution. David's language for his own suffering is vividly echoed in the Gospels to describe the crucifixion of Jesus: "My God, my God, why have you forsaken me?" (Matt. 23:46).

Jesus would utter these same words from the cross. When he took our sin, he was separated from the Father, for the first time in all eternity. Their perfect oneness and community was shattered, and it was incredibly painful for Jesus. "All who see me mock me; they make mouths at me; they wag their heads" (Ps. 22:7).

Matthew 27:39 describes Jesus: "And those who passed by derided him, wagging their heads." "He trusts in the LORD; let him deliver him; let him rescue him, for he delights in him" (Ps. 22:8).

In Matthew 27:43 we read: "He trusts in God; let God deliver him now, if he desires him. For he said, 'I am the Son of God.'"

"I am poured out like water, and all my bones are out of joint" (Ps. 22:14). This describes the physical collapse of Jesus's body on a cross. "They have pierced my hands and feet" (Ps. 22:16). For David, this was figurative language for an attack. For Jesus, this was literally true on the cross.

"They divide my garments among them, and for my clothing they cast lots" (Ps. 22:18). This exact event happened at the cross.

Psalm 22 is the psalm of the cross, which was figurative for David and literal for the Son of David. It was true for David in a limited sense, but true for the Son of David in the ultimate sense.

What a remarkable portrait of Christ's suffering on the cross, given that it was painted a thousand years before Christ even came and before crucifixion was even used. God is the sovereign

God, and he is working his plan, a plan that culminates with a savior dying for sinners.

Psalm 23:1

The LORD is my shepherd, I shall not want.

Psalm 23 is one of the best-loved psalms. It is a stunningly beautiful and powerful example of David's childlike trust in his God. We all long for this kind of trust.

It begins here with the very first line. David sees the Lord, the almighty, infinite, holy, and sovereign God, as his shepherd. Though he is the great and awesome God, David knew that God tenderly watched over him like a shepherd caring for his sheep. The Lord is a shepherd. In fact, David was more personal in saying, "The Lord is *my* shepherd."

What was David saying about God? He was saying that God cares about me. He knows me. He understands me. He watches over me. He protects me. He guides me. He is gentle with me. He nourishes me. He comforts me. He fights for me. He is attentive to me. He is for me. He stays near me. He will never leave me. He would die for me. He's my shepherd.

Whatever the need is, he can meet it. Whatever the burden is, he can carry it. Whatever the decision is, he can guide it. Whatever the problem is, he can handle it. Whatever the hurt is, he can heal it. He's my shepherd.

When the Lord is your shepherd, you can trust in God no matter what happens. He is watching over you. He is right there with you. He will see you through. He's your shepherd.

You won't lack anything you really need. If it is a good thing for you, you will get it. You will not be in want of anything when the Lord is your shepherd.

Perhaps David's greatness was in the way he saw God. "The LORD is my shepherd" (Ps. 23:1).

In a previous entry, A.W. Tozer taught us that how we see God shapes our entire life: "What comes into our minds when we think about God is the most important thing about us."

Do you see God this way? Is the Lord your shepherd?

Psalm 23:2

He makes me lie down in green pastures.
He leads me beside still waters.

God is a good God. God is like the shepherd who takes care of his sheep, who takes them to lush, green meadows so they can eat to their hearts' content and lie down and rest.

God is like the shepherd who leads his sheep to the quiet stream so they can drink the clear, cool mountain water.

That's what God is like. He's the good shepherd. He's the shepherd who provides for us, who nourishes us, who takes care of us, who gives us what we really need. He's the shepherd who refreshes us, restores us, and replenishes us.

The only questions for us are: Do we follow our shepherd? Do we follow him faithfully? Do we follow him even when the path is hard and the way is dark? Do we follow him even if we cannot see where we are going? Do we follow our shepherd no matter what because we see him as a shepherd? Do we follow him because we see him as the good shepherd and we trust him?

God is the God of the lush green meadow. He is the God of the clear mountain stream.

Do you see God the way David saw him? He is my shepherd and he is good to me.

Psalm 23:3a

He restores my soul.

God says to you: I will restore your soul. I will reach into the deepest part of your soul, to the place that nothing else can touch, and I will restore your soul. I will heal your heart. I will refresh your spirit.

You need that, don't you?

> When you are weary and burdened, you need your soul restored.
> When you are overwhelmed and undone, you need your soul restored.
> When you feel guilt and shame, you need your soul restored.
> When you are assailed by fear and worry, you need your soul restored.
> When you feel wounded and hurt, you need your soul restored.
> When you feel alone and rejected, you need your soul restored.
> When you feel angry and rejected, you need your soul restored.

At all of these times and more, you need God to do for you what you cannot do for yourself: heal your soul.

Nothing else can do it. Not entertainment. Not a weekend off. Not sports. Not exercise. Not television. Not a vacation. Not shopping. Not your hobby. Nothing else can restore your soul.

But the God who created the universe, the God who breathed life into Adam—he can do it. He can breathe life into your soul. He can make you alive again.

It happens when you meet with God. When you connect with God. When you draw close to God. When you are alone with God. When you gather with God's people and worship.

Jesus, the Good Shepherd, says to you even now, "Come to me, all who are weary and heavy-laden, and I will give you rest" (Matt. 11:28).

Christ can restore your soul.

Psalm 23:4

*Even though I walk through the valley of the shadow
of death, I will fear no evil, for you are with me;
your rod and your staff, they comfort me.*

In this classic expression of childlike trust, what is David saying to his God?

> Lord, because you are my shepherd, I will not fear. Lord, because you are watching over me, because you will protect me, because you will defend me, because you will fight for me, because you will take care of me, I will not fear.
>
> Lord, even if the valley is filled with darkness, difficulty, danger, or death, I will not fear.
>
> Lord, because you will be right there with me in that valley, I will not fear. Because you are beside me, behind me, above me, in front of me, under me, over me, in me, because you are right there beside me, invisible and yet more real than life, I will not fear.
>
> Lord, I will rest in you. I will not surrender to the fears that assail me. I will not fret and worry myself sick. I will not be afraid, because you are with me in the valley.

Are you in the valley right now? A valley of loneliness? Rejection? Failure? Divorce? Unemployment? Cancer? Depression? Addiction? Physical pain? Financial ruin? Overwhelming grief? Conflict? Mistreatment?

If so, then hear the voice of the Shepherd: "I will be with you. Whatever you are going through, I will be there. No matter how dark the valley, I am right there beside you. I will not leave you. Do not be afraid. I will see you through."

Hear the voice of your Shepherd.

Psalm 23:5b

You anoint my head with oil;
my cup overflows.

God loves a grateful heart.

David had such a heart. He could look at his life and smile at God's goodness to him and blessing on him. Yes, his life had been hard; at times, his life had been excruciating. But God had been good to him, so good. God had filled his cup to the brim, and it was overflowing.

David had a grateful heart.

What about you? Has your life been hard, even excruciating at times? It probably has. It's the way life is on this side of heaven. But God has been good to you, so good. Your cup overflows.

Could you not pray this prayer?

Lord, you have been a Shepherd to me.
You have cared for me and provided for me.
You have loved me even when I ignored you.
Your eye has always been upon me.
You have offered me unlimited grace.
You have sent your own Son to die for me.
You have freely given your Spirit to live in me.
You give me access to you at any time.
You have given me life and breath.
You have brought wonderful people in my life who care about me.
You freely forgive me when I fail you.
You strengthen me when I am weak and needy.
You hear my prayers.
You delight in my love.
You have given me a secure and eternal future with you.
You have rescued me from the pit of hell.
You have chosen me.
You have gifted me.
You have called me to a meaningful place in the great cosmic battle against the enemy.
You have protected me.

You want me.
You have given me food and shelter.
You have been so good to me.
My cup overflows.

Psalm 23:6

Surely goodness and mercy shall follow me
all the days of my life, and I shall dwell
in the house of the LORD forever.

The "Mount Everest" of Psalm 23 is in verse 6. What kind of person makes a statement like this? "Surely goodness and mercy shall follow me all the days of my life"? Only a person who knows his Shepherd would be able to make such a claim.

David is not naïve. He is not too young to understand. He knows, all too well, that life can be tough, unfair, and cruel. He has already lost three kids.

But David knows that God is not like life. God is never unfair or cruel.

Others may hurt us and do us harm. We may hurt ourselves with our own sin. But not God—God will pursue us in love.

God's goodness and mercy will follow us all the days of our lives. Not just some of the days, but all the days. Every single day, we will experience God's bounty. We will drink it in like refreshing water.

And beyond that, we will dwell in the house of the Lord forever. There is no doubt about our future. No uncertainty or insecurity. We have a secure destiny—with God.

What an expression of trust. Every phrase of this final verse oozes with trust. David had walked with God for all his life. He had learned, often through painful experience, that God is good, that God can be trusted, that God's goodness and love will follow him all his life. Surely, surely this will take place.

What kind of person talks this way? Only a person who knows his God.

Psalm 24:1

The earth is the LORD's and the fullness thereof,
the world and those who dwell therein.

Wise people understand the difference between the owner and the manager or steward. Wise people understand that the manager owns nothing; everything belongs to the owner and the manager is only there to take care of the owner's property.

When it comes to things in my charge, things in my possession, things in my life, I am the manager, not owner. It all belongs to God.

It all belongs to God for a very simple reason: He made it. He made it all. He made the world and everything in it. He made the universe.

It all belongs to God. Sun and stars. Oceans and mountains. Trees and flowers. Birds and fish. You and me. It all belongs to God.

All that I have does not actually belong to me. It belongs to God. I am its steward, not owner. God's the boss, I'm the servant. I take care of God's things, not my things. Money, house, car, retirement account, health, body, and abilities—all that I have belongs to God.

I am God's servant, holding things lightly, living for eternity, representing my King, desiring only to please him, traveling light and free.

Wise people understand the difference between the owner and the manager.

Psalm 27:4

One thing have I asked of the LORD, that will I seek
after: that I may dwell in the house of the LORD all
the days of my life, to gaze upon the beauty of
the LORD and to inquire in his temple.

This is David's heart for God. This is David's passion for God. "Lord, this is the one thing I long for, the one thing I yearn for. More than anything else, more than everything else, I want you. Lord, that may I be with you, may gaze at you, may draw close to you."

Because David had an enormous passion for God, he longed to meet God, to be with God.

We need to take time with God, plenty of time. We should take unhurried time with God daily.

Why should believers do this? This is why I do it: First, I want to. I love being alone with the Lord and drawing close. It's the highlight of my day. It's the highest privilege of my life.

Second, God wants it. Whether or not I want to be with God, God wants to be with me. Any parent of a teenager can relate. God wants to be with us because he loves us.

Third, I need it desperately. For my sanity, for my emotional and spiritual health, for my soul's restoration—I need it, or I will run dry.

Fourth, this is the purpose of human life: to know God and love him. And this won't happen apart from daily, unhurried time with God.

Finally, I need to be changed. I need to be rescued from pride, jealousy, self-centeredness, unbelief, hurry, worry, and much more. This won't happen without plenty of time with God.

A.W. Tozer wrote in his book *The Divine Conquest*:

> May not the inadequacy of much of our spiritual experience be traced back to our habit of skipping through the corridors of the kingdom like children through the market place, chattering about everything but pausing to learn the true value of nothing. In my creature impatience I am often caused to wish that there were some way to bring modern Christians into

a deeper spiritual life painlessly by short easy lessons. But such wishes are vain—no short cut exists. God has not bowed to our nervous haste, nor embraced the methods of our machine age. It is well that we accept the hard truth now. The man who would know God must give time to him.

O Lord, stir my heart. Move in my heart. Give me a passion for you. Give me a heart for you. The kind of heart for you that David had. Amen.

Psalm 27:8

You have said, "Seek my face."
My heart says to you,
"Your face, LORD, do I seek."

It is important to seek God's hand. In fact, it is essential. We seek God's hand to provide the things that we need. "Give us this day our daily bread."

We seek God's hand because we need him, because we are dependent upon him, and because we are desperate for him.

This dependence pleases God. It is the opposite of proud self-reliance. Over and over, the Bible tells us: ask, ask, ask. Ask for God's hand.

But there is something even more important than seeking God's hand: seeking God's *face*. That is, seeking God himself. We seek God for who he is, not for what he can do for us. We seek him in order to know him, to love him, to draw close to him, and to be intimate with him.

We worship. We adore. We give thanks. We sing to him. We tell him we love him. We pour out all that's on our heart. A.W. Tozer once wrote: "We are called to an everlasting preoccupation with God."

Stuart Sacks tell this story:

> While I was serving in Paraguay, a Maka Indian named Rafael came to sit on my porch. I was eating and went out to see what he wanted. He responded, "Ham, henek met." Again I asked what I could do for him, but the answer was the same. I understood what he was saying but not its significance: "I don't want anything; I have just come near." I later shared the incident with a local veteran missionary. He explained that it was Rafael's way of honoring me. He really didn't want anything; he just wanted to sit on my porch. He found satisfaction and pleasure just being near me. "What brings you here, my child?" the Lord asks. "Ham, henek met." Doesn't that reveal the heart of true worship?

Yes, we seek God's hand. But first and foremost, we seek God's face.

Psalm 42:1

As a deer pants for flowing streams,
so pants my soul for you, O God.

The deer is desperate for drink. In the dry, arid Middle East, perhaps during a drought, the deer searches and searches for a stream. The thirsty deer is so desperate for water that it pants out of its intense thirst.

The psalmist relies upon this vivid imagery to say, "Lord, that's the way I feel about you. Lord, I long for you. I thirst for you. I yearn for you. Lord, let me meet with you. Let me draw close to you."

The story of the Bible is a love story. It's a story that begins in the heart of God with a deep, unbound, unstoppable love for his people. It's a love that pursues us, woos us, and wins us. It's a love that awakens a responsive love in our hearts.

Never forget: it's not duty, not discipline, not philosophy, but love.

Writer David Bryant was once in Calcutta talking with Mother Teresa. There were great needs not being met, with pain and suffering everywhere. At one point, Bryant asked Mother Teresa, "With the crying needs of Calcutta, how do you keep going?" Mother Teresa replied, "I get up and spend four hours with the Lord every day because he is the deep well and I need to drop my bucket into the well every day."

Four hours may be a bit intimidating for nearly all of us. But we too need time, unhurried time, with the Lord every morning. Jesus is the deep well and we need to drop our buckets into the well every day.

Psalm 46:10

Be still, and know that I am God.
I will be exalted among the nations,
I will be exalted in the earth!

Psalm 46 speaks of a time of turbulence and upheaval, of fear and uncertainty. The psalm begins:

> God is our refuge and strength,
> a very present help in trouble.
> Therefore we will not fear though the earth gives way,
> though the mountains be moved into the heart of the sea,
> though its waters roar and foam,
> and the mountains tremble at its swelling. (Ps. 46: 1-3)

Perhaps this is a time of national calamity—a terrorist attack, a devastating hurricane, or widespread financial collapse.

Or it might be a time of personal calamity—the loss of a job, betrayal by a spouse, the death of a loved one, or a diagnosis of cancer.

At all of those times, hear the voice of God saying, "Be still, and know that I am God."

This is not a time for activity and noise. This is a time for stillness and silence. This is the time to be quiet enough to hear the still, small voice.

At these times, be still and hear the voice of God:

> Know that I am God.
> Know that I am the Almighty.
> Know that I am the infinite and eternal.
> Know that I am God and I rule the universe.
> Know that I am the sovereign God and nothing touches you that does not first pass through my hands.
> Know that I am God and I am bigger than your disaster.
> Know that I am God and I can see you through the valley.
> Know that I am God and I will be with you, right there beside you.
> Know that I am God and I will have the final word.
> Know that I am God.

When the earth collapses, when your world falls apart, be still and know that God is an ever-present help in trouble. Be still and know that God is God.

Psalm 55:22

Cast your burden on the LORD, and he will sustain you; he will never permit the righteous to be moved.

There are times when the burdens of life are so heavy, so difficult, and so onerous that I feel like I might suffocate. The burden is overwhelming. I don't know if I will survive. All I can do is cry out to God in desperation.

This promise in Psalm 55 has been a source of unending strength and encouragement over the years; for problems of all kinds, big and small, I have gone to this passage. How many times have I gone over this verse before the Lord?

"Cast your burden on the LORD." Here it is, Lord. You take it. I cannot carry it. It's too big for me.

"And he will sustain you." Yes, Lord, *you* will hold me up. You alone. Without you, I'm sunk.

"He will never permit the righteous to be moved." Lord, I have no righteousness of my own. But by your grace, I am righteous in Jesus. By your grace, you have made me righteous and right with you. I am one of your holy people and I want to live for you. This promise is for me, Lord, and what a promise it is. You will hold me tight, you will hold me up, and you will hold me steady.

Do you have a burden? When burdens come, don't carry them. Cast them upon the Lord. Let God carry your burdens.

This is a promise to memorize. This is a promise to claim. This is a promise to cling to.

Psalm 63:1

O God, you are my God; earnestly I seek you;
my soul thirsts for you; my flesh faints for you,
as in a dry and weary land where there is no water.

Do you hear David's heart for God in this prayer? His passion, longing, and desire for God? Does it stir you? Does it awaken something deep in your heart?

What makes this psalm especially remarkable is the situation behind it. David is on the run, fleeing from his own son, fleeing for his life. Can you imagine his broken, grief-stricken heart? His own son. And yet here he is, pursuing God with all his heart.

"O God, you are my God." David is saying, "My whole world has unraveled, but you are still my God. You are the Almighty God. You are my Shepherd. You are my God and you will see me through."

"Earnestly I seek you." Not casually, not half-heartedly, but passionately, fervently, and wholeheartedly. This is not religious ritual. This is not duty. This is a love affair. The whole kingdom is at stake, as is David's very life. And yet here he is, seeking God with all his heart. Is this not David's greatness, this passionate heart for God?

"My soul thirsts for you; my flesh faints for you, as in a dry and weary land where there is no water." There is no water in the Judean desert, and David's thirst for water is a picture of his thirst for God. He's saying, "Lord, only you can satisfy the deepest longings of my soul."

I think of Mother Teresa, who was going through a dry period in her spiritual life and yet still had such a passion for Christ that she prayed this prayer: "I want to love you, Jesus, like you have never been loved before."

What hearts for God.

Why do some people have such a rare passion for Christ? I don't know. Ultimately, this kind of heart for God is a gift. Every good thing is a gift from God, but you can ask for this gift. Lord, give me this kind of heart for you. This thirst for you. This love for you.

Psalm 63:2

So I have looked upon you in the sanctuary,
beholding your power and glory.

I find some of the psalms to be so rich. I think of psalms like Psalms 23, 27, 34, 46, 86, 103, 121, and 145, but I think of all psalms, my favorite has to be Psalm 63. Where else in the Bible do you find such a passionate heart for God, especially in the first five or six verses?

Verse 2 is a bit surprising. What does David mean by saying, "I have looked upon you in the sanctuary?" David is in the Judean desert, fleeing for his life from his own son. There is no sanctuary in the desert. Is David referring to the tabernacle back in Jerusalem?

I don't think so. A sanctuary is a place to meet God, and David must have had to find a sanctuary in the desert, a private sanctuary beneath the stars, a place where he could meet with his God and worship.

Above all, David was a worshipper. He could not wait to worship. He could not *not* worship. He would have to find a sanctuary in the desert, a place where he would encounter God, a place to see the power and glory of God.

What about you? Are you a worshipper? Wherever you are, whether at home, in the car, in an airport, on a golf course, or in a hotel room, do you find a sanctuary, a place to worship and pray and sing and listen? Do you find a place to draw close in holy wonder and meet with your God?

Psalm 63:3

Because your steadfast love is better than life,
my lips will praise you.

David had a profound sense of being loved by God. In fact, this was behind David's greatness. Because he felt so deeply loved by God, David was a passionate worshipper. Because he felt so loved by God, David could trust God with overwhelming problems, such as fighting the giant Goliath. Because David felt so loved by God, he could believe God's grace and forgiveness when he had sinned horribly.

Because David felt so loved by God, he could pen lines such as these:

> The LORD is my shepherd,
> I shall not want. (Ps. 23:1)
> Even though I walk
> through the valley of the shadow of death,
> I will fear no evil,
> for you are with me;
> your rod and your staff,
> they comfort me. (Ps. 23:4)
> Surely goodness and mercy shall follow me
> all the days of my life,
> and I shall dwell in the house of the LORD
> forever. (Ps. 23:6)

David's sense of deep love from God was the wellspring of his heart *for* God. David felt so loved by his God that he could pray: "Lord, your love is better than life. Lord, your love is more important to me than life itself. Lord, if I have to choose between your love and life itself, I choose your love. I would rather die than not have your love."

For David, this was not just religious talk. This was not theoretical. David's life was in danger. And yet he cries out, "Lord, your love means more to me than life itself."

St. Augustine once posed the question: If God came to you and offered to meet all of your needs, but told you that you would never see his face, how would you respond? For David, this would have been a no-brainer. To David, God's steadfast love was better than all the rest of life.

What about you? Have you tasted the rich, embracing love of God? Have you encountered the relentless tenderness of Jesus? Has his love overwhelmed you and dazzled you?

Lord, your love is better than life. Therefore, I will praise you.

Psalm 63:4

So I will bless you as long as I live;
in your name I will lift up my hands.

Perhaps this idea of raising your hands in worship is foreign to you. It's not in your background. You're not used to it, and it doesn't feel natural. You don't want to feel pressured to raise your hands. It's not you.

All of that is understandable, but there is more to be said. Deep down, there are times when you want to lift your hands to God. There are times when you want to raise your hands to God above because this is the natural expression of joy and worship in your heart.

You feel something, something deep in your heart. You feel something inside, and you want to give expression to these feelings of joy and praise. You want to give expression with your voice and with your hands. Your hands want to fly up to heaven, or you want to clap, stand, kneel, or dance. You want to express with all you are—heart, voice and body—what you feel inside, the depths of your praise and joy.

Think of a football game. It's the championship. It's a close game, a nail biter. The score is tied. The final seconds are ticking off. Your team throws a desperate pass to the end zone and scores. They win and the whole place erupts. Hands and arms fly up. People shout and holler, clap and roar.

This is no polite golf applause. No one is sitting on their hands. Of course not! We want to give expression to the feelings of our hearts. It's completely normal and appropriate. It's the way God made us.

When I gather in worship with God's people, there are times when I feel so deeply that I must lift my hands to God just as I lift my voice to God. It feels right. It feels good. It feels the way God intended it to feel. Don't feel pressured. Do feel free. Give full voice to the praise and joy that you feel in your heart.

Psalm 63:5

My soul will be satisfied as with fat and rich food,
and my mouth will praise you with joyful lips.

Worship satisfies your soul.

Worship satisfies your soul because God satisfies your soul. Just as delicious food satisfies the stomach, heartfelt worship satisfies the soul.

You are hungry for worship. You are hungry for worship because you are longing for God. In worship, you encounter God.

You are hungry for God because you are made in the image of God. You are an image bearer, an immortal being. Only God can satisfy the soul of an immortal being made in God's image.

In his *Confessions*, Augustine gave expression to his passion for God when he wrote:

> You flashed, you shone;
> and you chased away my blindness.
> You became fragrant;
> and I inhaled and sighed for you.
> I tasted, and now hunger and thirst for you.
> You touched me;
> and I burned for your embrace.

Nothing else will satisfy your soul cravings. Not marriage. Not a child. Not riches. Not things. Not a new car. Not a vacation. Not a dream house. Not a sport or hobby. Not sexual pleasure. Not food. Not alcohol. Not a sleeker body. Not plastic surgery. Not retirement. Not a getaway. Not anything.

Only God.

God alone.

Psalm 86:1

Incline your ear, O LORD, and answer me,
for I am poor and needy.

With these words, David expresses his deep dependence upon God. "Incline your ear, O LORD, and answer me, for I am poor and needy" (Ps. 86:1).

What? David is poor and needy? Isn't David wealthy and powerful beyond words? Is David not king over Israel at the height of Israel's glory?

Yes, David *is* king. So how can he cry out, "I am poor and needy?"

David is referring to spiritual poverty, not financial poverty. This is poverty of spirit. This is the first beatitude in the Sermon on the Mount: "Blessed are the poor in spirit, for theirs is the kingdom of heaven" (Matt. 5:3).

This is the first beatitude because it is the most basic beatitude. This is where our relationship with God begins: with dependence, with humility, with our deep sense of need for God.

David is saying, "Lord, how I need you. I'm totally dependent upon you. If you don't deliver me, I have no chance. If you don't rescue me, I'm sunk. O God, hear my prayer. Hear and answer." David is clearly desperate for God.

Do you feel this way? Do you feel desperate for God? Do you ever feel like saying, "Lord, if you don't intervene, I'm sunk"?

Jackson Senyonga is a pastor in Uganda who has seen revival and transformation in his country. On his trips to the United States, he commented, "You in America are not desperate enough. You are addicted to a spirit of ease and comfort."

O Lord, help us in America to realize how desperate we really are.

Psalm 90:1

LORD, you have been our dwelling place
in all generations.

Sometimes a husband who has been married to his wife for a long time and is deeply in love with her can truly say, "Home is wherever my wife is. I am home whenever I am with her. Wherever on the globe she happens to be, that's home."

That's the way I feel about my wife, Gayle.

But what this husband says of his wife is even truer in your relationship with God. For the deeply devoted believer, home is found in God. Home is found not in a place but in a person. Home is being with God. He is home.

Moses gives voice to this at the outset of Psalm 90. He is essentially saying, "Lord, you are our dwelling place. You are our home. You are our place of refuge. Indeed, you have been our dwelling place throughout all generations."

Because God is God, because he is the everlasting God, because he was God before the Rocky Mountains were formed, because he was God before the creation of the universe, because he has been God from everlasting and will be God to everlasting, God is our true dwelling place.

Home is being with God. He is your heart's true home. He is what you're looking for. He is what you're longing for.

Psalm 91:1

He who dwells in the shelter of the Most High
will abide in the shadow of the Almighty.

Many Christians around the globe cannot read this verse without thinking of the life of Jim Elliot.

Elliot was born in Oregon in 1927. Raised in a family devoted to Christ, he exuded a fearless resolve to follow Christ early on. A natural leader, he would not shrink back from speaking out for Christ.

He made it his practice to meet God daily in the Scripture. He knew and loved the Bible, and he loved the God of the Bible. In fact, he had a most uncommon hunger to know God.

He was also a gifted writer and kept a journal. He once wrote, "He is no fool who gives that which he cannot keep, to gain what he cannot lose." He wrote this as a college student.

As a young man, he went to Ecuador to reach people for Christ. He learned Spanish, then he moved to the edge of the Amazon jungle to minister to Quechua Indians. There he married Elisabeth, a woman he had known since college.

Elliot and four other young missionaries were drawn to the Huaorani, a small tribe that had never been reached for Christ. The tribe was known to be dangerous to outsiders.

In 1956, the Huaorani martyred Jim and his four friends. He was only 28. Fortunately, his wife Elisabeth compiled his letters and journal entries into a book on her husband. She decided to take the title for the book from Psalm 91:1 and called it *Shadow of the Almighty*. The book is powerful.

Jim Elliot epitomized Psalm 91:1. God was his shelter, his refuge. He lived his life, too brief by our standards, to its full capacity, resting in the shadow of the Almighty.

If I could choose one person in the last hundred years who best reflected the passion Paul had for Jesus, I would choose Jim Elliot. He is one of those few people who could say what Paul said and mean it just as much. "For to me to live is Christ, and to die is gain" (Phil. 1:21).

Psalm 96:3

Declare his glory among the nations,
his marvelous works among all the peoples!

From Genesis to Revelation, we see that God is a missionary God. God's concern was never *only* with Israel, but with all the nations of the earth.

Psalm 96 is one of the great mission passages in the entire Old Testament. With verse 3, we come to the very heart of God's missionary purpose.

What is the driving motivation behind mission work? It is not our love for people, as important as that is. It is *not* our concern for people's salvation, as essential as that is. No, the highest motivation for missions is God-centered, not man-centered. Missions must be fueled by a burning desire to see God's name exalted across the world.

Missions, first and foremost, are about the glory of God, not the salvation of people. Missions are about exalting the name, honor, and glory of Jesus Christ among all the peoples of the world. Every tongue, tribe, nation, and people must proclaim the glory of Jesus Christ as King of kings and Lord of lords.

Pastor John Piper wrote:

> The final goal of all things is that God might be worshiped with white-hot affection by a redeemed company of countless numbers from every tribe and tongue and people and nation. (Rev. 5:9 and 7:9)

Missions exists because worship doesn't. When the kingdom finally comes in glory, missions will cease. Missions are penultimate; worship is ultimate. If we forget this and reverse the roles, the passion and the power for both diminish.

Christian leader John Stott sounded a similar note:

> We should be "jealous" for the honour of his name— troubled when it remains unknown, hurt when it is ignored, indignant when it is blasphemed, and all the time anxious and determined that it shall be given the honour and glory which are due to it. The highest of all missionary motives is neither obedience to the

Great Commission (important as that is), nor love for sinners who are alienated and perishing (strong as that incentive is), but rather zeal–burning and passionate zeal–for the glory of Jesus Christ. Before this supreme goal of the Christian mission, all unworthy motives wither and die.

Psalm 103:1

*Bless the L*ORD*, O my soul,*
and all that is within me, bless his holy name!

Psalm 103 is one of the greatest psalms in the Bible. I consider Psalms 23, 63, and 103 the richest psalms in the Psalter.

Psalm 103 includes some of the most exalted language in the entire Bible for God's love, God's forgiveness, and God's goodness. If you have ever struggled to understand and feel how much God loves you, as I have, then Psalm 103 is a psalm to soak in over and over. This psalm is a "Mount Everest" of the Bible.

Psalm 103 begins with a charge to bless or praise God. Note carefully: David is telling himself to praise. He is talking to himself. Sometimes we need to talk to ourselves, especially when we feel discouraged, lonely, depressed, or guilty. Talk to yourself and remind yourself of the promises and commands in the Bible.

Why is it so vital that we praise God? Several reasons:

First of all, it is only right to praise God. He deserves our highest praise. He is worthy of our deepest adoration. Praise reflects reality. We live in a world ruled by a sovereign God who is unfathomably great and unutterably good. It simply would not be right for us not to praise God.

Second, praise is the language of love. Because we love God, we want to praise him and adore him. It is our privilege, our delight, and our desire. We express our love for God when we praise him. Moreover, praise not only expresses our love to God, it also nurtures that love. Think about it: when we are praising God for his grace, goodness, mercy, and faithfulness, we are moved to love our God all the more.

A third reason that praise is so vital is because in praise, we gain perspective on our problems and needs. When we begin praying with praise, we lift our gaze from a focus on our problems to a focus on our God. We see things from heaven's perspective, not earth's perspective. We are more likely to trust God. Praise is absolutely essential to a life of trusting God.

For each of these reasons, praise is vital to our praying. No wonder the pages of Scripture are peppered with praise. "Bless the Lord, O my soul, and all that is within me, bless his holy name!"

Psalm 103:2

Bless the LORD, O my soul,
and forget not all his benefits.

It is so easy to forget all that God has done for us. It is so easy to focus on our problems and needs rather than on all the good things God has given us. We are prone to forget.

Not surprisingly, all throughout the Old Testament, God calls his people to remember. Remember what God has done for you. Remember God's provisions for you. Remember God's gifts to you. Remember God rescues you. Remember!

The whole purpose of Passover is so that the Jews would remember what God had done when he rescued them from slavery in Egypt. Similarly, Jesus gave us communion so that we would regularly remember what he did for us on the cross in delivering us from our slavery to sin.

As humans, we can forget so quickly the things God has done for us. We must be deliberate and intentional in remembering how God has gifted us, rescued us, blessed us, and protected us.

So, dear child of God, remember. Remember with a grateful heart. Remember with gratitude. Remember and give thanks.

Sometime soon, you might carve out an unhurried period of time with the Lord and make a list of all God's gifts to you. Write down everything you can think of: big things and little things, distant things, recent things, routine things, and exceptional things. Write down as many blessings as you can, then get down on your knees and give thanks. "Bless the Lord, O my soul, and forget not all his benefits."

Psalm 103:8

The LORD is merciful and gracious,
slow to anger and abounding in steadfast love.

Do you see God this way? In your heart of hearts, do you see him as merciful, gracious, slow to anger, and abounding in steadfast love?

So many people see God as stern, harsh, demanding, joyless, and hard to please, like a cosmic Scrooge. But that's not the God of the Bible. That's not the real God who revealed himself in Jesus Christ.

The real God is merciful. He is bursting with tenderness and affection. He feels for you when you are hurting. All through the Bible, we see God's tender heart for the widow and the orphan. In Matthew 9:36, we read this of Jesus: "When he saw the crowds, he had compassion for them, because they were harassed and helpless, like sheep without a shepherd." That's God—full of compassion and mercy for you.

The real God is gracious. He extends grace to the guilty. He forgives all our sins. In fact, two verses later, in verse 10 of Psalm 103, we read, "He does not deal with us according to our sins, nor repay us according to our iniquities." And four verses later, in verse 12, we read, "As far as the east is from the west, so far does he remove our transgressions from us." God is so gracious to us.

The real God is slow to anger. Because we can be impatient and quick-tempered, we might feel that God is this way, but it is not so. God is so patient, so gentle, and so slow to anger. God never loses his temper. He is easy to live with.

The real God is abounding in love. He is not just a little loving— he abounds in love. He overflows with the most relentless love and affection. He is crazy about you. His love knows no bounds. Picture new parents tenderly gazing at their long-awaited baby, eyes brimming with love and compassion. That's God gazing at you.

We have no idea of how tender God's heart is. But if we did, would we not love him more? Would we not trust him more? Would we not obey him more? Would we not enjoy him more? Would we not rest in his love and care? Would it not transform our whole outlook on life?

A.W. Tozer once said of God, "He meant us to see him and live with him and draw our life from his smile." Do you draw your life from God's smile?

Psalm 103:11

For as high as the heavens are above the earth, so great is his steadfast love toward those who fear him.

God is saying to us:

> My love for you is so great. It is as high as the heavens are above the earth. It is higher than you could ever imagine. There is no limit to my love for you. My love for you is inexhaustible. I will never stop loving you. Never. In fact, I will never love you one bit less than I love you right now, no matter how much you mess up, because my love for you is perfect and unconditional. This is my love for you: as high as the heavens are above the earth.

There is a movie called *The Bear*. A young cub loses his mother to hunters and has little chance of surviving in the wild, but an enormous papa bear takes the cub under his care and begins to look after the cub, showing the little bear how to forage for food and survive in the wilderness. One day, the cub is ready to venture out on his own. He is off on an adventure. But a mountain lion spots the cub and begins stalking it. The mountain lion creeps up and attacks the cub. The cub escapes, but the mountain lion is stronger and faster. When things look the bleakest, when it looks like the cub is going to be killed, the little cub rears up on its hind legs like it had seen the papa bear do.

Just at that moment, the mountain lion inexplicably backs up and slinks away. What happened? A mountain lion is not frightened by a mere bear cub. The camera lens widens and you see what the cub couldn't see; the giant papa bear was 20 yards behind the cub, reared up on its hind legs, ready to pulverize the mountain lion.

You realize that the papa bear had kept his eye on the cub the entire time. Yes, he gave the cub space and the freedom to depart, but the papa bear still cared and kept his eyes on the cub he loved. And when the mountain lion attacked, papa bear came running.

You are that cub. God is that papa bear. Yes, God will give you space and the freedom to leave him, but he continues to love you and never takes his eyes off of you. And when you are desperate, God will rescue you from the prowling lion that seeks to destroy you.

For your entire life, every single day, God has never, ever taken his eyes off you.

Time to go home, back to God.

Psalm 103:12

*As far as the east is from the west,
so far does he remove our transgressions from us.*

This is a promise to claim. God is saying to you and me, "All your sin is gone. Gone forever, gone completely, gone never to return."

David, who wrote this psalm, had some big sins, but he believed that God's grace was bigger than his sin. Even if the sin was adultery, God's grace was bigger. Even if the sin was murder, God's grace was bigger. Even if the sin was rampant pride, God's grace was bigger.

David understood grace. And he lived before the time of the cross, before he could see the full wonder of a Savior dying in our place and paying for all of our sins.

For those of us who live after the cross, surely we too must grasp grace.

David would have loved John Newton, the former slave ship owner who discovered grace and penned the classic hymn "Amazing Grace." Newton had been responsible for ripping families apart: husbands from wives, parents from children. He had been responsible for unthinkable brutality on voyages across the Atlantic, when slaves suffered horribly. Many died and were thrown overboard into the sea.

Newton's sin was so big, but he discovered grace. Amazing grace. Grace that's bigger than all our sin. Grace that removes our sins as far as the east is from the west. All our sins: past, present, and future; thoughts, words, and deeds. All our sins.

Yes, David would have loved Newton.

The next time you wrestle with guilt and condemnation, turn to the great promise of grace in Psalm 103:12. Read it. Learn it. Revel in it. Believe it.

This is a promise to claim.

Psalm 103:13

As a father shows compassion to his children,
so the LORD shows compassion to those who fear him.

God is Father. He is the perfect father. Loving, kind, wise, gentle, fair, honest, dependable, and strong. He is all that a father should be. Father is the Christian name for God.

But perhaps your earthly father was not a loving father. Maybe he was absent, preoccupied, angry, or even abusive. The writer George MacDonald, who was a big influence on C.S. Lewis, offered wise counsel in his book *Unspoken Sermons*:

> In my own childhood and boyhood, my father was the refuge from all the ills of life, even sharp pain itself. Therefore I say to son or daughter who has no pleasure in the name Father, "You must interpret the word by all that you have missed in life. All that human tenderness can give or desire in the nearness and readiness of love, all and infinitely more must be true of the perfect Father—of the maker of fatherhood."

To see God as Father means so much. It means you see God as loving you deeply, tenderly, and fiercely, as committed to your greatest welfare.

It means you see him as strong and powerful. He can take care of you, rescue you, protect you, and provide for you.

It means you see him as wise. He knows what is best for you. He understands you completely. There is no wiser parent anywhere.

It means you are never confused about who you are. You are a child of Father, a child of Papa. Much loved. Joyfully adopted. Completely accepted. Delighted in.

That's who you are.

Psalm 103:15-16

As for man, his days are like grass;
he flourishes like a flower of the field;
for the wind passes over it, and it is gone,
and its place knows it no more.

Life is brief. It is oh so brief.
When we are 20, it seems that we will live forever.
At age 30, "Well, maybe not quite forever."
At age 40, "Whoa! I'm halfway there."
At age 50, "Time is racing by!" And it just speeds up from there.

Why do we humans, unlike animals, never quite adjust to the brevity of life? Because we were made for eternity. God has put eternity in our hearts. "He has made everything beautiful in its time. Also, he has put eternity into man's heart" (Eccles. 3:11).

How should we respond to life's brevity? There is only one solution: live for eternity. Accept the biblical truth that this world is not home. We were made for the next world, not this world. Like Paul, strive to long for the next world. "For to me to live is Christ, and to die is gain" (Phil. 1:21).

This means we decide that we will not live for money or possessions. We will live for Jesus Christ. We will surrender our life to him. We will love people and not things. We will invest our time and resources in reaching people and loving them. We will live our life for the next world.

In *Mere Christianity,* C.S. Lewis wrote, "Aim at heaven and you will get earth thrown in; aim at earth and you will get neither."

Psalm 119:1

Blessed are those whose way is blameless,
who walk in the law of the LORD!

Psalm 119 is a passionate love song in praise of Scripture. It is also a work of literary beauty. The first eight lines all begin with the first letter of the Hebrew alphabet, the next eight lines begin with the second letter, and so on throughout the psalm. The 22 stanzas take us through the entire Hebrew alphabet, eight lines at a time. Furthermore, Psalm 119 is the longest chapter in the Bible. This is one striking psalm.

Psalm 119 begins with a call to obey God's Word. God will bless us, the Bible says, not if we have God's Word, read God's Word, or study God's Word. No, God will bless us if we obey God's Word, if we walk according to it. "Blessed are those whose way is blameless, who walk in the law of the Lord!"

Obedience is a major theme of Psalm 119. Just a few of the examples:

> You have commanded your precepts
> to be kept diligently. (Ps. 119:4)
> Oh that my ways may be steadfast
> in keeping your statutes! (Ps. 119:5)
> I will keep your statutes;
> do not utterly forsake me! (Ps. 119:8)

If you want the blessing, favor, and protection of God in your life, there's no other way than to obey God's Word.

Obey Scripture whether you like the command or not. Obey whether you agree with the command or not. Obey immediately and completely. Obey no matter what. Obey because God is God and you are not. Understanding can wait, but obedience cannot.

To read a passage and not obey is to defy God. This includes commands on lying, gossip, charity, divorce, sexual purity, giving thanks, loving your wife, and respecting your husband.

The writer Flannery O'Connor observed, "The truth does not change according to our ability to stomach it."

Obey it! Obey God's holy Word and God will bless you.

Psalm 119:72

*The law of your mouth is better to me
than thousands of gold and silver pieces.*

The psalmist delighted in God's Word. To delight in God's Word is to love it, to treasure it, to value it, to regard it as priceless.

The remarkable thing is that the psalmist's Bible was Genesis through Deuteronomy. We've got so much more to delight in: Psalms, Isaiah, Proverbs, John, Acts, Romans, Ephesians, and more.

In his extraordinary book *The Heavenly Man,* Brother Yun tells this story:

> After his conversion as a young man, he found out about the Bible. He did not have one. He did not know anyone who had one. Bibles were scarce in China in those days. He was so hungry for the Bible. His mother had heard of an old man in another village who had been a pastor. They went to visit him. The old man told him to pray for a Bible. So, day after day, he knelt down with one simple prayer, "Lord, please give me a Bible. Amen."
>
> After a month nothing happened, so he went back to the old man's house and this time the pastor told him he needed to fast and weep for a Bible. So for the next 100 days, he fasted morning and noon and ate a little bit in the evening, weeping and praying for a Bible. Still no Bible.
>
> Then one morning at 4 a.m., he received a vivid vision in which two men give him a Bible. The vision was so real that he got up in the middle of the night and began looking for a Bible in the house. Not finding it he began weeping loudly and woke his parents. His parents rushed in to see what was wrong and they wept with him. Just at that desperate moment, they hear a faint knock at the door. He answers it and there are two strangers at the door, the same two men that he had just seen in his vision. They give him a bag containing a Bible.

In his own words, he wrote: "My heart raced as I opened the bag and held in my hands my very own Bible! The two men quickly departed into the still darkness. I clutched my new Bible to my heart and fell down on my knees outside the door. I thanked God again and again! I promised Jesus that from that moment on I would devour his Word like a hungry child."

That's what it means to treasure God's Word.

Psalm 119:92

If your law had not been my delight,
I would have perished in my affliction.

The psalmist says that at times in his life, the trials have been so difficult and the pain so great that he would not have survived without God's Word. He says that he would not have made it. He would have shriveled up and died spiritually, emotionally, and perhaps even physically—if it had not been for the Word of God.

Let me ask you. Do you understand what he's saying? Have you experienced what the psalmist experienced? Does this ring true in your life?

It does for me. There have been times in my life that were so difficult, so overwhelming, or so scary that I would not have survived if it had not been for God's Word. Certainly, this has applied to times of deep anguish due to a mental health issue: my obsessive-compulsive disorder. There have been other dark times: health crises for children and grandchildren, challenging seasons of marriage, periods in my ministry when I felt like a failure, and times of unrelenting financial pressure.

In all of these times, the Bible has been a rock in my life. It has been a foundation to stand upon. It has been a source of endless comfort, peace, and rest. Where would I be without it? I don't know that I would have survived.

This is not to say that Scripture offered a simple answer to a problem or provided a spiritual jolt each day. Rather, when you meet God in the scriptures, day in and day out over a long period of time, something happens to you. You feel an increasing connection and closeness to God, a bond that will not break. You find yourself changing. There is a strength and peace within you, and you breathe the breath of God. You have a rock to stand on. There is a solid foundation for life. God gives you all of this through his Word.

Begin today. Meet God in the pages of Scripture every day. You need it.

Psalm 119:97

Oh how I love your law!
It is my meditation all the day.

Psalm 119 calls us to meditate on God's Word. Don't merely read the Bible, but meditate on it. Ponder, reflect, consider, pray through, think it over. Chew on it like your dog chews on a bone.

> Oh how I love your law!
> It is my meditation all the day. (Ps. 119:97)
> I will meditate on your precepts
> and fix my eyes on your ways. (Ps. 119:15)
> I have more understanding than all my teachers,
> for your testimonies are my meditation. (Ps. 119:99)
> My eyes are awake before the watches of the night,
> that I may meditate on your promise. (Ps. 119:148)

George Müller oversaw an orphanage in England during the nineteenth century, in which he took care of more than ten thousand orphans. He never asked for money but relied on prayer alone. He did not just read God's Word, he meditated on it. He described his daily practice:

> The first thing I did...was to begin to meditate on the Word of God; searching...every verse, to get blessing out of it; not for the sake of the public ministry of the Word; not for the sake of preaching on what I had meditated upon; but for the sake of obtaining food for my own soul. The result I have found to be almost invariably this, that after a very few minutes my soul has been led to confession, or to thanksgiving, or to intercession, or to supplication; so that though I did not...give myself to prayer, but to meditation, yet it turned almost immediately...into prayer. When I have been for awhile making confession, or intercession, or supplication, or have given thanks, I go on to the next words or verse, turning all, as I go on, into prayer for myself or others.

When you read God's Word, be all there. Soak in it. Pray through it. Meditate upon it. Let it marinate in your heart all the day.

Psalm 119:105

Your word is a lamp to my feet
and a light to my path.

We are like pilgrims who find ourselves alone at night in a dense, dark forest. We are lost and we cannot see the way. We need light to guide us, a lamp for our feet and a light for our path.

The psalmist cries out, "Your Word, O Lord, is that lamp. Your Word is that light."

The Bible is a light that shines from heaven, revealing who God is and who we are. The Bible tells us what life is all about, how to live life well, and how to find joy, peace, and contentment. The Bible is a light that shines into the darkness of the world around us and makes sense out of the confusion.

Robert Coles is a Harvard psychiatrist and the author of more than eighty books. He is a Pulitzer Prize winner, and *TIME* once called him the greatest living psychiatrist. At some point on his pilgrimage, he became a follower of Christ. In an interview with Philip Yancey, Coles described the Bible as a source of light and wisdom: "Nothing I have discovered about the makeup of human beings contradicts in any way what I learn from the Hebrew prophets such as Isaiah, Jeremiah, and Amos, and from the book of Ecclesiastes, and from Jesus and the lives of those he touched. Anything I can say as a result of my research into human behavior is a mere footnote to those lives in the Old and New Testament."

If you want wisdom beyond your own, then get into God's Word.

If you want guidance for a thriving marriage, then get into God's Word.

If you want practical wisdom for raising kids, then get into God's Word.

If you want perspective on the trials and suffering in life, then get into God's Word.

If you want insight on relationships, then get into God's Word.

If you want understanding about God and his will for your life, then get into God's Word.

If you want guidance for all areas of life, then get into God's Word.

God's Word is a lamp for your feet and a light for your path.

Psalm 119:165

Great peace have those who love your law;
nothing can make them stumble.

Great peace. We want that, don't we? In the storms and confusions of life, we desperately want God's peace to flood our soul.

We also need protection from stumbling. We don't want to stumble in marriage, in parenting, in finances, in friendships, in work, in temptations, or in anything. We need God's hand of protection.

God grants peace and protection to those who love his Word. If you love God's Word, you will treasure it and read it and learn it and live it. It will be an endless delight to you.

In my freshman year at Rice University, I had been a Christian for six months. During the Christmas holidays, I attended a conference for college students sponsored by Campus Crusade for Christ.

The speaker, Howard Hendricks, challenged us to read the Bible every day. He exhorted us to make this an unrivalled priority in our lives if we wanted to know God and live for him.

I decided to accept his challenge. I thirsted to know God and be all that God wanted me to be, so in January 1973, I began to read the Bible every day. Every morning after breakfast, I would retreat to a lonely place in the basement of my dormitory and spend time alone with God, reading the Bible and praying.

That was more than forty years ago. I have continued to meet with God each day, praying and reading his Word. It has been the privilege and the foundation of my life. It has been oxygen to my soul. It has been a solid rock to stand upon when everything about me crumbled. It has been light in a dark world, life in a dead world, and glory in a dull world.

I cannot express what the Bible has meant to me. I cannot imagine it not being in my life.

It has not been a book of theology or a list of religious duties to me. It has been the living Word of God. It has been a draught of living water. It has been a time for God to meet with me, speak to me, and reveal his heart to me.

In *The Sign of Jonas*, Thomas Merton wrote, "By the reading of Scripture I am so renewed that all nature seems renewed…The whole world is charged with the glory of God and I feel fire and music under my feet." That's it exactly. Fire and music and the glory of God.

All through God's holy Word.

Psalm 131:1

*O LORD, my heart is not lifted up; my eyes are not
raised too high; I do not occupy myself with things
too great and too marvelous for me.*

David had so much going for him. He was the King of Israel
when Israel was at its zenith. He was a brilliant general, a
courageous warrior, a gifted musician and songwriter, and he was
enormously wealthy and powerful.

And yet David had a profound humility before God. He had
a soul-deep sense of humility and childlike trust before the Lord.

Part of David's humility, part of David's childlike trust, was to
admit: "Lord, some things are beyond me, above me, too big for
me, too hard for me. Lord, there is so much I do not understand
and *cannot* understand. Lord, you are so big, so vast, so immense.
How could I, a mere mortal, think that I could understand all that
you do?"

There is so much that we cannot fully understand about God:
the Trinity, that Jesus is fully God and fully man, the sovereignty
of God, free will of man, the suffering of children and babies, holy
wars in the Old Testament, and the reality of hell, to name a few.
Perhaps what is even harder to understand is our own pain and
suffering in an unfair world.

It's OK to ask God the hard questions, but we should not
assume that we will get answers to all of our questions on this
side of heaven. Part of our faith journey is to trust God when we
don't have answers and when we lack understanding.

> Trust in the LORD with all your heart,
> and do not lean on your own understanding.
> (Prov. 3:5)

David had enough humility to recognize that God was so
vast that he could not possibly understand everything about
him. David had enough humility to admit, "God is God and I am
not." David had enough humility to trust God in the face of life's
enigmas and pain.

What about you?

> O LORD, my heart is not lifted up;
> my eyes are not raised too high;

I do not occupy myself with things too great
and too marvelous for me.
But I have calmed and quieted my soul,
like a weaned child with its mother;
like a weaned child is my soul within me. (Ps. 131:1-2)

Psalm 139:14

*I praise you, for I am fearfully and wonderfully
made. Wonderful are your works;
my soul knows it very well.*

Have you ever felt like a failure?
I have. It doesn't feel very good. When I started Woods Edge
Community Church, I had gone through four tough years of ministry. These were years of struggle, frustration, hard work, personal conflict, and more. I had lost my confidence as a pastor and
as a preacher. I didn't feel good about myself. I felt like a failure.

Most of us go through seasons like this, when we feel like a
failure, a reject, or a nobody.

At those times, it is vital that we hear God's voice and not the
voice of the enemy. We must intentionally listen to God's truths
about us, not Satan's lies about us.

One of the best places for God's truths about us is Psalm 139.
There we hear God's voice telling us these essential truths:

> I know you. (Ps. 139:1-6)
> I am always with you. (Ps. 139:7-12)
> I carefully made you. (Ps. 139:13-16a)
> I have a plan for you. (Ps. 139:16b-18)

In other words, you matter to God. You matter more than you
know.

The centerpiece of the psalm comes in verses 13-14:

> For you formed my inward parts;
> you knitted me together in my mother's womb.
> I praise you, for I am fearfully and wonderfully made.
> Wonderful are your works;
> my soul knows it very well.

David is filled with awe and wonder and bursts out in praise:

> Lord, you fashioned me in my mother's womb. You
> intricately, carefully, personally fashioned me. You
> made every cell in my body. I am your handiwork.
> Your thumbprint is on me. Your eye has always been

upon me. Lord, I am fearfully and wonderfully made. Lord, I praise you for the way you tenderly made me. Indeed, I am special to you.

If ever you feel like a failure, if ever you experience rejection and disappointment, if ever you feel like a nobody, run to Psalm 139 and hear the voice of God. You matter to God. You are incredibly special and precious to the God who made you.

Psalm 139:23-24

Search me, O God, and know my heart!
Try me and know my thoughts!
And see if there be any grievous way in me,
and lead me in the way everlasting!

This may not be the safest prayer to pray. God may make you uncomfortable as he shines a spotlight on the inner recesses of your soul.

But this is a prayer that we need to pray. We need God to show us our hidden sins. We need God to expose our blind spots. We need God to rescue us from our sinful self-deceptions.

Confession, honest and humble confession, is powerful. It is vital to a healthy spiritual life. When we come to the holy God of the universe with a broken and contrite spirit, God responds. He draws near. He hears our prayer. He goes to work on our soul. He rescues us and transforms us.

Never forget: The holy God of the universe, who wields the razor-sharp scalpel for the soul, is Father. He's Papa. And all that he does, he does in love, with a gentle and tender touch.

We can trust him with our heart. So pray this prayer. It is a prayer we need to pray. We can trust Father on this:

> Search me, O God, and know my heart! Try me and know my thoughts! And see if there be any grievous way in me, and lead me in the way everlasting!

Proverbs 1:7

The fear of the LORD is the beginning of knowledge;
fools despise wisdom and instruction.

What does it mean to fear the Lord? Are we afraid of God? Is this a cringing fear?

Psalm 33 helps:

> Let all the earth fear the LORD;
> Let all the inhabitants of the world stand in awe of him! (Ps. 33:8).

This makes it clear: to fear God is to revere God. The idea is reverence, respect, and awe. This is a reverential fear, not a cringing fear. This is a healthy and holy fear that obeys God because he is God and he is to be obeyed. It is our solemn duty and our happy privilege to obey the Lord.

Abraham obeyed God when God called him to sacrifice his long-awaited son, Isaac. Why did he obey God? Because he feared the Lord. If we fear the Lord, then we will obey him. Genesis 22:12 states that God put a halt to the sacrifice of Isaac by saying, "Do not lay your hand on the boy or do anything to him, for now I know that you fear God, seeing you have not withheld your son, your only son, from me."

If we fear God, we will obey him. It's not that we are afraid of God but that we revere him because he is God. He is the Almighty, the King, the holy God, and we owe him our allegiance, our reverence, and our fidelity.

Perhaps the idea behind fearing God was captured best in the children's stories of C.S. Lewis. Aslan is a golden lion who represents Christ. When the children enter the fairytale land of Narnia, they learn of Aslan from the beavers:

> "Is he—quite safe?" Susan said, "I shall feel rather nervous about meeting a lion."
> "That you will, dearie, and no mistake," said Mrs. Beaver, "If there's anyone who can appear before Aslan without their knees knocking, they're either braver than most or else just silly."
> "Then he isn't safe?" said Lucy.

"Safe?' said Mr. Beaver. "Don't you hear what Mrs. Beaver tells you? Who said anything about safe? 'Course he isn't safe. But he's good. He's the king, I tell you."

That's why we fear the Lord. He's the King and he is not safe. But he is good.

All spiritual knowledge, all knowledge of God, begins right here, with the fear of the Lord, the healthy and holy longing to please him and obey him.

Proverbs 3:5-6

Trust in the LORD *with all your heart,*
and do not lean on your own understanding.
In all your ways acknowledge him,
and he will make straight your paths.

If I could only memorize one verse in the Bible, I might well choose this one. OK, it's actually two verses.

This is indeed a verse to learn, a verse to love, a verse to live. It applies to a thousand situations. It speaks to every problem, every decision, and every fear. It speaks to all of life.

"Trust in the LORD." The Lord God Almighty, the Sovereign Ruler of heaven and earth, the one who made you and loves you. He can take care of you.

"Trust in the LORD with all your heart." Trust is more of a heart matter than a head matter.

"In all your ways acknowledge him." Exactly what are you acknowledging? That he is the Lord, the Almighty God, and the King. That he is God and you are not. That he is worthy of your trust, the Shepherd who cares for you. You acknowledge all the truths of the Bible about God.

"And he will make straight your paths." Here's the promise of God: When we trust him, he will take care of us. He will bless us, lead us, and protect us. God will see us through.

So trust him with all your heart. Trust him when your teenager is wayward. Trust him when your college student drives back to school at night. Trust him when the doctor says "cancer." Trust him.

Trust him when you don't understand why you suffer. Trust him when you lose your job. Trust him when your spouse walks out. Trust him.

Trust him for your father's salvation. Trust him when you cannot get pregnant. Trust him when you face a major decision at work. Trust him.

This is your calling. This is your mandate. This is your life.

In every situation, in every decision, with every problem, you have a choice to make. Will you or will you not trust in the Lord with all your heart and lean not on your own understanding? Will you acknowledge that God is God and you're not? Will you acknowledge that he is in fact the Lord, the Lord God Almighty, and he is still in control of his universe?

Do it! Do it today and every day. Trust in the Lord with all your heart. Decide to trust in the Lord.

Proverbs 3:9-10

*Honor the L*ORD *with your wealth*
and with the firstfruits of all your produce;
then your barns will be filled with plenty,
and your vats will be bursting with wine.

This classic passage on giving says to "honor the Lord" and not just "give to the Lord." Yes, we do give to God, but we do so much more. We honor him. We worship him. We bring a heart of deep-felt gratitude to the God who made us and loves us. This perspective, to honor God with our giving, is everything.

Precisely because we are honoring the Lord and not just giving to him, we bring our firstfruits. We don't bring leftovers. We don't tip God with a token gift. We don't begrudgingly give out of obligation. No, we honor God with our firstfruits. We give to God first because he is first in our lives. We don't wait until the bills are paid. No, right off the top, before anything and everything else, we worship God with our giving, and thereby declare with our actions that God is first in our lives.

When we honor God this way, God gives us a promise. He says to us: I will bless you. I will take care of you. I will provide for you. I will pour out abundant blessings on you.

This may not happen immediately. But eventually, ultimately, in some way at some time, God will pour out abundant blessings upon you.

Down through the years and over the centuries, with all kinds of people in all kinds of situations, God has proven himself faithful. This is an adventure to experience, an adventure of faith, seeing God come through for you. Don't live your life and miss out on the great whitewater adventure of faith.

Honor the Lord. Don't merely give to him. Honor him! Honor the Lord and then watch what God does.

Proverbs 5:18

Let your fountain be blessed,
and rejoice in the wife of your youth.

Sex is God's idea. It is God's creation. It is God's gift. The Bible is completely positive about sex in marriage. Consider Proverbs 5:18-19, a passage that is almost embarrassingly candid and expressive:

> Let your fountain be blessed,
> and rejoice in the wife of your youth,
> a lovely deer, a graceful doe.
> Let her breasts fill you at all times with delight;
> be intoxicated always in her love.

God is saying to every married couple: "Enjoy your sexual relationship. This is my gift to you. Have fun! Husbands, take delight in the playful beauty and gracefulness of your wife's body. Be intoxicated, ravished, by her love."

This may not be the way you thought of God and sex, but this is the biblical perspective. Sex is God's gift. In itself, sex is completely good.

Yes, sex can be abused. It is like fire. In the fireplace, fire is a good thing, giving warmth and light. But out of the fireplace, fire can do great damage.

Sex is that way. It is completely good in marriage, but outside of marriage, it can do great damage. Sex needs the context of a loving, committed, trust-filled marriage. Sex needs this context because it is so powerful.

Sex is not just the merger of two bodies, but the merger of two hearts and two souls. Whenever a man and a woman have sex, there is a channel cut between their souls, a channel of emotional and spiritual intimacy. A channel intended by God to express tender love and deep oneness.

You cannot do that casually. You can only do that within the safety and security of lifetime love. No wonder people get so hurt when they abuse God's gift of sex.

Sex is good. Enjoy it to the hilt in marriage, but only in marriage. It is simply too powerful for any place other than a committed, loving, and secure marriage.

Proverbs 10:19

When words are many, transgression is not lacking,
but whoever restrains his lips is prudent.

The more we talk, the more we sin. That ought to sober us and cause us to slow down our talking, but many of us talk on.

There was a tombstone in an English churchyard. The faint etching read:

> Beneath this stone, a lump of clay,
> Lies Arabella Young,
> Who, on the twenty-fourth of May,
> Began to hold her tongue.

Far better if we heed Proverbs 10:19 and begin to hold our tongue while we live. The Bible says in James 1:19 that that's what wise people do. They are not incessant talkers. They talk, of course, but they are quick to hear and slow to speak.

Why do we talk too much? Maybe it's nervousness or insecurity, but a big reason for excessive talking is pride. We are self-preoccupied, self-centered, and self-enamored. Proverbs 18:2 says, "A fool takes no pleasure in understanding, but only in expressing his opinion."

One of my heroes is Theodore Roosevelt. Roosevelt was a courageous, fearless president with many incredible traits. But like the rest of us, he was one flawed individual, and talking too much was one of those flaws. One biographer, Edmund Morris, comments:

> He delights like a schoolboy in parading his knowledge, and does so loudly, and at such length, that less vigorous talkers lapse into weary silence. John Hay once calculated that in a two-hour dinner at the White House, Roosevelt's guests were responsible for only four and a half minutes of conversation; the rest was supplied by the President himself.

OK, maybe you're not that bad; I hope not. But Theodore Roosevelt is not the standard. God calls us to be careful, to hold back, to go slow when it comes to talking. Be slow to speak and quick to listen. Most of us get that backwards; we are quick to speak, slow to listen.

Words are a great resource. We can do so much good with life-giving words. But words can be abused. One way we abuse words is to talk too much and listen too little. In this time of cell phones, e-mail, and Facebook, perhaps the problem of excessive words is worse than ever.

Wise people hold their tongue. How are you doing at this rare discipline?

Proverbs 13:20

Whoever walks with the wise becomes wise,
but the companion of fools will suffer harm.

Pat Morley, the founder of the highly effective men's ministry Man in the Mirror, recounted a conversation about friendship:

> Once I boasted to an acquaintance, quite sincerely, that I had hundreds of friends. Without pause he said, "No you don't. You may have met hundreds of people, but there's no way you can really know more than a handful of people. You'd be lucky if you had three real friends."
>
> At first I was offended that he thought he knew so much about my situation. But as I reflected on what he said, I realized that I had a thousand acquaintances but, at that moment in time, less than three genuine friends. I've worked on this area of my life, and today I believe I have five real friends including my wife.

Morley is right. Friendship is a rare and precious gift. Friendship can be hard and frustrating, and it will cost us time and energy.

But friendship can be so good. It can be a source of incredible pleasure, encouragement, and comfort. Friendship is a priceless gift of God.

But friendship is much more. We become, to a large extent, like our friends. This may not be true of acquaintances, but with our friends, we tend to become like them over the years. We tend to adopt their values, their attitudes, their convictions, and their interests. For good or ill, we will become like our friends. "Whoever walks with the wise becomes wise, but the companion of fools will suffer harm" (Prov. 13:20).

If friendship is so life shaping, how vital it is that we choose our friends wisely. How vital it is that our kids choose their friends wisely.

What do you look for in a friend? What impresses you? Is it money? A charismatic personality? A great sense of humor? Unusual giftedness? These are not bad things, but they are not the traits you should look for in a friend.

Rather, the Bible says to look for wise friends. Look for friends with godly wisdom, friends who understand what really matters in life. Look for friends who know God and walk with God.

For God tells you that one day, you will become like the friends you choose.

Proverbs 15:1

A soft answer turns away wrath,
but a harsh word stirs up anger.

When you are in a dispute and your frustration is rising, when you feel hurt and angry and you want to lash out, the Bible has a simple, practical principle: be gentle. Use soft words, a soft tone, and gentle gestures, for the Bible teaches us, "A soft answer turns away wrath, but a harsh word stirs up anger."

You probably know what that's like. Most of us have responded with harsh words at one time. Some of us have done that more often than we care to admit. Harsh words don't help things, do they? They stir up anger. Whether you are right, wrong, or some mixture of both, harsh words don't help the conflict.

It's just the way life works. It's not just *what* we say, but *how* we say it.

Perhaps this principle applies to marriage more than anywhere else. When you live with someone and seek to merge two lives into one, there will be friction. There will be conflict. Oh, how valuable Proverbs 15:1 can be for conflict in marriage. Every couple ought to adopt this verse as a firm rule of thumb for conflict and decide, "We don't rant and rave. We don't shout and yell. We don't call each other names. We don't speak harshly. We obey God and speak softly. It doesn't matter if my parents yelled—we don't yell. We obey God, for a soft answer turns away wrath, but a harsh word stirs up anger."

Marriage may be the prime application, but the principle of Proverbs 15:1 applies to all of life. When you're upset at your high schooler, your grade schooler, or your preschooler: soft! When you are in a meeting at work and you feel disrespected and insulted: soft! When a careless, selfish driver cuts you off on the freeway: soft! When the clerk is a bit rude to you: soft!

In a thousand situations, in all of life, practice the Proverbs 15:1 principle: "A soft answer turns away wrath, but a harsh word stirs up anger."

By the power of the Spirit, make this the way you live your life.

Proverbs 16:18

Pride goes before destruction,
and a haughty spirit before a fall.

Strong words. A sober warning.

If we live in pride, God warns us, "You are headed for destruction. You are headed for a fall."

We may not know when, where, or how the fall will come. It may not come fully until we die, but the fall will come. Sooner or later, we will be humbled.

But what exactly is pride? Pride is when we rely upon ourselves rather than God. When we live for ourselves rather than God. When we are preoccupied with ourselves rather than God.

Pride is when we refuse to humble ourselves before God and obey his commands. When we draw attention to ourselves and promote ourselves. When we think we are responsible for the good things in our lives.

Pride is when we strut around and act as if we were God.

Unfortunately, none of us is immune to pride. All of us are infected by the insidious plague of pride—a malady that is self-destructive, for pride inevitably leads to destruction.

C.S. Lewis once described the sin of pride:

> According to Christian teachers the essential vice, the utmost evil, is pride. Unchastity, anger, greed, drunkenness, and all that, are mere fleabites in comparison: it was through pride that the devil became the devil: pride leads to every other vice: it is the complete anti-God state of mind.
>
> Pride is the mother hen under which all other sins are hatched.
>
> Pride is the essence of sin. Sin is fundamentally self-centeredness.
>
> Pride keeps more people out of the kingdom of God than anything else.
>
> The great jurist, Oliver Wendell Holmes, Jr., once remarked, "The great act of faith is when man decides that he is not God."

Well put. Recognize that *you* are not God, and decide to live your life for the one who is God, Jesus Christ.

Proverbs 17:17

A friend loves at all times,
and a brother is born for adversity.

The greatest test of friendship is loyalty.
A friend loves at all times, no matter what happens. In the best of times and the worst of times, through thick and thin, a friend will be there for you. Above all else, a friend is loyal.

A loyal friend will never betray you or undermine you. A loyal friend will never gossip about you, for a friend loves at all times.

If you lose your job and go through all your savings, a real friend will offer to help or anonymously get you money, for a friend loves at all times.

If you get a serious disease, your friend will be there. If you lose your marriage, your friend will be there. If a loved one dies, your friend will be there. He will call you, reach out to you, and come to be with you, for a friend loves at all times.

If you get too big for your britches, if you begin to wander from God, if you have a blind spot that is hurting you, your friend will be the one to confront you and challenge you, for a friend loves at all times, and your welfare is more important than his comfort.

If something wonderful happens to you, like a big promotion, a significant raise, or a huge bonus, your friend will be glad with you. Genuinely, deeply glad, for a friend loves at all times.

If you are discouraged, worried, or hurting, and you need someone who will just listen to you without being judgmental, even if it is 2 a.m., then you know you can call your friend, for a friend loves at all times.

This kind of friend, a loyal friend, a friend who loves at all times, is an incredible gift of God.

The question is not: Do I have friends like this? The question is rather: Am I a friend like this?

Proverbs 18:12

Before destruction a man's heart is haughty,
but humility comes before honor.

God exalts the humble. God humbles the haughty. He blesses the humble. He opposes the haughty. Who are the haughty? What do they look like?

> They are self-reliant.
> They are self-preoccupied.
> They are self-righteous.
> They refuse to submit to God.
> They don't have a broken and contrite heart.
> They draw attention to themselves.
> They are not servants.
> They incessantly talk about themselves.
> They flout God's Word.
> They are overly critical of others.
> They are not thankful people.
> They need no one.

Who are the humble? What do they look like?

> They are worshippers.
> They are Jesus-preoccupied.
> They don't focus on themselves.
> They are self-forgetful.
> They depend upon the Lord.
> They surrender to the Lord.
> They obey the Lord.
> They don't look down on others.
> They are not self-righteous.
> They don't draw attention to themselves.
> They are grateful people.
> They don't care who gets the credit.
> They know they need God.

The first group: God will humble them. He is able to do it.

The second group: God will save them, bless them, and honor them.

Proverbs 18:21

Death and life are in the power of the tongue,
and those who love it will eat its fruits.

Larry Nettles is a close friend. We went to college together at Rice University. He once told me this story:

> When I was growing up, I desperately wanted to be an athlete. My dad played basketball at the University of Texas. But I was terrible at sports. I was horrible at football, basketball, and baseball.
>
> When I got to high school, my dad encouraged me to try cross-country running. I did. After a time, the coach, Coach Dunlap, said to me, "I think you are going to be good."
>
> I was astounded. No one had ever said that to me. So I asked him, "Why do you say that?"
>
> "Because you have rhythm when you run. You have mental toughness. You have self-discipline."
>
> I thought to myself, "I could be good!" I doubled my mental toughness and self-discipline. I worked hard. I rose to the expectations. I got better and better. I set school records. I became one of the best runners in Texas. I got a full athletic scholarship to Rice University.

Then, Larry paused and looked intently into my eyes. "Those words changed my life in more ways than you can imagine."

He went on to tell me that Coach Dunlap's words gave him confidence in every area of his life. He began to see himself differently. He said it changed the path of his life.

"Death and life are in the power of the tongue." With our words, we can breathe life into people. And with our words, we can bring death into people.

Wise is the man or woman who speaks words that breathe life, build up, encourage, and affirm. Wise is the person who is forever alert to speak words of life to a child, a spouse, a friend, a student, a neighbor, a coworker, a stranger, a clerk at Wal-Mart, or someone who looks troubled.

Life-giving words. We can change lives forever.

Words like these: I love you. I respect you. I believe in you. I am so proud of you. You can do this. You are so good at painting. I love the way you shared your toys with your brother. Could I pray for you right now? You are going to get through this, for God will see you through. I have been praying for you every day. I am so sorry; will you forgive me? Thank you so much for that gift.

When words like these are spoken from the heart, they breathe life into people.

You can make such a difference with your words.

Proverbs 27:5-6

Better is open rebuke than hidden love.
Faithful are the wounds of a friend;
profuse are the kisses of an enemy.

An enemy may tell us what we want to hear. A real friend will tell us what we need to hear.

All of us have blind spots. All of us have flaws, weaknesses, and sins. We need people in our lives who will challenge us gently and lovingly. People who know us. People we trust.

All of us need people like this in our lives. In fact, if we do not have people like this, we are in trouble. We might be headed for a disaster. Certainly, we will never become the man or woman that God intends us to become.

If you are married, surely your spouse challenges you—hopefully, in a gentle and loving way. But you need more than your spouse. You need friends, real friends, who love you enough to confront you. You need a small group, a group where there is genuine community and not pseudo-community. We all need people like this in our lives. It is simply God's way of transforming people.

To challenge someone is an act of love. It's never fun, but you don't do it because it's fun, you do it because you care about the person. That's why parents have no problem confronting their kids. They care. Parents are more concerned with loving their kids than pleasing their kids. They are lovers, not pleasers, when it comes to their children. If you are a lover, you confront. If you are a pleaser, you shrink back in cowardice.

I offer two cautions:

1. If someone is not open to challenge or not teachable, don't go to them. "Do not reprove a scoffer, or he will hate you; reprove a wise man, and he will love you" (Prov. 9:8).
2. Go directly to the person. If you go to someone who is not part of the problem or part of the solution, that's gossip, not love. "If your brother sins against you, go and tell him his fault, between you and him alone" (Matt. 18:15).

Don't get carried away with challenging people. God has not given you the spiritual gift of criticism.

But if you love someone, there will be times when you need to challenge them. Perhaps it's a problem with pride, a problem with honesty, a problem with drinking, or a problem with the way they treat their spouse.

When these occasions arise, go to the person. Lovingly, gently, and humbly go for their sake because you care.

"Better is open rebuke than hidden love. Faithful are the wounds of a friend; profuse are the kisses of an enemy" (Prov. 27:6).

Proverbs 27:17

Iron sharpens iron, and one man sharpens another.

No one wants to be a dull axe. We want to be a sharp axe, effective in the hand of God.

This will not happen if we're apart from certain people in our lives. Wise people, godly people, humble people. People who care.

We need people in our lives who love Jesus and love us. We need people who will love us enough to challenge, affirm, and encourage us. We need people who care enough to listen to us and understand us. We need people who will pray for us and pray with us. We need people who will model what it means to passionately pursue Christ.

For example, if you want to love God more, it helps immensely to be around people who are great lovers of God. Or, if you want to be a better husband or wife, it helps tremendously to spend time with people who are great husbands or wives. We need to see the life of Christ incarnated in our midst. It's just the way God has made us.

Furthermore, this sharpening does not happen at a distance. It does not even happen at arm's length. It happens when people get close. It happens when we let people into our lives and into our hearts. It happens when we take a risk and get real. It happens when we let people get close enough to see our struggles and our fears.

Iron doesn't sharpen iron from a distance. Iron doesn't sharpen iron unless there are a few sparks along the way. It might even get heated at times.

This is not the easy way. If you want the easy way, don't let people get too close.

But you will never be sharp in the hands of God. You'll never be effective for the kingdom. You won't be all that God intended you to be.

So what can you do? Be intentional. Let people into your heart. Care enough to reach out to others. Join a small group and raise the bar in it. Find a mentor. Find someone to mentor. Be real. Open your heart. Take a risk. Invite people to speak into your life. Do life with other people. Love boldly.

"Iron sharpens iron, and one man sharpens another."

Song of Solomon 8:6

*Set me as a seal upon your heart, as a seal upon
your arm, for love is strong as death, jealousy is
fierce as the grave. Its flashes are flashes of
fire, the very flame of the LORD.*

Only one book of the Bible is devoted exclusively to courtship and romance, to love and marriage. That book is called Song of Solomon, which is a fitting title because its love has inspired countless love songs over the centuries. But this song is *the* love song, and this book is *the* book of romance. It is the story of young King Solomon and his chosen bride, the beautiful Shulammite. We see, encapsulated in this love story, God's delight in marital love and romance.

Near the end of the book, we see several traits of romantic love.

First of all, it is exclusive.

"Set me as a seal upon your heart." In the ancient world, a person's seal signified ownership, saying, "this belongs to me." Shulammite is saying to Solomon, "I am the seal on your heart. You belong to me and I belong to you. We belong to each other." The wedding ring is a symbol for us of this idea. It means, "I am taken. I belong to another." True love is exclusive. It is for one man and one woman only.

Second, love is strong and constant.

"For love is strong as death." Love is strong, unyielding, and powerful. It survives the tough times that accompany every life and marriage. But how can we make love last? Throughout the western United States, forest fires are common. Most forests in the West don't last very long. But there is one region, the Pacific Northwest, where there are old growth forests that are hundreds of years old. They are beautiful, with towering Douglas firs and massive redwoods, and the ferns grow everywhere on the forest floor.

The reason these trees survive without fires is because the ground is saturated with rainfall much of the year. Gentle and continual rainfall. In the same way, saturate your marriage with God's love—gentle, continual love. Then you too can withstand the fires of life, and your love will grow strong and powerful, like the redwoods. Each day, drink in God's love for you; then you will find a wellspring of love inside. True love is strong and powerful.

Third, love is passionate.

"Its flashes are flashes of fire, the very flame of the LORD." True love is passionate and intense. Put all your heart into it. Too often this happens during courtship, but not after the wedding. The couple gets busy with life and careers, maybe a new house, maybe children, and they slowly drift apart, often not even aware of it until it's too late.

Whenever a couple takes their marriage for granted, love begins to die, so be on your guard. Give each other priority with your attention. Give marriage your best energy. Be fervent in loving one another.

The Notebook was a good movie built on a great book. Nicholas Sparks based the story on the wife's grandparents' love story. At the start of the book, the husband, looking back on his life, says, "I am nothing special, of this I am sure. I am a common man with common thoughts. I've led a common life. There are no monuments dedicated to me, and my name will soon be forgotten. But I've loved another with all my heart and soul, and to me, this has always been enough."

When it comes to marriage, love this way, with all your heart and soul.

Song of Solomon 8:7

*Many waters cannot quench love, neither can floods
drown it. If a man offered for love all the wealth of his
house, he would be utterly despised.*

Song of Solomon is the love song above all love songs, for it is
the love song inspired by God to give us his perspective on love
and romance, on courtship and marriage. Near the end of the
story, we read these words spoken by Shulammite, the bride of
young King Solomon:

> Set me as a seal upon your heart,
> as a seal upon your arm,
> for love is strong as death,
> jealousy is fierce as the grave.
> Its flashes are flashes of fire,
> the very flame of the LORD.
> Many waters cannot quench love,
> neither can floods drown it.
> If a man offered for love
> all the wealth of his house,
> he would be utterly despised. (Song of Sol. 8:6-7)

Love is not only exclusive, strong, and passionate (verse 6), it
is also invincible and priceless.

In verse 7, we see that true love endures. It is invincible.
"Many waters cannot quench love; neither can floods drown it."

When I was a little boy, my parents moved my four sisters
and me to Niagara Falls, New York. There, for the first time, I saw
snow, learned that I spoke with an accent, and saw the stunning
Niagara Falls. The falls are so powerful—an avalanche of water.
Yet the Bible says that all the water in the world cannot quench
love.

Love never ends. It's invincible. It endures until the end of
time. There will be challenges in marriage, but be undeterred,
unflagging, and unmovable. Be tenacious. No matter what, refuse
to throw in the towel.

There is a story from World War II that I especially like.
The Queen of England was asked if she planned to evacuate

her children from London because the bombing of the city was so severe. She replied, "The children won't leave unless I leave. I won't leave unless the King leaves. And the King won't leave under any circumstances whatsoever."

That's the way to think of marriage. "I won't leave under any circumstances whatsoever." True love is invincible.

True love is not only invincible, it is also priceless beyond compare. "If a man offered for love all the wealth of his house, he would be utterly despised."

Is that not true? Is love not invaluable? Is it not a gift from God to treasure beyond the greatest Rembrandt masterpiece?

There is a classic passage on love in 1 Corinthians 13. It describes the glory, beauty, and supremacy of love, and then closes with these immortal words, "So now faith, hope, and love abide, these three; but the greatest of these is love."

Love is simply the greatest thing in the world. And of all human loves, the crown jewel is marital love, a love that is exclusive, strong, passionate, invincible, and priceless beyond measure. That's real love.

This is the kind of love that God wants for every married couple. Pursue it! Pursue this love with all your heart. Settle for nothing less.

Isaiah 6:3b

Holy, holy, holy is the Lord of hosts;
the whole earth is full of his glory!

God appears to the prophet Isaiah in a vision. Isaiah sees the Lord on his throne, high and exalted. Seraphim are singing God's praises, calling out, "Holy, holy, holy is the Lord of hosts; the whole earth is full of his glory."

These two lines could be the motto for the entire Old Testament. We often think of holiness as referring to purity or being sinless, but that's only part of the meaning. The essence of the word "holy" is that God is separate, not just from sin, but from everything. He is separate from all creation, different than all creation, transcendent over all creation. He is so far above everything and everyone that nothing can even be compared to God. He is the incomparable God.

That's what it means to say God is holy. Holiness is not just one attribute of God. More precisely, it is the sum of all God's attributes because God is infinite, sovereign, eternal, omniscient, and much more. He is different. He is holy. Holiness refers to the God-ness of God. All that makes him not human, but God is involved in his holiness. So holiness refers to God being separate from us, different from us, far above us. God's holiness is so important because it is the sum of all God's attributes, all that makes God who he is. No wonder the seraphim cry out. We cry out with them. "Holy, holy, holy is the Lord of hosts; the whole earth is full of his glory" (Is. 6:3).

Isaiah 6:8

And I heard the voice of the Lord saying,
"Whom shall I send, and who will go for us?"
Then I said, "Here I am! Send me."

"Here I am." Available to God.

You see it in Isaiah (Is. 6). You see it in Abraham (Gen. 22). You see it in Mary (Luke 1).

It is the response God looks for in his people. It is the response God longs for in his children.

It is the response of faith. It is the response of trust. It is the response of a servant. "Here I am. Here I am, Lord, ready to do your bidding. Whenever, wherever, whatever. Send me."

But there's a downside, or should I say a hard side? The hard side is risk. If you say "yes" to God's call, where will it take you? Where will you end up? What desert will you have to cross?

You don't know. Isaiah didn't know. He didn't know he would face rejection and end up being sawed in two. Abraham didn't know. He didn't know God would ask him to slay his own son. Mary didn't know. She didn't know she would watch her own son be nailed to a cross.

You don't know the what, the why, or the how. All you know is God.

But that's enough. It's enough for people of faith. It's enough for people who know their God. It's enough for people who've trusted his love. It's enough for people who've felt his grace.

Yes, there is a hard side. There may be pain, there may be sacrifice, but God will see you through. If you could ask Isaiah or Abraham or Mary, they would tell you, "We have no regrets. God can be trusted. It is always best to trust the Lord."

Just as God called Isaiah, God will call you. How will *you* respond?

God is not looking for great ability but great availability. God is looking for people who will say, "Here I am! Send me."

For to us a child is born, to us a son is given;
and the government shall be upon his shoulder,
and his name shall be called Wonderful Counselor,
Mighty God, Everlasting Father, Prince of Peace.
Of the increase of his government and of peace there
will be no end, on the throne of David and over his
kingdom, to establish it and to uphold it with justice
and with righteousness from this time forth and for-
evermore. The zeal of the LORD of hosts will do this.

In 700 BC, the nation of Israel had overwhelming problems. There were vicious enemies around. People had forgotten their God. Darkness, death, and despair filled the land.

What was the solution? A new government? A new leader? Economic reform? Military strategy? A new education system?

Isaiah declares that the only hope will be in a coming baby. How could that be? The baby wouldn't be a regular baby—he would be a king. Indeed, he would be the King of kings and would rule the world.

This baby king would have four titles, describing what he can do for us.

"Wonderful Counselor." This king has all wisdom and understanding. Life may be too complicated for us. Life's complexities are beyond us, but they are not beyond Jesus. Do you need wisdom? Go to the Wonderful Counselor. He knows what to do.

"Mighty God." Now we know: this king is none other than God in the flesh. He is the mighty God, mighty enough to save us. Whatever the need is, he can do it. He can rescue you.

"Everlasting Father." The baby is like a loving father in the way he cares for us. He provides. He protects. He shepherds. He cares. He understands. He listens. What is your biggest burden right now? Bring it to him. *He cares about you.*

"Prince of Peace." Jesus can take your fears, your worries, your guilt, and your hopelessness and replace them with his peace. He can flood your heart with peace. He can envelop you in peace because he is the Prince of Peace.

The ultimate solution to the needs of ancient Israel was this most unusual baby, the baby who was King. He is your solution too. Call out to him. Look to him. Run to him.

He knows what to do. He can rescue you. He cares about you. He can flood your heart with peace.

Run to him now.

Isaiah 40:31

*But they who wait for the L*ORD *shall renew their*
strength; they shall mount up with wings
like eagles; they shall run and not be weary;
they shall walk and not faint.

Isaiah 40 is one of the most striking passages in the Bible on the greatness, the majesty, and the power of God.

It was written to a discouraged people. The Babylonians had taken Israel captive. They had been uprooted from their homes, their communities, and their land. They were discouraged, disheartened, and despondent. They were wondering, "Where is God? Does God care? Does God see? Does God notice? Has God abandoned us?"

We understand. At times, we feel discouraged and wonder if God sees, if God cares. Maybe you feel that way right now.

Through the prophet Isaiah, God reminds his people of how big he is, how vast he is, how great he is.

In Isaiah 40:12-14: God is so much bigger than nature—the oceans, the skies, the deserts, and the mountains.

In Isaiah 40:15-17: God is so much bigger than the nations, nations like Babylon that terrorize and destroy.

In Isaiah 40:18-20: He is so much bigger than idols—the created things that so many worship, anything that is more important to us than God.

In Isaiah 40:21-23: He is so much bigger than the rulers of the earth. We may be impressed by the powerful rulers of nations, but not God. They are like grasshoppers to him.

Finally, God points us to the most awe-inspiring, humbling thing in all creation: the stars. God created the stars and calls them by name. He is so much bigger than even them.

In light of all this, in light of the sheer greatness and power of God, he says to us:

> Put your hope in me. Look to me. Wait upon me. I have not abandoned you. I have not ignored you. I can take care of your biggest problem–addiction, unemployment, teenage rebellion, depression, loneliness, or cancer. Whatever it is, however big it is, I am bigger. So wait upon me. Look to me. Put all your hope in me. I will come through for you!

Isaiah 41:10

Fear not, for I am with you;
be not dismayed, for I am your God;
I will strengthen you, I will help you,
I will uphold you with my righteous right hand.

When you lose your job, when a close friend betrays you, when your teenager runs away, when your marriage falls apart, when you hear the diagnosis "cancer"; in all of these crises and a thousand more, hear God's Word to you: "Fear not, for I am with you; be not dismayed, for I am your God; I will strengthen you, I will help you, I will uphold you with my righteous right hand."

When you feel overwhelmed by life's problems and you are not sure you will survive, hear God's Word to you: "Fear not, for I am with you; be not dismayed, for I am your God; I will strengthen you, I will help you, I will uphold you with my righteous right hand."

When you visit a friend in the hospital who faces surgery or life-threatening disease, let them hear God's Word for them: "Fear not, for I am with you; be not dismayed, for I am your God; I will strengthen you, I will help you, I will uphold you with my righteous right hand."

Every line breathes life and hope and peace.

"Fear not." The fears may come, but do not give way to them. Refuse to give way to fear.

"For I am with you." If you know God is right there with you, you can bear it. You might need to remind yourself over and over. *He is with me.*

"Be not dismayed." Do not be alarmed. Refuse to be shaken. Do not fret yourself.

"For I am your God." This is the bottom line: he is our God and he is bigger than our burden.

"I will strengthen you, I will help you." God's strength is poured out upon our weakness. Feel God's strength rise within you. He is our strength.

"I will uphold you with my righteous right hand." This is deeply encouraging. God will not let you fall. He will uphold you. He will never let you go, never.

Let these words wash over you. Hear them. Hear the voice of God.

"Fear not, for I am with you; be not dismayed, for I am your God; I will strengthen you, I will help you, I will uphold you with my righteous right hand."

Isaiah 53:6

All we like sheep have gone astray;
we have turned–every one–to his own way;
and the LORD has laid on him
the iniquity of us all.

The book of Isaiah is sometimes referred to as the Fifth Gospel because there are so many passages about Jesus Christ, the coming Savior. Of those passages, one of the greatest chapters is Isaiah 53, which is a powerful portrait of the events surrounding the cross, penned seven centuries before Christ came.

In Isaiah 53, the central verse is verse 6: "All we like sheep have gone astray; we have turned—every one—to his own way; and the LORD has laid on him the iniquity of us all."

The first two lines underscore our sin problem. We see the universality of sin; "All we like sheep have gone astray." We also see the essence of sin is when we go our way rather than God's way. "All we like sheep have gone astray; we have turned—every one—to his own way." This is the essence of sin: independence from God, rebelling against God, or seeking to please oneself rather than God.

If the first two lines describe our sin problem, the last two lines give God's solution to it. God took our sin, all our sin, and laid it on Christ. When Christ hung on the cross, God took all our sin and placed it on Christ so he could die in our place.

So here, in the middle of Isaiah 53, is a powerful statement. First, man's basic sin problem is stated to be going our way rather than God's way. Then there's God's solution: a substitute who will bear our sin.

It's amazing when you think of it—all your sin and rebellion paid for by another, who died for you.

Amazing Grace.

*For as the rain and the snow come down from heaven
and do not return there but water the earth, making
it bring forth and sprout, giving seed to the sower and
bread to the eater, so shall my word be that goes out
from my mouth; it shall not return to me empty, but
it shall accomplish that which I purpose, and
shall succeed in the thing for which I sent it.*

God's Word never fails to fulfill its intended purpose. We may not fully understand God's purpose, but whatever God's purpose is when his Word goes out, you can count on it being fulfilled.

God's Word is like the rain and the snow. They fall. The earth is watered. Plants grow. Life flourishes. The rain and the snow always fulfill their purpose. It is the same for the Word of God.

Perhaps you are talking with a troubled friend and John 14:1 comes to mind: "Let not your hearts be troubled. Believe in God; believe also in me."

Or you are facing a big decision in your life and you repeat aloud the promise of James 1:5: "If any of you lacks wisdom, let him ask God, who gives generously to all without reproach, and it will be given him."

Or a friend is grieving a loss, and you remember the unforgettable words of Psalm 23:4: "Even though I walk through the valley of the shadow of death, I will fear no evil, for you are with me; your rod and your staff, they comfort me."

Perhaps you are feeling overwhelmed by life's pressures and you recall Jesus's promise in Matthew 11:28: "Come to me, all who labor and are heavy laden, and I will give you rest."

In all of these instances and a thousand more, God's Word will have its way. The Bible is powerful. The Bible is fruitful. The Bible always accomplishes God's purposes.

That is why it is absolutely essential to read it, study it, learn it, memorize it, cite it, and share it. Saturate your soul with God's Word until it spills over.

When I was a young Christian in the 1970s, Francis Schaeffer was perhaps the leading Christian writer for college students and intellectuals. He once wrote of the Bible:

I don't love this book because it has a leather cover and golden edges. I don't love it as a 'holy book.' I love it because it is God's book. Through it, the Creator of the universe has told us who he is, how to come to him through Christ, who we are, and what all reality is. Without the Bible, we wouldn't have anything. It may sound melodramatic, but sometimes in the morning I reach for my Bible and just pat it. I am so thankful for it. If the God who is there had created the earth and then remained silent, we wouldn't know who he is. But the Bible reveals the God who is there; that's why I love it.

Isaiah 66:1-2

Thus says the LORD: "Heaven is my throne,
and the earth is my footstool; what is the house that
you would build for me, and what is the place of my
rest? All these things my hand has made, and so all
these things came to be," declares the LORD. "But this
is the one to whom I will look: he who is humble and
contrite in spirit and trembles at my word."

The almighty Creator, the great and holy God, vast and eternal, delights in the man or woman who is humble, who is contrite in spirit, and who trembles at his Word. God loves to see these three traits in us.

The three traits go together. If you are humble, then you will be contrite in spirit, and you will tremble at God's Word. If you are contrite in spirit, then you will be humble, and you will tremble at God's Word. If you tremble at God's Word, then you will be humble, and contrite in spirit. The three traits go together and reflect a profound surrender and submission to God.

Who are the humble? Humble people know that everything good in their life comes from God. The humble are dependent on God, even desperate for God. There is no sense of self-reliance, self-promotion, or self-exaltation. These are the people who humble themselves before God in surrender and humble themselves before other people in service. The humble person is focused not on himself but upon God and other people.

What about the contrite in spirit? People who are contrite in spirit are broken because of their sin. When the Spirit of God gently exposes some sin in their life, there is not a hardened defiance before God but a tender brokenness. There is the same spirit that the tax collector exuded in Luke 18, when he felt too broken to even lift his eyes toward heaven, but simply cried out, "God, be merciful to me, a sinner!" The contrite in spirit are quick to confess their sins to God.

What does it mean to tremble at God's Word? These are the people who have a deep reverence and respect for the Bible as the living Word of God. They know that this is not a human book, but God's book; therefore, they treasure it. They prize it. They savor it. And, most importantly, they obey it. They feel such a responsibility before a holy God to obey whatever they read in his Word.

Is this you? Humble? Contrite in spirit? Trembling at God's Word?

These are the people who delight the heart of our God.

Jeremiah 9:23-24 (NASB)

Thus says the Lord, "Let not a wise man boast of his wisdom, and let not the mighty man boast of his might, let not a rich man boast of his riches; but let him who boasts boast of this, that he understands and knows Me, that I am the Lord who exercises loving kindness, justice and righteousness on earth; for I delight in these things," declares the Lord.

God is looking for the man or woman who thirsts to know him. He is looking for the person who longs to be close to him, to be one of his intimates, to know him personally.

This is not the person who is enamored by wisdom, money, or riches. This person will not be enamored by the things the world is enamored with. He will not be overly impressed by the wealthy and the powerful, by the Larry Ellisons and the Warren Buffetts of the world. He will not be awed by those who are mighty in athletic performance, by the Kobe Bryants and the Usain Bolts of the world. Nor will this person be unduly moved by scholars and writers who accumulate degrees and publish works.

No, this is the person who has caught a glimpse of glory and who breathes the breath of eternity. This is the person who has seen God and never recovered. This is the person who is impressed with God himself, the Creator, not with his creatures. This is the person who longs to know God, understand God, and be close to God. This is the person who knows that God is the Lord, the almighty and sovereign God. This is the person who knows that God is the God of steadfast love, justice, and righteousness in the earth. This is the person who knows that God is good and great, and it is the privilege of our lives to know this God.

Where are the people like this? The people who thirst to know God?

To know God is our highest good and deepest joy. To know God is more life-giving and soul-thrilling than anything else. To know God is our purpose, our mission, and our life. To know God is the glory of a human life.

Jeremiah 29:11

For I know the plans I have for you, declares the
LORD, plans for welfare and not for evil,
to give you a future and a hope.

These words were first given to the prophet Jeremiah so that he could deliver them to the people of Israel, who had been exiled to Babylon. They were frightened and hurting, and they needed this life-giving encouragement. Though the promise is not given directly to us, we see the heart of God for his people, which includes us.

Life is so hard and overwhelming at times. How deeply encouraging it is to know that God is a sovereign God and that he has a plan for our lives. How comforting it is to remember that God has a heart to bless us and not harm us, especially when the storms of life come and we are not sure we will survive. How meaningful it is to know that God will give us a future and a hope, no matter how bleak things look in that moment.

If we know that God is the sovereign God, that God is on his throne, that God has his eye upon us, and that God will see us through, then we can bear it. Whatever it is, we can bear it.

Dear Christ-follower, whatever you are going through today, know that God has a plan for you. You may not understand that plan. Indeed, you will not understand that plan, not fully. But God's heart means to bless you and do you good. Look into the face of Jesus and you will see what God is like. You will see that God is good and he will do you good.

Whatever you are going through, whatever it is, God will have the final word. And it will be good.

Just you wait and see.

Daniel 3:18

But if not, be it known to you, O king, that we will
not serve your gods or worship the golden
image that you have set up.

For me, Daniel 3 ranks as one of the most moving stories of courage and obedience in the entire Bible.

Babylon, led by its proud and powerful King Nebuchadnezzar, is the reigning superpower of the day. Nebuchadnezzar arrogantly commands his government officials to bow down before a golden image or else be thrown into a fiery furnace.

Nebuchadnezzar gathers all of his officials together. When the signal is given, they all fall to the ground to worship the image. That is, all except three Jews: Shadrach, Meshach, and Abednego. Nebuchadnezzar, who is accustomed to complete obedience, is furious. He threatens them with their lives. Their response is a classic.

"O Nebuchadnezzar, we have no need to answer you in this matter" (Dan. 3:16). They have no need to answer because worshipping an image is not even an option for them.

"If this be so, our God whom we serve is able to deliver us from the burning fiery furnace, and he will deliver us out of your hand, O king" (Dan. 3:17). God can deliver them. God will deliver them. Nebuchadnezzar may be a mighty king, but they serve God, who is so much bigger. God is able to take care of them.

"But if not, be it known to you, O king, that we will not serve your gods or worship the golden image that you have set up." (Dan. 3:18). Even if their God does not rescue them, they want to be clear on one thing: they are not worshiping that image.

Shadrach, Meshach, and Abednego are facing the threat of an excruciating death. But they are undeterred and not intimidated by this fearsome dictator. They fear God more. They would rather suffer and die than displease their God.

What loyalty. What courage. What obedience. What fearlessness.

How about you? Does Daniel 3 strike a chord in your heart? Have you joined the "company of the committed," the men and women throughout history who have decided to go all out for the only cause that matters? Have you made the resolute decision that you will obey the Lord regardless of the consequences? Is there any area of compromise you need to surrender to Jesus Christ?

Rise up, O man of God, O woman of God, and fully surrender to Jesus Christ. Hold nothing back.

Micah 6:8

He has told you, O man, what is good; and what does
the LORD require of you but to do justice, and to love
kindness, and to walk humbly with your God?

Micah 6:8 is a clear, crisp, and simple summary of what God expects from you and me. These three things that matter so much to God are the three things God wants to see in us: justice, kindness, and humility.

To act justly is to treat people fairly and respectfully. You do not oppress or mistreat others. You do not abuse your power by taking good things God has given people, such as life, freedom, and property.

There is a quote at the Holocaust Memorial Museum in Washington, D.C., that reads, "Thou shalt not be a victim. Thou shalt not be a perpetrator. Above all, thou shalt not be a bystander."

That's justice. What about kindness? To show kindness is to help the poor, the downtrodden, and the hurting. Kindness is like the Good Samaritan rescuing the wounded traveler.

Jack Jezreel, founder of JustFaith Ministries, illustrates the difference between kindness and justice:

> Suppose one morning I wake up, look out my window, and in the stream that runs behind my house I see a man who is unconscious, wet, and bleeding? Of course I'd rush to his aid and give him medical attention and get him to the hospital. What if the next day I find another man in the stream in the same condition? Well, I'd also take care of him. But if on the third day I found another person, after getting that person to the hospital, I'd better walk upriver and find out how and why these bodies are getting into the stream!
>
> Both justice and kindness are important, but kindness deals more with symptoms and justice deals more with causes.

The third requirement is humility. "Walk humbly with your God." This is the person who thinks, "It's not about me. It's all about Jesus. I don't think less of myself, but I think about myself less. I want to be more of a listener than a talker, more of a giver than a taker, more of a servant than a boss."

How do these three traits fit together? They all express what it means to love your neighbor as yourself. Justice is when you see someone mistreated and you respond in love to rescue them. Kindness is when you see someone in need and you respond in love to help them. Humility is when you see someone and you focus on them and not yourself. All three traits—justice, kindness, and humility—reflect a heart of love.

And all three traits delight our God in heaven.

Malachi 3:10

*Bring the full tithe into the storehouse, that there may
be food in my house. And thereby put me to the test,
says the LORD of hosts, if I will not open the windows
of heaven for you and pour down for you a
blessing until there is no more need.*

Malachi 3 is a hard-hitting passage, perhaps the strongest
passage on giving in the entire Bible. God is a bit like a mother
bird pushing us off the limb so that we can experience the joys
of flying.

"Will man rob God? Yet you are robbing me. But you say,
'How have we robbed you?' In your tithes and contributions."
(Mal. 3:8). If we do not return the first tenth of our income to
God, God looks at that as robbing him. We are not robbing the
church or the pastors. We are robbing God.

"You are cursed with a curse, for you are robbing me, the
whole nation of you" (Mal. 3:8). God simply will not pour out his
favor and blessing upon us if we will not trust him with our tithe.
When we steal from God, we forfeit the blessing of God. No one
cheats God without cheating themselves in the process.

Which would you choose: living on 100 percent of your
income without God's blessing on your life, or living on 90 percent
of your income and having God's favor on your life? I guess the
better question is: Which do you choose?

"Bring the full tithe into the storehouse, that there may be
food in my house. And thereby put me to the test, says the LORD
of hosts, if I will not open the windows of heaven for you and
pour down for you a blessing until there is no more need." This is
an unusual challenge, found only here in the Bible. God is saying,
"Try it. Test me. Bring the first tithe of your income and see if I
will not open the windows of heaven."

There is something special about giving. It is *the* test of the
heart. Are we serving God or money? Are we trusting God or
money? Who is our real master?

This brief life is your only opportunity to trust God with your
finances. Don't miss your one opportunity to fly.

And when Jesus was baptized, immediately he went up from the water, and behold, the heavens were opened to him, and he saw the Spirit of God descending like a dove and coming to rest on him; and behold, a voice from heaven said, "This is my beloved Son, with whom I am well pleased."

Can you imagine standing on the bank of the Jordan River and watching this scene? First, John baptizes Jesus, which is shocking enough. Then heaven opens, and a dove descends that's more than just a dove. And there's this voice. What a voice! Like thunder, speaking to Jesus. "This is my beloved Son, with whom I am well pleased."

Can you imagine standing there, eyes wide, jaw open, and heart racing?

In one fell swoop, the triune God. Father, Son, and Holy Spirit. One God, three persons.

It's not one person who changes forms. It's not like liquid water becoming ice and then becoming vapor. The Father doesn't become the Son and later become the Spirit. Oh no. One God (underscored throughout the Bible), yet three distinct persons, each eternally and equally God.

The baptismal charge found at the other end of Matthew's Gospel places the unity and the plurality of the Godhead side by side. "Baptizing them in the name of the Father and of the Son and of the Holy Spirit." One name, singular, because there is only one God. Yet this is the name of the Father, the Son, and the Spirit, indicating that there are three persons in the one Godhead.

Does this make sense? Not fully.

Is it logically tidy and neat? Hardly.

Is there any precedent or analogy elsewhere? Not that I know of.

Would any person have dreamed this up? I doubt it.

Is there mystery here? Yes! Mystery abounds.

Am I surprised that God transcends and baffles my little finite reason? Not at all.

One God, yet three persons. That's what the Bible assumes. And this truth is crucial. It means that God did not need to create humans or angels in order to love. God has always loved. There has always been perfect love between the persons of the Trinity. God did not become a lover at a point in time, because he has always loved. Our God *is* love. If God was not triune, then he would not be love in his essence.

Triune God. We would never have thought this up, but now that God has revealed his Trinity, we see how wonderful and necessary it is. Our great triune God is a lover.

"This is my beloved Son." And he always has been.

Matthew 4:4

But he answered, "It is written, 'Man shall not live by bread alone, but by every word that comes from the mouth of God.'"

Like a wounded bear enraged, he keeps charging. Jesus's attacker, the devil, charges again and again, claws bared. Three times he attacks.

Each time Jesus fights him off. Each time Jesus resists the bear. Each time Jesus stands firm, unyielding and unmovable.

The devil questions Jesus's position as Son of God. Then he quotes Scripture deceptively. Then he offers Jesus the world.

And how does Jesus fight back? What weapon does Jesus wield? His sword, sharp and deadly. The sword of the Spirit, God's piercing Word.

Three times Jesus answers, "It is written."

The wounded bear, enraged, will come after you. He will tempt, accuse, lie, deceive, and bluster. Be ready. Stand firm, resist, and fight him off.

Jesus teaches us how to fight the battle. Know the scriptures. Quote the scriptures. Obey the scriptures. Wield your sword, sharp and deadly, for the battle rages on, and to be victorious, you too must stand on God's Word. Know it. Study it. Memorize it. Cite it. Obey it. Treasure it.

This book is your lifeline.

Matthew 4:19

And he said to them, "Follow me, and I will make you fishers of men."

God loves to use ordinary people.

When Jesus chooses the twelve disciples, he begins with four fishermen. Not scholars, not rabbis, not priests. Fishermen.

Peter and Andrew, along with James and John, drop everything and follow Jesus:

They follow Jesus immediately.
They follow Jesus wholeheartedly.
They follow Jesus unreservedly.
They follow Jesus with glad and full hearts.
They follow Jesus without reservations or conditions.
They follow Jesus not knowing where he will take them.
They follow Jesus no matter the costs of following him.

These are the kind of followers Jesus is still looking for—not casual, half-hearted followers living for themselves, but fully devoted followers living for their King. Going for broke. Going all out for their Savior.

Jesus does not tell you, "Go make yourself a fisher of men." No, your job is simply to follow Jesus with all your heart. Fall in love with Jesus, and he will make you a fisher of men.

Matthew 5:3

*Blessed are the poor in spirit, for theirs is
the kingdom of heaven.*

Writer Lee Strobel relates the story of Dr. Alexander Zaichenko,
who was a prominent economist in the former Soviet Union. He
was an atheist from a family of atheists living in a country of atheists.
But he began to ask himself the kinds of questions that many people
ask themselves as they get older. "What's life really all about? Is this
all there is?"

As he groped for answers, he obtained a black-market Bible and
began reading it with an open mind. He started at the beginning of
Matthew and was surprised by how boring it was. After reading the
genealogy of Jesus, which began with, "Abraham was the father of
Isaac, and Isaac the father of Jacob, and Jacob the father of Judah
and his brothers," and so forth, he began to think, "Maybe atheists
are right. Maybe there's nothing to this stuff." But he kept reading,
and finally he reached Matthew 5, where Jesus delivers the Sermon
on the Mount.

This towering intellect, who had studied all the classics, all the
philosophers, all the great thinkers, later declared, "It took my breath
away." When Zaichenko read the words of Jesus in the Sermon on
the Mount, he realized that those words were not the words of a mere
man, and he came to Christ.

The Sermon on the Mount, which is commonly considered the
greatest speech in history, begins with the simple line, "Blessed are
the poor in spirit." Not the poor in resources or money or body; the
poor in spirit.

The poor in spirit are those who recognize how much they need
God. They recognize that they need God desperately. They are dependent on God. They are spiritually poor, spiritually bankrupt. Poor in
spirit is the opposite of self-sufficient, self-reliant, and self-righteous.

Why did Jesus begin here with spiritual poverty? Perhaps because the root sin is pride, and the worst form of pride is spiritual
pride or self-righteousness. Spiritual poverty is the opposite of spiritual pride, so Jesus begins with the poor in spirit.

The first beatitude focuses on recognizing how desperate you
are for God, how much you need God, and how dependent you are
upon God.

Matthew 6:1

Beware of practicing your righteousness before other
people in order to be seen by them, for then
you will have no reward from your
Father who is in heaven.

God is concerned not just with what you do, but why you do it. Motives matter to God.

For me, that's a challenge, because I don't think I have ever had pure motives in anything. Take preaching, for example. I have never preached a message without some trace of human pride. Not once.

But that's no excuse. We may not have perfect motives, but our motives still matter. They matter to God, so they must matter to us.

Note that Jesus does not say it is wrong to do good deeds before people. Rather, it is wrong to do good deeds in order to be seen by people. The issue is not if your act is private. Rather, the issue is: Is this act prideful?

Why do you do what you do? Is this for God or is this for me? Is my concern to exalt Jesus or to exalt myself?

Jesus gives three examples in the following verses: giving, praying, and fasting. But Jesus's principle applies to everything in life. Motives matter.

A.W. Tozer once wrote, "It is not what we do that makes a thing sacred, it is why we do it."

Matthew 6:9

Pray then like this: "Our Father in heaven."

When Jesus taught the disciples how to pray, he began with the startling title, "Our Father." The Jews never called God Father, nor did anyone else. Michael Green noted, "You can search Islam and you will not find that name of Father among the ninety-nine names of God. You will search Hinduism or Confucianism in vain. This is unique."

The Hebrew term *abba* is a tender, affectionate, loving name for a father. It has the sense of "daddy" or "papa." In many ways, the main New Testament name for God is Father.

Perhaps you had bad experiences with your earthly father. Perhaps you had an absent father, an alcoholic father, or an abusive father.

If you had a good father, then you understand God as Father by comparison. But if you had a bad father, then you understand God as Father by contrast. Since no one has a perfect father, to some extent everyone understands God by contrast, but all of us understand the idea of the Father that is good.

What is a perfect Father like? He is wise, loving, kind, and gentle. He is strong, powerful, fair, and forgiving. He protects us and he provides for us. He is good. That's the perfect Father.

But he is not merely our Father. He is our Father in heaven. This is not God's location, for God fills the universe. The point is that God is glorious, majestic, exalted, and all-powerful. He is sovereign, infinite, and incomprehensible. He is great.

Never forget the goodness of God, for he is our Father. Never forget the greatness of God, for he is our Father in heaven.

This may be the most important thing about prayer: remember the person you are talking to. When you keep in mind whom it is you are talking to, when you remember whom is right there with you, when you consider that God is Father and God is in heaven, then your prayer life will never be dull and boring. It will be vibrant and exciting.

Just remember whom it is you are talking with.

Matthew 6:9c

Hallowed be your name.

The point of this prayer is: Lord, may your name be honored. May your name be exalted. May your name be glorified. Lord, may you get the honor due to your holy name.

The spirit behind this request is a blazing passion for the glory of God. Our concern in prayer is God's name, not our name; God's reputation, not ours. For self-centered humans like us, that's easier said than done.

Do you notice how God-centered this prayer is? Think of the first four lines:

> Our Father in heaven,
> hallowed be your name,
> your kingdom come,
> your will be done,
> on earth as it is in heaven.

Jesus is teaching us how to pray, and his model prayer exudes one striking trait: making your prayers God-centered, not self-centered. It's not wrong to bring your needs to God. In fact, it's a good thing. But put the focus on God's glory, not your problems.

If you begin to pray by honoring the glory of God, it lifts your gaze off yourself and onto God. The perspective on your problems becomes correctly sized. You are reminded that however big your problem is, God is bigger.

Are your prayers more God-centered or self-centered? Pray God-centered prayers.

Matthew 6:10a

Your kingdom come.

The kingdom is how God rules in the lives of people. It is not a kingdom of territory or land, but a kingdom of human beings. Whenever someone trusts Christ as Savior and whenever people submit to him, there is the kingdom of God.

Christ's kingdom is not a political kingdom, with armies, parliaments, and capital buildings. Rather, Christ's kingdom is a spiritual kingdom, a kingdom of the spirit. It is not a visible kingdom but an invisible one.

It is not a kingdom of force and coercion, but a kingdom of love and grace. It is a kingdom not of words but of power, the power of the Holy Spirit.

The kingdom is an international community made up of people from every tribe, tongue, group, and nation. There are no barriers of race or gender or rank in this kingdom. This is a kingdom of joy, peace, power, and love. In this kingdom, the people don't die for the king; he dies for them and then he rises again. And now the servants of the king spread throughout the earth to rescue people from the kingdom of darkness.

The kingdom is wherever someone bows a knee to King Jesus. But the kingdom will come to its fullness when the king returns to earth. All of this we pray for when we pray, "Your kingdom come."

Come, Lord Jesus! Come and reign in all the earth. Come and reign in all my life.

Matthew 6:10b

Your will be done on earth as it is in heaven.

Prayer that pleases God is prayer that is focused on *God's* will, not *our* will. Lord, may your will be done in my life, in my family, in my church, in my community, in my country, in the whole earth.

And we mean it when we pray this way. We really want God's will more than our own will. This is our heart.

Prayer is not getting what we want from God. Prayer is not trying to get God to change his mind. Rather, prayer is aligning our will with God's will, because God is the sovereign and holy God and he knows what's best. Prayer is getting on board with what God is doing and surrendering all that we are and all that we have to a loving Father. Prayer that pleases God is focused on God's plans, God's desires, and God's agenda for our life, rather than our plans, our desires, and our agenda for our life.

Jesus exemplified this heart in the Garden of Gethsemane when he prayed in his agony, "My Father, if it be possible, let this cup pass from me; nevertheless, not as I will, but as you will" (Matt. 26:39).

This is the way Jesus prayed, and this is the way God wants us to pray.

Matthew 6:11

Give us this day our daily bread.

The first three requests in the Lord's Prayer focus on God's glory. The last three requests focus on our needs.

"Give us this day our daily bread" is a petition for God's provision day by day. Lord, I depend on you for daily bread. My bread ultimately does not come from a grocery store, but from a loving Father.

Bring all your needs to God. If there is something you need, ask for it. From Genesis to Revelation, God teaches us to ask, repeatedly. Ask, ask, ask. "You do not have, because you do not ask" (James 4:2).

This doesn't mean we get whatever we want whenever and however we want it. But your Father tells you to ask.

In fact, the asking itself glorifies God. Think about it: every time you ask God for something, you implicitly declare:

> Lord, I believe you are God.
> I believe you are God, I'm not, and I need you.
> I am not sufficient on my own.
> Lord, I may not have perfect faith, but I have enough faith to come to you and ask.
> Lord, help! Lord, rescue! Lord, deliver!
> Lord, I believe that you care, that you can do this for me if you choose, and that you are my Papa. Amen.

Every time you ask God for something, you glorify your Father in heaven.

Asking God for things is not a sign of selfishness. It's a sign of dependence.

Papa likes it, so ask.

Matthew 6:12a

And forgive us our debts.

The Lord's Prayer begins with three God-centered petitions, concerning God's name, God's kingdom, and God's will. Following this are three personal petitions concerning provision for the present, pardon for the past, and protection for the future.

In the Lord's Prayer, Jesus teaches us to bring our sins to God and ask for forgiveness. If you want forgiveness from God, then you must extend forgiveness to others.

Matthew 6:14-15, just after the Lord's Prayer, underscores this command: "For if you forgive others their trespasses, your heavenly Father will also forgive you, but if you do not forgive others their trespasses, neither will your Father forgive your trespasses."

Does Jesus mean we earn grace by giving grace? Not at all. Grace is, by definition, unearned and undeserved. A gift. Furthermore, the Bible is emphatic that Christ paid for all our sins and that there is no condemnation for those in Christ Jesus.

We could call this "legal" forgiveness. It concerns our right to stand before God.

But there is also a "family" forgiveness or a "relational" forgiveness, and we find that in the Lord's Prayer. If I speak to my wife, Gayle, with a harsh tone, she doesn't sever the relationship. We don't have to get remarried when I apologize. However, there is a barrier between us, and I need to apologize to her to restore the relationship.

This is what Jesus addresses in the Lord's Prayer, and it is crucial. If we want to be close to our God and have no barriers between us, if we hope to enjoy his love, peace, and tenderness, if we want him to hear our prayers, then we must forgive people who hurt us. Forgive just as God forgives you.

Matthew 6:13ab

And lead us not into temptation,
but deliver us from evil.

Jesus begins with two personal petitions: provision for the present and pardon for the past. In the third petition, Jesus teaches us to ask for protection for the future.

From Genesis to Revelation, the Bible teaches us that there are unseen spiritual beings all around us. There are angels led by Michael and demons led by Satan engaged in a cosmic spiritual battle. Demons oppose God in every way and are out to destroy your soul and ruin your life.

Many Christians pretty much ignore the spiritual battle. They are a bit too sophisticated for such things. But not Jesus. He did not ignore the raging battle fueled by fear and pride. Rather, he courageously fought the battle.

Perhaps the best statement about biblical balance in spiritual warfare was given by C.S. Lewis in the preface to his book *The Screwtape Letters:* "There are two equal and opposite errors into which our race can fall about the devils. One is to disbelieve in their existence. The other is to believe, and to feel an excessive and unhealthy interest in them. They themselves are equally pleased by both errors and hail a materialist or a magician with the same delight."

It is noteworthy that in the only sample prayer that Jesus gives us, one of the three requests concerns the spiritual battle. This suggests that prayer concerning the battle is important and should be a significant part of our daily prayer lives.

Fight the battle. In Christ's strength, fight the battle.

Matthew 6:21

For where your treasure is,
there your heart will be also.

Addison Leach was a college professor. He knew two young women who became followers of Jesus.

They went to their parents and said, "We've become Christians, and we want to be missionaries." Each of their parents said, "Now dear, you had a religious experience. How wonderful. But you need some security. Before you go off to have a missionary experience, which is fine, we want you to have a master's degree. We want you to have taken a job or two so you've gotten your career off the ground. And we want you to have some money in the bank for some security."

The women went to Dr. Leach and said, "What do we say about that?" He replied, "Here's what I would say to your parents. Tell them we're on a little ball of rock spinning through space. It's called Earth, and who knows if we're going to run into something. But even if we don't, some day, under each one of us is going to open a trap door, and everybody's going to fall off. At the end of your life, a trap door will open up underneath you, and you will fall off the little ball of rock. And underneath will be the everlasting arms or nothing at all. And you think a master's degree is going to give you some security?"

This story raises the issue: Is our security in money or is it in God? Money is powerful. It reveals our heart.

Jesus does *not* say where you heart is, there is your treasure. He does not say your money follows your heart.

Rather, he startles us with the opposite truth: "Where your treasure is, there your heart will be also." Money is powerful. If you invest it in God and his kingdom, it will pull your heart along with it. You will love God more.

However, if you put all your money into accumulating and hoarding, then your money will pull your heart away from God. You will love God less.

Maybe you thought that the gateway to a spiritual life was prayer or Bible reading, serving or community. All of these are absolutely vital, but the gateway to the spiritual life is your money.

There's something about money; it's tied to your heart in some profound way. It shows where your heart is, who you really are, and where your trust really is.

Matthew 6:24

No one can serve two masters,
for either he will hate the one and love the other,
or he will be devoted to the one and despise the other.
You cannot serve God and money.

Money is the rival to God in the human heart. Our significance, our sense of worth, our sense of security and safety will be found in money and things, or they will be found in God.

Which is first in your life: Money or God? A related question: Are you generous, or are you greedy?

Tim Keller, a writer and pastor in Manhattan, comments, "It is astounding that we live in the place we live, in the time we live, and we won't think about the possibility that we're greedy. That shows the power of greed. It shows the power of money."

Keller points out that hardly anyone thinks that they are greedy. This is why: we always find someone else who has a lot more money or stuff than we do, and we say to ourselves, "They're greedy. Not me!"

We live in a country of great affluence. In fact, the United States has 6 percent of the world's population and 50 percent of the world's wealth. We have astronomical personal debt. And yet hardly anyone in our country feels they are greedy.

Greed means that we're always wanting more. More stuff, more things, and more money. Greed means I feel good about myself and I feel secure if I have money. Greed means I spend on self, accumulate for self, and focus on self. Greed is the opposite of generosity.

No wonder Jesus talked so much about money. It is the rival to God in the human heart.

Matthew 6:33

*But seek first the kingdom of God and his righteous-
ness, and all these things will be added to you.*

Jesus tells us that if we put God first in our lives, God will provide
for our needs. Not our wants, but our needs.

How do we seek God first? It means we seek God in his
Word and prayer each day. We obey God even when it's difficult.
We worship God regularly with the community of faith. We
give joyfully and generously. We pursue God's dreams and not
our dreams. We consider that our life belongs not to us, but to
another, to the one who died for us.

It means I recognize that my life is not about me but about
Christ. I live to exalt his name, not my name. I live for his
kingdom, not my kingdom. I live for his will, not my will.

No matter what happens, I put Jesus Christ first. Here's an
example.

A hundred years ago, William Borden, heir to the Borden
dairy fortune, graduated from a Chicago high school. His father
gave him three things: money for a trip around the world, a
servant to go with him, and a new Bible.

Borden traveled through Africa, parts of Asia, and Europe,
and saw much suffering and pain. He turned to the back page of
his Bible and wrote two words: "No Reserves."

After graduating from Yale University, he turned down
offers from Wall Street and the family business. Jesus Christ had
captured his heart and called him to the mission field. He decided
to enter Princeton Theological Seminary and wrote two more
words: "No Retreats."

Three years later, he graduated and sailed for China to work
with Muslims. While in Egypt, he was stricken with cerebral
meningitis and died in thirty days. He was twenty-five years old.
His father, later leafing through his son's Bible, found a third
phrase: "No Regrets."

This was the perspective of a young man who put Christ first,
who went all out for Christ. Penned on the back page of his Bible:

No Reserves.
No Retreats.
No Regrets.

Matthew 7:7

Ask, and it will be given to you; seek, and you will find; knock, and it will be opened to you.

This is an astounding promise. "Ask, and it will be given to you." But it is also puzzling. Perhaps you're thinking, "I ask for a lot of things that I don't get. How is this true?"

We should ask two questions to clarify: Who is this a promise to? What is this a promise of?

First, who is this a promise to? Anybody and everybody? No; in the context of the Sermon on the Mount, Jesus is addressing his believers, who can call God "Father," who have trusted Christ as Savior.

However, Jesus is not talking to believers in general, but to those believers who are going all out for Christ. They are poor in spirit, gentle, merciful, and persecuted. They are salt and light. They obey God. They are not perfect people, but they are surrendered people.

So this is an astounding promise to you if you are fully surrendered to Jesus, if you are going all-out for Christ.

The second question, "What is this a promise of?" Jesus clarifies in verses Matthew 7:9-11: "Or which one of you, if his son asks him for bread, will give him a stone? Or if he asks for a fish, will give him a serpent? If you then, who are evil, know how to give good gifts to your children, how much more will your Father who is in heaven give good things to those who ask him."

What is Jesus's point here? God is more ready to give good gifts to his children than we are. If you have children or grandchildren, then you like saying yes to them. You like to give them good things.

But sometimes our children ask for things that are not good for them, and we say no for their sakes. Moreover, sometimes we ask for things, and they are good things, but we don't need them yet. God intends to give them to us, but not yet.

We don't like waiting. We don't want to wait three seconds for our slow computers. But God uses waiting. It's one of the main things God uses to shape our souls, to teach us dependence, endurance, faith, and gratitude.

This passage shows us the heart of a father. Whenever we ask, God's heart is to say "yes" to us. So ask, ask, ask. And, if it's a good thing for you, at this time, you can know that your loving Father will say "yes."

See the heart of a Father, and ask.

Matthew 7:12

*So whatever you wish that others would do to you, do
also to them, for this is the Law and the Prophets.*

The Sermon on the Mount is not just one the greatest messages
in the Bible; it is the greatest message in all history. No other
speech or message has had the impact, the influence, and the
power of this brief speech. Two thousand years later, it continues
to reach both uneducated people and learned scholars.

When you read the world's great philosophers and then
read the words of Jesus, you cannot miss the stark contrast.
Jesus's words, especially in the Sermon on the Mount, have an
otherworldly resonance of truth, wisdom, and authority. To
compare the world's great philosophers to Jesus is like comparing
the local fifth-grade football team to the Green Bay Packers.

One of the most notable declarations in the Sermon on the
Mount is verse Matthew 7:12, commonly known as the Golden
Rule: "So whatever you wish that others would do to you, do also
to them, for this is the Law and the Prophets."

This succinctly summarizes what it means to love people.
Bishop J.C. Ryle remarked, "It settles a hundred different points.
It prevents the necessity of laying down endless little rules for our
conduct in specific cases."

If you want people to be patient with you, then be patient with
others. If you appreciate it when people listen to you with eye
contact, seeking to understand you, then listen that way to them.
If you appreciate when people tell you the truth, then speak the
truth to others. If you want others to pray for you, then pray for
others. If you appreciate it when other people give you the benefit
of the doubt, then give others the benefit of the doubt. If someone
is upset at you—especially someone close to you, like a spouse,
a child, or a close friend—if you appreciate that person coming
directly to you, rather than giving you the silent treatment, the
cold shoulder, or talking about you to a third party, then do the
same for them.

If you want people to forgive you, then be a big-hearted
forgiver of others. If you appreciate when people affirm you and
build you up, then affirm and build up others. If you appreciate
it when people speak to you with a kind and gentle tone, rather
than a harsh and demanding tone, then do the same for them.
If you appreciate it when people take the trouble to learn your
name, then learn their names. If you appreciate it when a spouse

or a friend keeps their promises to you, even about the little things, then be a promise keeper yourself. If you appreciate it when someone defends you and is loyal to you, then be loyal to other people.

In any and every way, let Matthew 7:12 be your touchstone: "So whatever you wish that others would do to you, do also to them, for this is the Law and the Prophets."

Matthew 9:36

When he saw the crowds, he had compassion for them, because they were harassed and helpless, like sheep without a shepherd.

See as Jesus saw. Feel as Jesus felt. Love as Jesus loved.

Jesus saw people. He looked deeply into their eyes and into their souls. He saw each person as someone who mattered to God. He saw people as those who were special in the sight of God. Jesus saw people like no one has ever seen people.

Jesus felt for people. His heart was bursting with tender compassion. He felt for those people who were especially needy. He felt for people who were helpless. He felt for people who were harassed by an onslaught of problems. Deep, visceral feelings flooded Jesus's heart whenever he encountered human beings in pain. Jesus felt for people like no one has ever felt.

Jesus loved people. How he loved people. He cared. He wept. He healed. He touched. He taught. He rebuked. He forgave. He died. No one has ever loved people the way Jesus loved people.

See as Jesus saw. Feel as Jesus felt. Love as Jesus loved.

This is true for all the people in your world. Your spouse. Your children. The cranky coworker down the hall. Your difficult boss. The man who dries your car at the carwash. The reclusive neighbor down the street. The showoff in your gym class. The friend who let you down. Your father who still tries to control you. The rude clerk at the mall. The loud, know-it-all coach of your son's soccer team. Your non-Christian friend who has the weirdest ideas. The woman in your small group who is offended by the smallest things. Each and every person in your world.

See as Jesus saw. Feel as Jesus felt. Love as Jesus loved.

Matthew 11:28

*Come to me, all who labor and are heavy-laden,
and I will give you rest.*

Each one of us at times feels weary, burdened, and overwhelmed. Jesus speaks to us at those times.

If you are weary because of busyness and a hectic, harried lifestyle, if you have filled your life with too much activity and noise, and too little quiet and stillness, then Jesus says to you, "Come to me, all who labor and are heavy-laden, and I will give you rest."

If you are burdened with guilt because of a past failure that torments you, then Jesus says to you, "Come to me, all who labor and are heavy-laden, and I will give you rest."

If you feel burdened by fear and worry constantly harassing you and stealing your joy, then Jesus says to you, "Come to me, all who labor and are heavy-laden, and I will give you rest."

If you are wrestling with some sin that is plaguing and attacking you, ruining your joy in the Lord, then Jesus says to you, "Come to me, all who labor and are heavy-laden, and I will give you rest."

If you feel overwhelmed by an addiction that has you in its grasp, if you feel helpless to break free from this addiction that is ruining your life and hurting those you love, then Jesus says to you, "Come to me, all who labor and are heavy-laden, and I will give you rest."

If you are burdened by anger and resentment because you have been mistreated, and the bitterness is slowly poisoning your soul, then Jesus says to you, "Come to me, all who labor and are heavy-laden, and I will give you rest."

If you feel overwhelmed with discouragement, a sense of failure, and a black cloud of depression, then Jesus says to you, "Come to me, all who labor and are heavy-laden, and I will give you rest."

If you have lost a close family member or friend, and your heart feels so completely broken that it will never heal, then Jesus says to you, "Come to me, all who labor and are heavy-laden, and I will give you rest."

If you feel like you are always on a religious treadmill and you can never quite measure up or please the Lord, then Jesus says to you, "Come to me, all who labor and are heavy-laden, and I will give you rest."

At times, we all grow weary and heavy-laden. It is part of our humanness in this world. But whatever the burden, big or small, Jesus says to you, "Come to me, all who labor and are heavy-laden, and I will give you rest."

What is the burden you face today? Pause now and hear the voice of Jesus, "Come to me, all who labor and are heavy-laden, and I will give you rest."

Matthew 16:26

*For what will it profit a man if he gains the whole
world and forfeits his soul? Or what shall a man give
in return for his soul?*

What if you had Bill Gates's or Warren Buffett's money?
What if you had Beyoncé's or Angelina Jolie's fame?

What if you had Barack Obama's or Vladimir Putin's power?

What if you had the whole world, but you did not have God?
Thirty seconds after your death, you would be filled with remorse
and regret for all eternity.

Charlemagne was King of the Franks (768-814) and Emperor
of the Romans (800-814). He built the Frankish Kingdom into an
empire that covered much of Western and Central Europe. Pope
Leo III crowned him Imperator Augustus on Christmas Day 800.

Before his death in 814, he gave careful instructions about
how he wanted to be buried.

He would be seated on his throne in the royal crypt with his
cape on his shoulder, holding the royal scepter. A book would be
sitting on his lap, with his finger pointed to a certain verse. Two
hundred years later, another emperor, Otto, wanted to see if the
instructions had been followed. He sent a team into the crypt.
They found a skeletal body, his crown tilted, his cape moth-eaten,
the scepter fallen to the ground, but with the book still on his
lap, bony finger pointing. The book was the Bible, and the finger
pointed to Matthew 16:26: "For what will it profit a man if he
gains the whole world and forfeits his soul?"

Here was a great emperor, who gained much of the world,
making his statement about what really matters: not all the
money, fame, and power in the world, but your own soul.

Matthew 18:19-20

Again I say to you, if two of you agree on earth about anything they ask, it will be done for them by my Father in heaven. For where two or three are gathered in my name, there am I among them.

Clearly, God loves it when we pray together. God is thrilled when his children come to him in unity and pray with one heart and one voice.

This does not mean that we are in the same room while one person prays and everyone else daydreams. No, that's not what Jesus is talking about.

When we pray with hearts together, hearts aflame for Christ, bringing our united petitions together to the Father's throne— that's what Jesus wants to see. At that moment, we are *agreeing* in prayer.

Why is this? Why do the united prayers of God's people move him so? I don't know for sure. God loves our unity. He loves our oneness. He loves when we pray together. But ultimately, we do not fully know why this means so much to God.

But we know this: God is delighted when we come together in prayer. He is delighted. And so, Jesus adds another promise: "For where two or three are gathered in my name, there am I among them."

We already know that Jesus is with us, that Jesus will never leave us. So what does he mean when he says, "For where two or three are gathered in my name, there am I among them?

Jesus must mean that he will be with us in a special sense, in a profound way, in a powerful way. If we gather together and seek the face of God, then count on it. Jesus is there, big time.

So, at every opportunity, pray together. Husbands and wives. Parents and kids. Friends. A small group. A ministry team. A band of brothers. The whole church. Or, better still, Christians throughout the city.

Come together before Almighty God in prayer. And know God will be right there with you in some special way.

Matthew 22:37-38

And he said to him, "You shall love the Lord
your God with all your heart
and with all your soul and with all your mind.
This is the great and first commandment."

When Jesus was asked, "What is the greatest commandment in the Law?" he didn't hesitate. He didn't equivocate. He didn't say, "They are all important."

No, Jesus responds with a strong, clear answer. He responds immediately and emphatically.

The most important commandment, the very first and foremost commandment, the reason you are on the planet, is simple: love God with all your heart.

Can you believe it? The sovereign, infinite, holy God, the God who created 300 billion galaxies with his mere word; that God wants to be loved by you.

What he wants from you, more than anything else, is your love. He wants to be a priority to you. He longs for you to love him back. He wants to be wanted by you. It's absolutely incredible, but it's true.

So love him with all your heart, with all you have, with all you are. Love him fiercely, love him affectionately, love him obediently, and love him passionately.

The essence of the Bible is not do's and don'ts. It's not rules and regulations. It's not religious rituals.

No, the essence of the gospel is love. Love the Lord, your God.

Augustine, the great theologian of the early church, once wrote, "Love God and do what you please." His point? If you love God, you will want to please him, so do what you want.

Bernard of Clairvaux once said, in response to a question about why and how God is to be loved, "The reason for loving God is God himself, and the measure in which we should love him is to love him without measure."

Not a half-hearted, lukewarm, casual, and convenient love, but a wholehearted, passionate, fully devoted love.

That's why you exist.

Matthew 22:39

And a second is like it: You shall love
your neighbor as yourself.

Jesus was asked, "What is the greatest commandment?" He was not asked, "What are the two greatest commandments?" but it didn't matter. Jesus gave two commandments: Love your God, love your neighbor. Loving God and loving your neighbor go together. If you love God, it will spill over to people.

What does it mean to love people? What does it look like?

Love for people begins in the heart. It begins with affection for people. We've got to *care*. But it doesn't end there. If we care about people, then we will express that care in concrete, tangible ways, in ways that people can feel, taste, and touch.

We will listen to the friend who is hurting. We will pray for the acquaintance whom needs healing. We will reach out to encourage someone in our small group who is struggling with their teenage son. We might take a meal to a single mom or go to serve the homeless weekly, treating them just as respectfully as anyone else. We will use a kind and gentle tone with family members.

This is what it means to love your neighbor as yourself: You focus on others more than yourself. You become more others-centered than self-centered. You become more of a giver than a taker.

This kind of love, Christ's kind of love, does not go just to those who are easy to love. Christ's kind of love goes to people who don't deserve it, people like us. It goes to people without expecting anything in return.

In the 1998 movie *Les Misérables*, Liam Neeson plays an angry ex-prisoner, Jean Valjean. Valjean assaults and robs a priest who had taken him in for the night. The next morning, Valjean is captured with the priest's silver.

When he is brought back to the priest, Valjean is undone by the priest's love, for the priest says he gave Valjean the silver. He defends him, forgives him, and believes in him.

Valjean was never the same again. This kind of love, Christ's kind of love, sacrificial love, is love that can change the world.

What if you loved people this way the rest of your life? What if every Christ follower loved people the way Christ loved people?

Matthew 23:12

*Whoever exalts himself will be humbled, and
whoever humbles himself will be exalted.*

Just as there are physical laws of the universe, such as the law
of gravity, there are spiritual laws of the universe, such as the
law of humility. The law of humility is crystal clear: If we exalt
ourselves, God will humble us. If we humble ourselves, then God
will exalt us.

Either way, every single person in history will be humbled.
Either we humble ourselves now, in this life, or God will humble
us forever, in the next life. Our choice.

John Ruskin, the renowned English poet and philosopher,
described humility thus: "I believe that the first test of a truly great
man is his humility. I don't mean by humility, doubt of his power.
But really great men have a curious feeling that the greatness is
not of them, but through them. And they see something divine in
every other man and are endlessly, foolishly, incredibly merciful."

Ruskin brings two of the essential characteristics of humility
to light. Humble people understand that any good thing within
them is a gift; "the greatness is not of them, but through them."
Also, they are not overly critical and judgmental of other people,
"and they see something divine in every other man and are
endlessly, foolishly, incredibly merciful."

How do you do on Ruskin's simple test for humility?

One of the most remarkable examples of humility is Michael
Faraday, the British physicist and chemist who discovered
electromagnetic induction in the nineteenth century. He was also
a devout follower of Jesus Christ.

In his book *Five Equations That Changed the World*, Michael
Guillen describes Faraday:

> He had labored for forty-plus years, filling up seven
> large volumes of detailed laboratory notes; he had
> turned down the presidency of the Royal Society not
> once but twice; and he had declined the queen's offer
> of knighthood. "I must remain plain Michael Faraday
> to the end," he had explained politely.
>
> Queen Victoria had offered Faraday his final honor
> – to be buried with Isaac Newton and other British

luminaries in Westminster Abbey. But predictably, the famous scientist had demurred, opting instead to be given "a plain, simple funeral, attended by none but my own relatives, followed by a gravestone of the most ordinary kind, in the simplest earthly place."

In three-quarters of a century, Faraday had gone from being a poor, hard-working errand boy to being a poor, hard-working scientist. No one before had changed science and society in such profound and permanent ways, or has since. For that reason, Michael Faraday—the son of paupers and the confidant of princes—always would be remembered for being in a class by himself.

"Whoever humbles himself will be exalted."

Matthew 24:35

Heaven and earth will pass away,
but my words will not pass away.

This is quite a statement, isn't it? Some people say Jesus was a great religious teacher, immensely wise but merely human. But is this the sort of thing that a mere human would say? Can you imagine Socrates, Plato, or Aristotle making this statement: "Heaven and earth will pass away, but my words will not pass away?"

It wouldn't fit, would it? If a great philosopher or teacher talked this way, we would immediately conclude that this person is a raving lunatic or a deluded megalomaniac. The person would immediately lose all credibility. We would no longer take him seriously.

Yet this is the way Jesus continually talked. He talked about forgiving people's sins, about judging the living and the dead, about being the light of the world, about giving people eternal life, and much more.

Jesus spoke this way, and he did it in the most natural, assured, even humble way. He wasn't bragging. He wasn't exalting himself. He was just stating the facts. This is the way it is, and you need to know it.

Jesus said the sort of things that only a lunatic or a megalomaniac would say. Except, of course, he was God in the flesh. These statements on the lips of Jesus are the most natural things in the world.

And two thousand years later, can anyone doubt that the words in Matthew 24:35 are true? The words of Jesus are published in endless Bibles around the world, in thousands of languages. The words of Jesus are read, studied, memorized, copied, taught, and published continually. The words of Jesus are ubiquitous, despite the fact that Jesus lived in an agrarian, pre-industrial, pre-technological, and pre-computer society. And he never wrote a word.

Yet Jesus could say without a trace of pride or self-centeredness, "Heaven and earth will pass away, but my words will not pass away."

Matthew 25:40

And the King will answer them, "Truly, I say to you, as you did it to one of the least of these my brothers, you did to me."

In a sermon at the Richard Manthe Center for Faith, the writer and college professor, Anthony Campolo, tells this story:

> I walked down Chestnut Street in Philadelphia. There was a filthy bum, covered with soot from head to toe. He had a huge beard. I'll never forget the beard. It was a gigantic beard with rotted food stuck in it.
>
> He held a cup of McDonald's coffee and mumbled as he walked along the street. He spotted me and said, "Hey, Mister. You want some of my coffee?" I knew I should take some to be nice, and I did.
>
> I gave it back to him and said, "You're being pretty generous, giving away your coffee this morning. What's gotten into you that you're giving away your coffee all of a sudden?" He said, "Well, the coffee was especially delicious this morning, and I figured if God gives you something good, you ought to share it with people."
>
> I figured, "This is the perfect set up." I said, "Is there anything I can give you in return?" I'm sure he's going to hit me for five dollars. He said, "Yeah, you can give me a hug." I was hoping for the five dollars.
>
> He put his arms around me. I put my arms around him. And I realized something. He wasn't going to let me go. He was holding onto me. Here I am an establishment guy, and this bum is hanging on me. He's hugging me. He's not going to let me go. People are passing on the street. They're staring at me. I'm embarrassed. But little by little my embarrassment turned to awe. I heard a voice echoing down the corridors of time saying, "I was hungry. Did you feed me? I was naked. Did you clothe me? I was sick. Did you care for me? I was the bum you met on Chestnut Street. Did you hug me? For if you did it unto the least of these, my brothers and sisters, you did it to

me. And if you failed to do it unto the least of these, my brothers and sisters, you failed to do it unto me."

In *The Jesus I Never Knew*, Philip Yancey relates the story of Mother Teresa telling a rich American visitor who could not comprehend her fierce commitment to the dregs of Calcutta. She said, "We are a contemplative order. First we meditate on Jesus, and then we go out and look for him in disguise."

This statement by Jesus astounds me, convicts me, and challenges me. Do I see people, do I treat people, do I love people, as if they were Jesus?

Matthew 28:19-20

Go therefore and make disciples of all nations,
baptizing them in the name of the Father and of the
Son and of the Holy Spirit, teaching them to observe
all that I have commanded you. And behold, I am
with you always, to the end of the age.

This challenge, spoken by Jesus to his disciples, is commonly known as the Great Commission. Coming at the end of his life, shortly before he returns to heaven, the charge has special importance.

Jesus commissions each of his disciples, and each one of us, to make disciples. These are our marching orders, our mission, and our mandate.

"Go." More specifically: as you are going. That is, whenever you go, wherever you go, be making disciples.

"Make disciples." This is the central command of the sentence. Here is our basic mission in life: Make disciples. Make disciples of Jesus Christ. Make followers of Jesus Christ. Reach them, love them, shepherd them, teach them, and empower them.

"All nations." This was a huge change. For two thousand years, the Jews focused on one nation, Israel. But now Jesus calls them to an expanded vista. Now go to all nations, all people groups, and the entire world.

"Baptizing." After you become a follower of Christ, the next step is to get baptized. Note: baptism follows conversion. Also, baptism is in the name (singular) of the Father and of the Son and of the Holy Spirit (plurality). Three Persons, yet one name. We are baptized in the name of our triune God.

"Teaching them to observe." Jesus does not tell us to teach all that he commanded. He does tell us to teach people to obey all that he commanded. Discipleship to Jesus is always obedience-based discipleship.

"I am with you always." The Great Commission comes with a great promise: I will be with you. Wherever you are, whatever you experience, whenever this might be, count on it: "I will be right there to guide you, protect you, strengthen you, empower you. Surely, surely, I will be with you always."

This is your mission. This is your promise.

Mark 2:17

And when Jesus heard it, he said to them, "Those who are well have no need of a physician, but those who are sick. I came not to call the righteous, but sinners."

The religious crowd in Jesus's day did not care about lost people. In fact, they resented Jesus's concern for and attentiveness to lost, mixed-up people. *For heaven's sake, he even eats with them!* they thought. Lost people didn't really matter to the religious crowd.

The religious crowd in our day largely feels the same way. Lost people don't really matter.

John Ortberg, in his book *Love Beyond Reason*, tells the story of his friend John:

> Several years ago a friend of mine in Chicago began what's called the Emmaeus ministry. The people they are trying to help are young men in their late teens or early twenties who come to Chicago, having no families—in fact, they almost never even know who their fathers are. They are trapped in drug abuse and end up surviving by becoming street hustlers—male prostitutes. This is not a group to whom many people are likely to extend love.
>
> So these people with Emmaeus simply walk the streets of Chicago from ten until two or three in the morning, looking for the most ragged of rag dolls. Every once in a while some man trapped in hustling will say, "I can't take it anymore. Is there any way out of this hell?" And then John and his friends will offer shelter or training and try to help him find the way.
>
> John was sitting in his living room one night with a young man named Joseph. John's wife and some other members of their little community were setting the table, and they invited Joseph to have dinner with them. Joseph whispered to John as they sat down, "I've never done this before." John was confused. "Done what?"
>
> "This family dinner thing around a table. I've never done that."

Joseph was typical of the young men in his world. He didn't know his father, his mother was a crack addict and abusive, he was removed from his home when he was four months old. He had been shuttled from group home to group home in the child-care system. He was in a gang by age eleven, in prison by sixteen. Now he was in his mid-twenties and never once in his life had he sat down to eat a meal around a table with a real family. Never had he participated as a father and mother and children passed the food and looked each other in the eye and talked about their day.

He was embarrassed. "I've never done this, but I've seen it on TV."

Lost people, mixed-up people, and hurting people mattered to John and his community. They also matter to Jesus. May they also matter to us.

"Those who are well have no need of a physician, but those who are sick. I came not to call the righteous, but sinners" (Mark 2:17).

Mark 10:45

*For even the Son of Man came not to be served but to
serve, and to give his life as a ransom for many.*

Speechwriter Peggy Noonan tells a fascinating story of Ronald
Reagan in her book *When Character Was King:*

> When I try to tell people what Reagan was like I tell
> the bathroom story. A few days after he'd been shot,
> when he could get out of bed, he wasn't feeling well one
> night and went to the bathroom connected to his room.
> He slapped water on his face, and water slopped out of
> the sink. He got some paper towels and got on the floor
> to clean it up. An aide came in and said, "Mr. President,
> what are you doing? We have people for that." And
> Reagan said oh, no, he was just cleaning up his mess, he
> didn't want a nurse to have to do it.

It may seem a bit incongruous for a wounded president of
the United States to be down on the floor cleaning up a mess,
but here is something far more jarring: the God of the heavens
stooped to become a human so that he could serve us. He served
us in many ways, but primarily by dying on a cross to pay for sin.

Jesus did not become a servant at the Incarnation or at the
cross. No, Jesus has always been a servant. His nature as God is to
serve, because to serve means to love, and God is a lover beyond
imagination. God is a servant, and when he came to earth, he
came to serve us. He came to serve you.

We who are his followers must be a community of servants.
That's what we do, that's who we are. We are servants of the
servant.

In every situation, whether it's home, work, or play, we are
thinking of others' needs, not our own. We focus on others, not
ourselves. We are givers more than takers, listeners more than
talkers, the ones looking to serve and not be served.

If you count yourself as a follower of Jesus, that means you are
a foot-washer. You are a servant. So in every situation, serve, just
as he has served you and serves you still.

Luke 9:23

And he said to all: "If anyone would come after me,
let him deny himself and take up his
cross daily and follow me."

Jesus did not call us to a life of comfort and ease. He did not call us to accumulation and then retirement. He did not call us to self-indulgence and self-aggrandizement. He did not call us to the American Dream.

No. Jesus called us to come and die. Dietrich Bonhoeffer penned that verse as his last words, and later, by order of Adolf Hitler, he was executed because of his faith in Christ. His words were fulfilled literally by his own life.

Jesus gives us three specifics. First, deny yourself. This does not mean we give up things, but that we give up self—needs, wants, dreams, plans, and happiness. As C.S. Lewis said, "Self-centeredness is the national religion of hell."

Second, Jesus tells us to take up our cross daily. In the Roman Empire, if you saw a man trudging along the road surrounded by soldiers and carrying a crossbeam, you knew he was on his way to die. Jesus says to us: You do that, every day. Sacrifice your very life for me. That's a far cry from a life of luxury and ease.

Third, Jesus says to us, "Follow me wherever I lead you, whatever I command you, however I call you. Follow me." This includes forgiving people. This includes gentle love. This includes generous giving. This includes sexual purity. Whatever Jesus commands us, whether or not we feel like obeying, we obey.

John Mott commented, "Let it be repeated, there are two views of one's life. One is that a man's life is his own, to do with as he pleases; the other is that it belongs to another and that the other to whom it belongs is Christ himself."

What about you? Is your life your own, to do with as you please? Or does your life belong to another, to Christ himself?

If you dare, here is a prayer of surrender:

> Lord, because you are my God,
> Because you have made me,
> Because you have saved me by the blood of Jesus,
> Because you have loved me fiercely, forgiven me

completely, and accepted me eternally,
I surrender my life to you.
Gladly I surrender.
I am trusting Jesus as my savior from sin. I bow to him as my king.
All that I am I give to you–my dreams, my hopes, my fears, my family, my relationships, my health, my career, my future, my money, my time, my talents, my hobbies. My whole life belongs to you.
Though I will struggle and sometimes fail, I choose to rest in your grace, which is greater than all my sin.
Lord, I love you. And I want to love you more. May I fall in love with you, Jesus.
Lord, I am your blood-bought servant.
I am your passionate worshipper.
I am your fully devoted follower.
I am your much-loved child.
Have all of me, Jesus. Have all of me.

Luke 15:20

And he arose and came to his father. But while he was still a long way off, his father saw him and felt compassion, and ran and embraced him and kissed him.

I love this verse. It comes from my favorite picture of God in the Bible, the parable of the prodigal son. Jesus is telling us what God is like.

God longs for you. When the prodigal son was a long way off, his father saw him. He saw him because he was looking for him, longing for him, yearning for him. God looks for you, longs for you, and yearns for you.

God's heart is bursting with compassion for you and your hurts. When the father saw his son, there was no anger, there was no indignation, there was no rejection. Only love. Welcoming, embracing love. That's God's heart for you when you come home.

The father ran to his son, even though dignified men in that culture never ran in public. It was beneath their dignity, but his father did not care. He humbled himself and *ran* to his son. Jesus is telling you, "God will humble himself to rescue you. God will humble himself to the point of taking on manhood and even dying a death on a cross for you."

When the father reached his son, he embraced him and covered him with kisses. Jesus is telling you, "You want to know what God is like? He is the God who will welcome you with open arms and smother you with kisses. He loves you. He is the God who yearns for you, the God who humbles himself for you, the God who restores you, the God of endless compassion, the God of amazing grace."

Forget those other voices in your head. This is the voice of Jesus, speaking to you: "This is what God is really like. This is his heart for you."

Believe it. Believe it and begin to live.

Luke 19:10

For the Son of Man came to seek and to save the lost.

This verse, from the well-known story of Zacchaeus the tax collector, summarizes the mission of Jesus. This is why he came: to seek and to save the lost. The lost are the people like you and me.

Jesus did not come for good people. He did not come for perfect people. He did not come for people who had it together—there are none. We are all flawed and sinful strugglers.

Jesus came looking for you.

Imagine this scene: You have a four-year-old daughter. You no longer hear her. You go to her room. Not there. You go through the house, calling her name. Not there. You begin to panic. You look in the backyard. Not there. The front yard. Not there. You go up and down the street, calling her name. Nowhere. You get other neighbors to look with you. You are getting more and more emotional, more and more desperate. *She's not there.*

Then you hear a commotion behind you. You whirl around, and there comes your daughter with a neighbor, who found her in her backyard with her puppy. You dissolve in tears. You hug her so tightly and just cry.

This is the way Papa feels about you.

It's time to come home.

John 1:1

*In the beginning was the Word, and the Word was
with God, and the Word was God.*

Jesus is called the Word because he shows us what God is like. He reveals the unseen, invisible God. Just as words reveal thoughts, Jesus reveals God.

Jesus is the Word, the Word made flesh. He shows us what God is like.

Jesus is eternal. In the beginning, in eternity past, long before Genesis 1:1, Jesus already was. "In the beginning was the Word." Jesus is eternal, and only God is eternal.

Jesus is distinct from God, or to be more precise, from God the Father. "And the Word was with God." The Greek preposition has the nuance of face-to-face. Jesus was face-to-face with God. He was co-eternal with the Father and yet distinct from the Father.

Jesus is God. "And the Word was God." There it is, plain as day, the crescendo of the majestic verse. The Word was God.

That's how John's Gospel majestically begins, and it reaches its fitting climax in Thomas's exclamation: "My Lord and my God!" At the beginning and at the end, Jesus is God.

God speaks to you. God speaks to you through the Word, through Jesus.

Pay close attention.

John 1:3

*All things were made through him, and without him
was not any thing made that was made.*

Jesus created all things. Delicate wildflowers, towering mountains, diverse wildlife, intricate humans, immense oceans, burning stars, and staggering galaxies. All things.

Was Jesus just a great teacher? Was Jesus just a religious philosopher? Is Jesus just one of the ways to God?

Hardly! Jesus is none other than God, God Incarnate, and God the Creator.

To think that this infinite and eternal Creator became a mere man, a wrinkled baby, buckles the knees. What staggering humility.

What are the implications for us that Jesus is our Creator? At least these four things:

1. Worship. We must worship a God so great.
2. Trust. A God so powerful can intervene in my life and take care of me.
3. Obedience. Since he created me, I am his and not my own.
4. Gratitude. To think that my Creator died to save me is amazing. Amazing grace.

John 1:11-12

He came to his own, and his own people did not re-
ceive him. But to all who did receive him, who
believed in his name, he gave the right to
become children of God.

Rejection is so hard for us. It always hurts. Sometimes it hurts so badly that we don't know if we will survive the wound. The fact is that we spend a lot of energy avoiding the pain of rejection. How do we do this? We don't let people get too close. We don't take risks. We play it safe. We wear masks.

Ah, the pain of rejection! It can hurt so badly. Think with me, no, feel with me, a few examples, big and small:

· A little boy is the last one chosen for the baseball game.
· A fourth-grade girl isn't accepted by the cool girls in her school.
· A high school girl is not invited to the prom.
· A teenage boy is afraid to call a girl because he fears rejection so badly.
· A young girl feels so hurt because her parents never have much time for her.
· A young man's girlfriend breaks up with him.
· A high school senior is not accepted to the college where her closest friends are going.
· Your friend betrays you by telling someone your secret.
· The forty-year-old man cannot find a job after losing his last one.
· Your spouse leaves you for someone else, and your heart feels like it is ripped right out of your body.

Rejection. The human heart can barely survive it. Sometimes it doesn't survive.

Jesus knows all about it. He understands. You see, Jesus was rejected. By millions. By his own people. By the very people he created, the very people he loved, the very people he died for. "He came to his own, and his own people did not receive him. But to all who did receive him, who believed in his name, he gave the right to become children of God."

Jesus understands our rejection. He will never reject us. He will always welcome us and embrace us with open arms. In fact, he will pour so much love and acceptance into our hearts that we can risk rejection again, because we have found acceptance in the one whom matters most.

John 1:14

The Word became flesh and dwelt among us, and we have seen his glory, glory as of the only Son from the Father, full of grace and truth.

Picture John, the aging apostle, closer to Jesus than any of the disciples. He reflects back on those three incredible years with Jesus, spending day and night in his presence. He smiles. He marvels. Then, guided by the Spirit, he pens the next words: "The Word became flesh and dwelt among us, and we have seen his glory, glory as of the only Son from the Father, full of grace and truth."

Yes! That's it—glory. That's the only word for it. That's what we saw in Jesus: the glory of God.

Can you see Jesus, full of glory?

See his love, his immense and powerful love. See him heal the hurting people. See him touch the untouched leper. See him weep at the death of his friend Lazarus. See him die for the sins of the world.

See his wisdom. Listen as he teaches like no man ever taught. See the crowds when he gives the Sermon on the Mount, for they are amazed at the teaching of the wisest teacher of all time.

See his power. Oh, what power! He calms the storm. He walks on water. He heals the sick. He defeats the demonic. He feeds the thousands. He raises the dead.

See his grace. See his love for the undeserving, the downtrodden, and the guilty. Watch the spurned tax collectors and prostitutes clamor around him. Hear him protect the woman caught in adultery: "Neither do I condemn you; go, and from now on sin no more" (John 8:11).

See his fearlessness. See him as he challenges the religious and political powerbrokers of his day. See him as he strides into a den of thieves to clear the temple grounds of the merchants. See him as he travels to Jerusalem to face a certain death.

See his truth. He never flinches from the truth, even when it is hard. No soft-pedaling for Jesus. He embodies truth: "I am the way, and the truth, and the life. No one comes to the Father except through me" (John 14:6).

See his holiness, his radiant and shining holiness. Even his jealous enemies could find no fault, no blemish, and no sin. He modeled full devotion and total obedience to the Father.

See his humility. He is always making outrageous claims, such as "He who has seen me has seen the Father" (John 14:9). He claims to be the Creator, the Judge, and the Lord. Any other person who made such claims would be discounted as a megalomaniac or lunatic. But not Jesus. He has the peace-filled aura of humility.

Love. Wisdom. Power. Grace. Fearlessness. Truth. Holiness. Humility. And so much more.

Glory!

John 1:18

No one has ever seen God; the only God, who is at the Father's side, he has made him known.

The face of God is seen in the face of Jesus.

What is God like? Look at Jesus.

Can I trust God? Will he take care of me? Does he want good for me? Look at Jesus. Look at Jesus care for his followers with a heart full of grace and truth.

Does God really hear me when I pray? Look at Jesus. Hear Jesus as he repeatedly tells us to pray and ask.

Does God care about sin? Will God actually bring judgment on evil and rebellion? Look at Jesus. Watch Jesus as he denounces sin and unequivocally speaks of the reality of hell and certain judgment.

Can God deliver me when life seems overwhelming? Can God intervene in my life to do the impossible? Look at Jesus. Watch Jesus as he calms the sea, stills the wind, heals the leper, and delivers the demonized. Watch Jesus as he repeatedly intervenes to do the impossible.

When I fail miserably, when I feel shrouded in a fog of guilt and condemnation, will God forgive me? Look at Jesus. Look at Jesus hanging on a cross, paying for the sin of the world, saying to the Father, "Father, forgive them, for they know not what they do" (Luke 23:34). Hear Jesus say to the woman caught in adultery, "Neither do I condemn you; go, and from now on sin no more" (John 8:11).

When I wonder about the hard questions, questions about babies dying, questions about those who have never heard of Jesus, what should I do? Look at Jesus. Look at Jesus, know that he cares more than I do, and will do what is right, fair, and good.

In every situation, in every dilemma, in every doubt, in every fear, in every question, in every tear, whenever I need to know what God is like, what do I do? Look at Jesus.

The face of God is seen in the face of Jesus.

John 1:29

The next day he saw Jesus coming toward him, and said, "Behold, the Lamb of God, who takes away the sin of the world!"

At the outset of his ministry, John the Baptist understood who Jesus was. John understood that Jesus came to this earth as the Lamb of God to die on a cross and take away the sin of the world.

This simple title, Lamb of God, has a rich background in the Old Testament. In Genesis 22, Isaac asks his father Abraham, "Where is the lamb for a burnt offering?" Abraham, knowing that Isaac would be sacrificed, simply replies, "God will provide." Little did Abraham know that God would provide a lamb for sacrifice to spare Isaac, and that both Isaac and the slain lamb would foretell of the Lamb of God, who would one day die for our sins.

In Exodus 12, we come to the Passover in Egypt, when the blood of lambs was smeared on the doorposts of Israelite homes so that their firstborn children would not die. The blood of these lambs again pointed to the blood shed by the future Lamb of God. God passes over our sins because he sees the blood of Jesus shed for us.

In Exodus 29, we read that every morning and every evening, a lamb is to be sacrificed as an offering. Every one of these lambs, day after day, week after week, month after month, year after year, decade after decade, century after century—every one of these lambs would point to the Lamb of God who would one day come and be a sacrifice.

In Isaiah 53, we see that the suffering servant will be like a lamb led to slaughter. This is, of course, a picture of Jesus Christ, the Lamb of God, who would in fact be led to slaughter for our sakes.

With all of this rich background in his mind, as well as his knowledge of the entire sacrificial system of the Old Testament, John says upon seeing Jesus, "Behold, the Lamb of God, who takes away the sin of the world!" Jesus is the fulfillment of all these countless sacrifices for sin.

Jesus's death on the cross was not a mistake or an accident; rather, it was the whole purpose of Jesus's coming. He died as a substitute. He died as a substitute to atone for, or to pay for, your sins and mine. All of our sin was placed upon Jesus on the cross, and he paid for it. All that we do is to receive the incredible, out-landish gift of forgiveness by trusting Christ as our savior.

No wonder that the biblical story comes to a crescendo in Revelation 5, when all of creation will sing to Jesus: "Worthy is the Lamb who was slain, to receive power and wealth and wisdom and might and honor and glory and blessing."

John had it just right: Jesus is the Lamb of God who takes away the sin of the world.

John 3:3

Jesus answered him, "Truly, truly, I say to you, unless one is born again he cannot see the kingdom of God."

The phrase *born again* has become well-known in our culture. It comes from a conversation one night between Jesus and a man named Nicodemus. Nicodemus was one of seventy rulers of Israel and a prominent teacher in the land. One night, under the cover of darkness so no one would see him, Nicodemus came to Jesus and simply said, "Rabbi, we know that you are a teacher come from God, for no one can do these signs that you do unless God is with him" (John 3:2).

Though the Pharisees opposed Jesus, Nicodemus could not deny that Jesus was a teacher sent from God. Jesus ignores the statements of Nicodemus and goes to the motive for his visit. He goes to the question that is buried deep in Nicodemus's heart—too deep, perhaps, for even Nicodemus to be aware of it. Jesus declared, "Truly, truly, I say to you, unless one is born again he cannot see the kingdom of God."

Jesus is saying: Nicodemus, you must be born again, born anew, born from above. You need a new birth. If any person is going to see God's kingdom, if any person is going to be saved and go to heaven, then that person must be born again. Nicodemus, you may be quite religious. You may be a member of the Sanhedrin. You may be the teacher of Israel. You may have great theological training. But, you must be born again.

With one simple statement, Jesus swept away all that Nicodemus stood for, all of his learning and religious efforts. He did not need religion, reformation, or knowledge—Nicodemus needed to be born again. Two verses later, Jesus clarified what it means to be born again when he said, "Unless one is born of water and the Spirit, he cannot enter the kingdom of God." Jesus is simply reiterating what he just said about being born again. We must be born again—that is, born of water and the Spirit. We must have a new birth, a new spiritual birth. It is the work of the Spirit. Think about how much you contributed to your physical birth. That's the precise amount that you contribute to your spiritual birth. It is the work of God for you.

John 3:16

For God so loved the world, that he gave his only Son,
that whoever believes in him should not perish but
have eternal life.

Martin Luther called John 3:16 a Bible in itself, the miniature gospel. In his dying moments, he repeated the words of this verse three times. It is perhaps the most famous verse in the Bible.

So much truth is packed into one sentence, but we will not begin to understand it if we see the word "God" as simply the subject of a sentence.

We find in the magazine *New Horizons* that B.B. Warfield once said:

> When we pronounce the word we must see to it that our minds are flooded with some wondering sense of God's infinitude, of his majesty, of his ineffable exaltation, of his holiness, of his righteousness, of his flaming purity and stainless perfection. This is the Lord God Almighty whom the heaven of heavens cannot contain, to whom the earth is less than the small dust on the balance. He has no need of aught nor can his unsullied blessedness be in any way affected...by any act of the creature of his hands. What we call infinite space is but a speck on the horizon of his contemplation: What we call infinite time is in his sight but as yesterday when it is past...It is this God, a God of whom to say that he is the Lord of all the earth is to say so little that it is to say nothing at all, of whom our text speaks....Now the text [John 3:16] tells us of this God—of this God, remember—that he loves.

This God, vast, immense, and amazing beyond all comprehension, loves you. And because he loves you, he gave to you his own Son. He gave the supreme gift, the outrageous gift, the stunning gift. Jesus, the eternal Son of the Father, became a mere human so he could die on a cross. For you. And all you have do is to believe in him, put your trust in him, take him as your Savior.

See the love of this great God. See the love of this great God in his son Jesus. See it. Receive it. Thrill to it. Exult in it.

John 3:30

He must increase, but I must decrease.

When John came preaching in the wilderness, the crowds flocked to him. People came from everywhere to hear John and to be baptized by him. He was an overnight success. God's favor was on him.

But when Jesus began his ministry, the crowds started leaving John and going to Jesus. John's disciples were concerned: "Rabbi, what do we do? They're all going to Jesus!" John's response: "The one who has the bride is the bridegroom. The friend of the bridegroom, who stands and hears him, rejoices greatly at the bridegroom's voice. Therefore this joy of mine is now complete. He must increase, but I must decrease" (John 3:29-30).

In other words, John exclaims: "Not only am I not worried that the crowds are going to Jesus, but I am overjoyed. I am thrilled. That's the whole reason I came. He, Jesus, must increase. I, John, must decrease."

Here is John's greatness: profound and genuine humility. No wonder Jesus would later say: "Among those born of women none is greater than John" (Luke 7:28).

John understood that he was not the point of the story. Jesus was the point. It's all about Jesus. So if the crowds left John, no big deal. "They don't belong to me. The point is Jesus, not me."

When we learn that nothing belongs to us, that everything we have belongs to Christ, that we are not the point, that it's all about Jesus, when we have the heartfelt attitude that Jesus must increase and I must decrease; then, like John, we will find real joy, and we will experience the favor of God.

"He must increase. I must decrease."

John 4:23

*But the hour is coming, and is now here, when the
true worshippers will worship the Father in
spirit and truth, for the Father is seeking
such people to worship him.*

One of the most well-known conversations in the life of Jesus is his interaction with the Samaritan woman in John 4. In the context of that conversation, Jesus makes what is perhaps the most profound statement on worship in the Bible.

First of all, the sovereign, infinite, holy God of the universe is seeking worshippers. He doesn't need worshippers, but he wants them. He wants them because worshippers of God are lovers of God, and God yearns for us to love him back.

Lots of people are workers for God. Fewer people are worshippers of God. Worshippers are lovers, and God is looking for worshippers.

Second, we must worship God in spirit. That is, we must worship from our hearts. If we go through the motions of worship or mouth the words of praise, but our heart is not in it, then the worship means nothing. In fact, it's not even worship. It's religious ritual. Worship in spirit—from your heart, with all your heart, with heartfelt sincerity and passion.

Third, we must worship God in truth. That is, worship God according to who he is and what he has commanded. We find out who God is and what he has commanded in the Bible. The Bible is crucial if we are going to worship God in truth.

If we worship with spirit but without truth, we have enthusiastic heresy. If we worship with truth but without spirit, we have dead orthodoxy. God is longing for worshippers who have both spirit and truth. Indeed, God delights in this kind of worshipper. He's seeking them.

Can he count you in?

John 4:34

Jesus said to them, "My food is to do the will of him who sent me and to accomplish his work."

Jesus's disciples had been walking on the road all day, and they were exhausted and famished. So they leave Jesus at a well and go into town to buy food.

When they return, they pull food out of their leather bags. They can hardly wait to dig in. The problem is that they are waiting for Jesus, their teacher, to begin eating, and he isn't taking a bite.

Finally, they urge him, "Rabbi, eat!" Jesus responds, "I have food to eat that you do not know about." The disciples are puzzled, thinking, *You do? How? Where? Who gave you this food?* They are entirely focused on the physical, not the spiritual. They are more concerned about food than God.

So Jesus clarifies: "My food is to do the will of him who sent me and to accomplish his work." Jesus is saying, "This is my real food. This is the food I hunger for, the food I must have or I cannot live. I simply must please my Father and do his will. I simply must obey my Father."

The way Jesus lived life is the way we must live life. He is our model and example.

Pleasing God, living for God, obeying God is our life. It is our joy. It is our liberation.

It is more important than food and drink.

John 5:19

*So Jesus said to them, "Truly, truly, I say to you, the
Son can do nothing of his own accord, but only what
he sees the Father doing. For whatever the
Father does, that the Son does likewise."*

Henry Blackaby, in his acclaimed workbook *Experiencing God*,
taught us:

> Don't go out and do things on your own for God, with
> your own strength and resources. Rather, do what Je-
> sus did. Jesus watched the Father and did what he saw
> the Father doing. Jesus was completely dependent on
> the Father, completely surrendered to the Father. He
> only did what he saw the Father doing.

Jesus is the model for all ministry. Find out what God is doing and do that. Find out where God is at work and get on board.
God is not looking for originality, but faithfulness. The Father is
looking for complete dependence and surrender.

Dwight Edwards, in his book *Revolution Within*, has a superb
summary of John 5:19:

> Jesus did nothing of his own initiative but joined in
> with what God was already doing. God the Father
> was always in the lead.
>
> Jesus did nothing of his own invention. He was de-
> pendent upon his Father's example and sought only
> to mirror what he saw his Father doing.
>
> Jesus did nothing of his own will. He didn't come
> to establish and fulfill his own ministry but the one
> designated for him by the Father.
>
> Jesus did nothing in his own strength. The min-
> istry he unleashed upon the world was done wholly
> through the power of his indwelling Father.
>
> In true New Covenant ministry, each of these will
> be true about us as well. "As the Father has sent me,"
> Jesus said, "I also send you." Our ministry is as tied to
> Christ as Christ's was to his Father!

That's the calling of a disciple: a life of dependence and
surrender.

John 5:24

Truly, truly, I say to you, whoever hears my word
and believes him who sent me has eternal life.
He does not come into judgment, but has
passed from death to life.

This verse is simple, strong, and emphatic. If one hears the Word of Jesus, the message of Jesus, and if one believes this message from the Father, then one has eternal life.

This is a clear statement of salvation by faith. How does anyone get eternal life? Believe the message of Jesus. Trust in Jesus and his work on the cross. Put your faith in Jesus. Belief, trust, and faith: all three of these English words reflect the same Greek term in the New Testament, translated in John 5:24 as "believes."

Note that eternal life is given when one believes in Jesus. At that moment, he or she has eternal life. Eternal life, by definition, is life that never ends. If we have eternal life, we will never lose it. If it could be lost, then it was not eternal life. It was conditional life or probationary life, but it was not *eternal* life.

To have eternal life means that we never come into judgment or condemnation. Elsewhere, the New Testament does speak of a believer's judgment, but this refers to a judgment to assign rewards to believers. It is not a judgment about one's eternal destiny in heaven or hell. Believers in Christ never experience a judgment about our eternal destiny.

That issue is settled the moment we trust in Christ. At that moment, we cross the Rubicon. We pass from death to life. We pass into eternal life, life that never ends.

So how do we get eternal life? Not by earning it. Not by being good. Not by going to church. No, we get eternal life by believing in Jesus to save us.

If you have never done so, put your trust in Jesus. Do it now! Breathe a prayer: "Jesus, I put all my trust in you to save me from my sin."

John 7:37b-38

If anyone thirsts, let him come to me and drink. Who-
ever believes in me, as the Scripture has said, "Out
of his heart will flow rivers of living water."

The answer to my thirstiness is Jesus. The answer to my thirst-iness is not more money. It is not a bigger house. It is not a different job. It is not marriage, or a better marriage, or children, friends, or health.

It is not that these are not good things. Some are very good things, but they won't quench my thirst. Only Jesus can do that. Only Jesus can quench my deepest longings. "If anyone thirsts, let him come to me and drink."

If I need love, the answer is Jesus. If I need security, the an-swer is Jesus. If I need forgiveness, acceptance, power, freedom, significance, comfort, peace, or anything else, the answer is Jesus. "If anyone thirsts, let him come to me and drink."

Jesus will quench my thirst. Not just with water, but with streams of living water. Ever-flowing, ever-bubbling, and ev-er-refreshing streams of living water, for Jesus gives me his Spir-it. That's right! The Spirit of God, God himself, on the inside, quenching my thirst, giving me life, satisfying my longings, and flowing inside me.

Ah! I need that water, Jesus. Fill me with that water, Jesus. Let the river flow.

John 8:32

And you will know the truth,
and the truth will set you free.

Over the massive front doors of the University of Texas Tower are engraved the words of Jesus in John 8:32 (King James Version): "Ye shall know the truth, and the truth shall make you free." I am thrilled that there is something pointing to Jesus Christ and his teachings at such a prominent place on a large university campus. However, I do wish people understood the verse in its context.

The suggestion of the verse standing alone in an academic environment is this: In the acquisition of knowledge and truth, there is freedom, freedom of all kinds. In learning information, you gain freedom.

Unfortunately, that was simply not the point Jesus was making. First of all, he was talking about spiritual freedom, not political or physical freedom. Jesus was talking about freedom from sin. Freedom from the power of sin, freedom to live the life that, deep down, we long to live.

And there is a condition to experiencing this freedom. The condition comes in the previous verse, John 8:31: "If you abide in my word, you are truly my disciples." The condition is abiding in the words of Jesus, obeying his commands, and following his teachings. If we obey Jesus, then we are his disciples. We will know the truth, and the truth will set us free. The Bible teaches us that we can live a life of freedom from the tyranny of sin. We will never be free from all sin in this life, but we can be free from slavery to sin.

In a paradox, this freedom, true freedom, only comes with slavery—slavery to Jesus Christ. If we surrender our will to Jesus Christ and do what he wants us to do, rather than what we want to do, we will know the joy and peace of true freedom. In slavery to Jesus, we find true freedom.

John 10:10

The thief comes only to steal and kill and destroy. I came that they may have life and have it abundantly.

John 10:10 is a window to the heart of Jesus, his heart for you. Jesus is saying to you: The whole reason I came was to give you life; real, full, eternal, abundant life. Life that is full, rich, and soul-satisfying. This is my heart for you. This is my desire for you. In fact, I died so that you may have life.

Satan will try to mislead you. Satan and his minions will try to deceive you into doubting Jesus's heart for you. The deceiver will point to your problems and blame God, he will point to the world's suffering and revile God, or he will point to difficult questions and accuse God.

But don't listen. Satan is a liar and a deceiver. His intent is to harm you. He comes only to steal and kill and destroy. He comes to devour your soul and ruin your life. Resist him. Stand against him.

Cling to Jesus. You can trust Jesus because his heart for you is completely good. He wants you to have life abundantly—rich, full, and meaningful. He wants you to have as much joy and peace and purpose as you can hold. He is good, and he wants good for you all your days. "I came that they may have life and have it abundantly."

John 10:28

I give them eternal life, and they will never perish, and no one will snatch them out of my hand.

I am secure in Jesus. You are secure in Jesus. He will never disown us. He will never reject us. He will never abandon us.

Others may reject, abandon, or betray us, but not Jesus. He is different. We are safe in his arms, completely safe. There is no reason to fear.

We are not holding on to him. Rather, he is holding on to us. He will not let us go, no matter what.

In one brief sentence, Jesus underscores four times how safe we are in him.

First, "I *give* them eternal life." Eternal life is a gift. We don't receive salvation by earning it. We don't hold onto our salvation by earning it. It is a gift. From first to last, salvation is a free gift.

Second, "I give them *eternal* life." By definition, eternal life never stops. If we could ever lose our salvation, then the life we had was not eternal life, was it? It was conditional life, probationary life, or ten years, three months of life. But it was not eternal. Jesus gives us life eternal, life unending.

Third, "They will *never* perish." In case we still don't get it, Jesus states the same truth negatively. We have life eternal and we will never perish. Never means never, at no time, not ever. If someone who had eternal life ever perished, then that would mean that Jesus's statement here was untrue, and that's impossible. This is emphatic.

Fourth, "No one will snatch them out of my hand." No one—not Satan, not an angel, not a demon, not you, not any human. No one.

And, just in case we still struggle to believe the amazing gift of eternal life, check the very next statement in verse 29: "My Father, who has given them to me, is greater than all, and no one is able to snatch them out of the Father's hand."

Could Jesus be more emphatic? You will never lose your salvation. You cannot undo your salvation. It just can't happen. We are secure, eternally secure, in Jesus's love.

Some folks say, "That's a dangerous teaching! If that is true, people won't be motivated to obey God. They will take advantage of grace." Perhaps. For some, grace can be dangerous. But for most people, the opposite is true. If God loves me this much, then I *want* to please him and live for him with all my heart.

Fear doesn't motivate me to obey. Love does.

John 10:30

I and the Father are one.

This statement is a blockbuster.

Jesus places himself on parity with the Father. The Father and the Son (we could add the Spirit) are one in action, purpose, and power, all of which implies that they are one in nature. The Father and the Son are one in their essential natures. That is exactly how the Jews understood him, for they immediately picked up stones in order to stone him for blasphemy.

"The Jews picked up stones again to stone him. Jesus answered them, "I have shown you many good works from the Father; for which of them are you going to stone me?" The Jews answered him, "It is not for a good work that we are going to stone you but for blasphemy, because you, being a man, make yourself God" (John 10:31-33).

Long ago, Augustine pointed out that this brief statement refutes two errors. One error is associated with Sabellius. Sabellius taught that the three Persons of the Godhead were actually only one Person, and that the Father became the Son, died on the cross, and then returned as the Holy Spirit. Many Christians, even today, think of the Trinity in this way. But the Bible teaches that there are three distinct Persons. Think, for example, of the baptism of Jesus, when in one scene we have Jesus in the water, the Spirit descending as a dove, and the voice of the Father in heaven. There is one God, but three Persons.

Much more serious is the heresy of Arius, who denied the deity of Jesus. The word "one" points to the fact that Jesus and the Father have the same nature, thereby refuting the Arians, as well as the Mormons, the Jehovah's Witnesses, and other similar cults.

Again, this is exactly how the Jews understood Jesus—the Jews who heard it, knew his language and culture, and who were looking at his face. "It is not for a good work that we are going to stone you but for blasphemy, because you, being a man, make yourself God."

John 10:35

Scripture cannot be broken.

In the midst of a discussion with Jewish religious leaders, Jesus quotes part of Psalm 82. Then he makes this parenthetical comment, almost as an aside: "Scripture cannot be broken." The brief comment speaks volumes about the way Jesus saw Scripture. "Scripture cannot be broken."

First of all, the expression sounds odd. Scripture cannot be broken. We do not normally think of books or writing in the context of brokenness. Broken or not broken is not a category that applies to books, but that doesn't deter Jesus. He says that Scripture cannot be broken. He is making the point, in a quite graphic way, that every word of Scripture will prove true. No error will be found. No fault will appear. No weakness will come out.

Whatever Scripture predicts will happen, whatever Scripture reveals will occur, whatever Scripture promises will be fulfilled, for Scripture cannot be broken.

It is not merely that Scripture has not been broken or will not be broken, but that Scripture cannot be broken. It is impossible. The veracity of God guarantees it.

People may doubt the Bible. People may attack it, may attribute errors to it, may call the Bible just a human book, may ignore and neglect the Bible. You may neglect the Bible.

But not Jesus. He treasured this book.

He studied it. Memorized it. Learned it. Loved it. Taught it. Obeyed it. Believed it. In fact, every single time in the gospels that Jesus referred to the Bible, he refers to it with complete confidence, even if he is referring to Adam and Eve, Jonah and the whale, or other controversial things. He has total confidence in Scripture.

There are so many words that have been written down through the centuries, and no doubt we're adding countless billions of words daily to that written record. Most of those words are shallow and superficial, while some are wise and insightful. But a very small percentage of those words are special. They are different than all the rest of the words in the universe, because these words are the breath of God.

And breathed out by God, they are unbroken. Unbroken and unbreakable. Alive and packed with power.

Hear those words.

John 11:25-26

Jesus said to her, "I am the resurrection and the life. Whoever believes in me, though he die, yet shall he live, and everyone who lives and believes in me shall never die. Do you believe this?"

Jesus's close friend Lazarus had died too young. Lazarus's sisters, Mary and Martha, were heartbroken with grief.

If it had been us, we might have said, "I am so sorry" and prayed with them, but not Jesus. He makes the stunning statement: "I am the resurrection and the life. Whoever believes in me, though he die, yet shall he live, and everyone who lives and believes in me shall never die. Do you believe this?"

I am the resurrection and the life. Not, "I have resurrection and life." Not, "I can find resurrection and life." Not, "I can give resurrection and life." But, "I am the resurrection and the life." In other words: "I embody resurrection and life. Resurrection and life are found in me. If you want resurrection, if you want life, physical life, spiritual life, any kind of life, here it is. I *am* the resurrection and the life."

By the way, who talks this way? Who in history talked this way? Do great religious teachers talk this way? No. Someone who talks this way is either a lunatic or the Lord of glory.

If Jesus embodies resurrection and life, the obvious question is: How do I get that resurrection and life?

He tells us. And it is so simple. So simple that sophisticated, I-can-do-it-myself types miss it. How do you get it? "Believe in me." That's it. Believe in Jesus. Trust Jesus. Put all your hope in Jesus.

If you do that, Jesus says, though you die (physically), you will live (spiritually). Moreover, everyone who lives (physically) and believes in Jesus shall never die (spiritually).

Jesus conquers death. Jesus crushes death because Jesus is the resurrection and the life. At some point, Jesus says to Martha, "Do you believe this?" That is exactly the question he asks you now: "Do you believe this?"

There is no more important question.

John 13:34-35

A new commandment I give to you, that you love one another: just as I have loved you, you also are to love one another. By this all people will know that you are my disciples, if you have love for one another.

Jesus places extraordinary emphasis on the call to love one another.

First, there's the setting: the eve of his death. Last words are important words. Then he calls it a new commandment. New in what sense? New in the call to love as Jesus has loved us.

Furthermore, there is the emphasis of repetition: love one another, love one another, and have love for one another. Three times.

Also, Jesus reminds the disciples of his love for them: "As I have loved you." Jesus is their model. Having been loved, they must love.

But the main way Jesus emphasizes love is when he says that love is the mark of his disciples. Not a mark, but the mark. This is it: loving one another. Nothing more, nothing less, nothing other than love is the distinguishing mark of a disciple.

It would be a lot easier if the identifying mark of Christ's disciples was something else: church attendance, Bible knowledge, memorizing verses, giving money, or serving the poor. Any of those would be easier, but the mark is something grander, deeper, and stronger.

Love each other. Care about people. Care about others so much that you will inconvenience yourself to help them. See people as precious, eternal, and specially made by God. Be patient, gentle, and kind. Forgive. Serve. Pray. Listen. Weep. Laugh.

Love people when they don't deserve to be loved. Love people when they don't love you back. Love people when they can't love you back.

Love people with all your heart and all your soul. Above all else, love one another.

There is no other mark of a disciple.

John 14:1

Let not your hearts be troubled. Believe in God;
believe also in me.

I don't know how many times I have repeated this verse to myself. When I've been worried, when I've been burdened, when I've felt overwhelmed, I would say these words to myself: "Let not your hearts be troubled. Believe in God; believe also in me. Let not your hearts be troubled. Believe in God; believe also in me."

Perhaps I have said these words more than any other verse in the Bible. They have been a source of endless comfort and peace.

In commanding us to not let our hearts be troubled, Jesus assumes that worry is a choice. We can let our hearts be troubled, We can give way to worry and fear. Or we can choose to trust our God. We choose fear and worry, or we choose faith and peace.

Jesus looks deeply into your eyes and speaks to your soul: "Let not your hearts be troubled. Believe in God; believe also in me."

When you are fearful for your child's safety, hear Jesus say to you, "Let not your hearts be troubled. Believe in God; believe also in me."

When you are worried about finances, hear Jesus say to you, "Let not your hearts be troubled. Believe in God; believe also in me."

When you have failed spiritually and feel guilty, hear Jesus say to you, "Let not your hearts be troubled. Believe in God; believe also in me."

When you are out of work and feel overwhelmed by fear and failure, hear Jesus say to you, "Let not your hearts be troubled. Believe in God; believe also in me."

When you are sick with worry over your teenager's choices, hear Jesus say to you, "Let not your hearts be troubled. Believe in God; believe also in me."

When you fear that you'll never find the right mate, hear Jesus say to you, "Let not your hearts be troubled. Believe in God; believe also in me."

When you hear the doctor say, "It's cancer," hear Jesus say to you, "Let not your hearts be troubled. Believe in God; believe also in me."

When you think about your own death, hear Jesus say to you, "Let not your hearts be troubled. Believe in God; believe also in me."

For worries, fears, and burdens, these are words to know, to memorize, to claim. These are words to stand upon.

John 14:6

~ⅠⅠ~

Jesus said to him, "I am the way, and the truth, and the life. No one comes to the Father except through me."

Did Jesus ever say anything quite so astounding as this? Did he ever say anything so controversial? So difficult?

Who talks like this? Can you imagine any religious teacher, any political leader, any military leader, any great man saying this?

"I am the way." Not just that I know the way or point to the way, but I am the way, the only way.

"I am the truth." Not just that I know the truth or have the truth, but I am the truth. I embody truth. Truth is found in me.

"I am the life." Not just a way to life or a source of life, but life itself. All life is found in me, and there is no life apart from me.

"No one comes to the Father except through me." Jesus is not trying to be exclusive or narrow. It's just the way it is. There is no other sacrifice for sin, no other source of life, no other way to God.

There is a striking scene in C.S. Lewis's *The Silver Chair*:

> "Are you not thirsty?" said the Lion. "I'm dying of thirst," said Jill.
>
> "Then drink," said the Lion.
>
> "May I–could I–would you mind going away while I do?" said Jill.
>
> The Lion answered this only by a look and a very low growl. And as Jill gazed at its motionless bulk, she realized that she might as well have asked the whole mountain to move aside for her convenience.
>
> The delicious rippling noise of the stream was driving her nearly frantic.
>
> "Will you promise not to–do anything to me, if I do come?" said Jill.
>
> "I make no promise," said the Lion.
>
> Jill was so thirsty now that, without noticing it, she had come a step nearer. "Do you eat girls?" she said.
>
> "I have swallowed up girls and boys, women and men, kings and emperors, cities and realms," said the Lion. It

didn't say this as if it were boasting, nor as if it were sorry, nor as if it were angry. It just said it.

"I daren't come and drink," said Jill.

"Then you will die of thirst," said the Lion.

"Oh dear!" said Jill, coming another step nearer. "I suppose I must go and look for another stream then."

"There is no other stream," said the Lion.

John 14:21

*Whoever has my commandments and keeps them, he
it is who loves me. And he who loves me will be
loved by my Father, and I will love him
and manifest myself to him.*

The point of spiritual life is not knowledge, but obedience. The goal is not that we know Jesus's commands, but that we do Jesus's commands, that we obey Jesus's commands.

Why is obedience so vital to God? It's simple. Obedience to God shows our love for God. If I truly love God, then I will want to please him. I'll want to obey him. It won't be drudgery but a delight.

If you love someone who is an equal, a fellow human being, then that love will always be expressed through servanthood. We will want to serve that person and meet their needs if we can. It's just natural.

But when it comes to loving God, someone who is above us, then that love will always be expressed in obedience. It's just natural. We will want to please God. This does not mean that obedience is easy—some of God's commands are tough. But our deepest heart is to obey God, even when it is neither convenient nor comfortable.

Now here's the good part. When we obey God, when our settled attitude is to obey him no matter what, what happens? Jesus gives us stunning promises: The Father will love us. Jesus will love us. Jesus will show himself to us.

But wait a minute. Doesn't God already love us? Yes, he does. He loves us perfectly. Infinitely. Unconditionally.

But God holds in his heart a special tenderness, a special closeness, a special intimacy for his children who long to please him.

A.W. Tozer put it well when he purportedly said, "God doesn't have favorites, but he does have intimates." God's intimates are those who obey him because they love him.

The Father pours out his Spirit on those who obey. The Father pours out his love on those who obey. The Father draws close to those who obey. The Father reveals himself to those who obey.

There is a road that leads into the very heart of God. Only those who obey God, only those who lovingly obey God, will travel that road.

John 14:27

Peace I leave with you; my peace I give to you. Not as the world gives do I give to you. Let not your hearts be troubled, neither let them be afraid.

It is incredible how much the God of the universe wants us to have his peace. Or, to be more direct and personal: it is incredible how much the God of the universe wants *you* to have his peace.

We see this so strongly in John 14. It's the eve of Jesus's crucifixion. Jesus is leaving his disciples, and they are more than a little upset. They are heartsick and worried. They have left everything to follow Jesus, and now all their hopes and dreams have come crashing to the ground. Besides that, they are in considerable physical danger. They are very troubled.

Jesus cares. He cares deeply. His heart goes out to them, just like his heart goes out to you.

The chapter began with the tender words of Jesus saying, "Let not your hearts be troubled. Believe in God; believe also in me" (John 14:1). Now, in verse 27, he again addresses their troubled souls. "Peace I leave with you; my peace I give to you. Not as the world gives do I give to you. Let not your hearts be troubled, neither let them be afraid."

How strong and emphatic is the heart of Jesus that you rest in his peace. "Peace I leave with you; my peace I give to you."

Jesus offers it. We only need to receive it. "Yes, Lord! I receive your peace. Flood me with your peace."

When you are assailed by worry and fear, don't take it. Say no, then choose to receive the peace of Jesus. "Let not your hearts be troubled, neither let them be afraid." This is the heart of Jesus for you.

John 15:7

If you abide in me, and my words abide in you, ask whatever you wish, and it will be done for you.

This is one incredible promise. "Ask whatever you wish, and it will be done for you." Whatever.

Jesus, is this really true? Of course it's true. It is spoken by the one who embodies truth, the one who said, "I am the truth."

But you may be thinking that it doesn't seem to be completely true to you. Maybe you are missing the first part of the sentence: "If you abide in me, and my words abide in you."

With the striking promise comes a striking condition: abide in Jesus.

How do we abide in Jesus? What does this mean? Abide is one of those big words in the Bible that is obviously an important word, but it is not obvious what it means.

Literally, the word *abide* means to remain. Jesus is telling you: "Remain in me. Remain close to me. Stay connected to me, dependent on me, and attached to me. Make yourself at home with me, intimate with me. Rest in me."

All of this is what it means when Jesus says to you, "Abide in me."

Not working harder to please God, not endless effort to please God, not religious duty and obligation.

No; resting in Jesus, drawing close to Jesus, intimacy with Jesus is what he wants. Trusting, not trying. Absolute dependence.

Like a vine and its support, stay connected to Jesus. Depend on him.

Is this you? If it is, to the extent that it should be, his promise is stunning. "If you abide in me, and my words abide in you, ask whatever you wish, and it will be done for you."

John 16:24

Until now you have asked nothing in my name.
Ask, and you will receive, that your joy may be full.

The disciples had asked things of God, but they had not learned to ask in Jesus's name. This was new for them. Followers of Jesus must learn to pray in Jesus's name.

To pray in Jesus's name does not mean to tack his name on to the end of a prayer, like a magic formula to make your prayer valid. Rather, to pray in Jesus's name is to come to a holy God through the blood of Jesus, and it means we pray the same sorts of things that Jesus would pray.

To pray in Jesus's name is to pray Christ-centered, Christ-focused, Christ-enthralled prayers. My will means nothing, Christ's will means everything. My glory means nothing, Christ's glory means everything. When we pray this way, in the name of Jesus, then those prayers will be answered.

So ask. Ask freely. Ask without hesitation. Ask.

This is Jesus's repeated call to you: ask, ask, ask. Don't get to heaven and find out you could have had so much more if only you had asked. "You do not have, because you do not ask" (James 4:2).

And why does Jesus want you to ask? For your joy. That's how good God is; he is zealous to give you as much joy as you can hold.

You must see God as wanting your deepest joy. C.S. Lewis wrote, "The ultimate purpose of God in all his work is to increase joy. Joy is the serious business of heaven." Similarly, Dorothy Sayers remarked, "The greatest sin of the Christian is to be joyless." And Julian of Norwich said, "The greatest honor we can give Almighty God is to live gladly because of the knowledge of His love." God wants you to experience full joy.

So ask. Ask freely. Ask for the glory of Jesus, and the Father will grant it. He will grant it so that you have joy.

John 16:33

I have said these things to you, that in me you may have peace. In the world you will have tribulation. But take heart; I have overcome the world.

Jesus never hides the truth from us. He gives it to us straight. There will be tribulation for us in this world. There will be heartache, suffering, pain, grief, and devastation.

There will be tribulation. Not just for those who sin, not just for those who don't trust God.

There will be tribulation for all of us. No exceptions. No contingencies. No maybes. No escape plans. Not if, but when. This is earth, not heaven. This is a sin-soaked world, with broken lives, broken hearts, and broken people.

Face reality. There will be tribulation for you in this world.

However, Jesus will triumph. And in him, you too will triumph. He has overcome the world, so the pain, hurt, and grief are only temporary. It's not permanent, not final.

Jesus Christ defeated sin, Satan, and death on the cross. Jesus overcame the world.

Face current reality, but never forget that Jesus wins, and one day, all pain and suffering will be vanquished.

Black Friday's here. But Easter Sunday's coming.

John 17:3

And this is eternal life, that they know you the only true God, and Jesus Christ whom you have sent.

In the true Lord's Prayer, Jesus gives the essence of eternal life. What is eternal life?

First of all, eternal life is not unending existence—life that never ends. Every human has that. We all will live on after death.

No, eternal life is not a quantity of life, but a quality of life. Eternal life is life with God. It's the life of God. It's the life of God in us.

When we know God, we have eternal life, the life of God, pulsating within us. This does not happen when we know about God. This only happens when we know God personally, experientially, actually. We know God with our heart and not just our head.

When we know God personally, we have the life of God within us, and that life will never end. It's eternal.

One more thing: eternal life is when we know God and Jesus Christ. The Father and the Son go together, and to know one is to know the other, for they are both equally God.

To have eternal life means that you are connected, personally, to the God of the universe.

John 17:4

*I glorified you on earth, having accomplished the
work that you gave me to do.*

What glorifies God? Doing his work. Doing the work he has
called you to accomplish.

When Jesus came to earth, he glorified the Father by accomplishing the work he was called to. That work was to die on a cross and pay for our sin.

Yes, Jesus had other tasks to accomplish, but primarily, Jesus came to die. "For even the Son of Man came not to be served but to serve, and to give his life as a ransom for many" (Mark 10:45).

How about you? What is your work that God has called you to do? This is how you will glorify God in the greatest way. You won't glorify God by doing the work he's called others to do, but by doing the work he's called you to do.

What is your calling?

William Wilberforce was a gifted young politician in the British Parliament when he came to Christ at age 25. He thought he needed to leave politics and become a pastor. But a close family friend, the pastor John Newton, the converted slave trader who wrote "Amazing Grace," persuaded Wilberforce that God had called him to stay in government. So Wilberforce stayed, and God used him to end slavery in Britain and to do enormous good for the kingdom.

What is your calling? Ponder these:

- Howard Hendricks wrote, "Your career is what you're paid to do; your calling is what you're made to do."
- Frederick Buechner wrote, "The place that God calls you is the place where your deep gladness and the world's deep hunger meet."
- John Ortberg stated, "American society does not talk much about calling anymore. It is more likely to think in terms of career. Yet, for many people a career becomes the altar on which they sacrifice their lives. A calling, which is something I do for God, is replaced by a career, which threatens to become my god. A career is something I choose for myself; a calling is something I receive. A career is some-

241

thing I do for myself; a calling is something I do for God. A career promises status, money or power; a calling generally promises difficulty and even some suffering – and the opportunity to be used by God. A career is about upward mobility; a calling generally leads to downward mobility."

What is your calling?
Ask God and keep asking until you know.

John 17:17

Sanctify them in the truth; your word is truth.

Jesus's request to his Father is brief but pregnant with implication. "Sanctify them in the truth; your word is truth."

The truth liberates. The truth transforms. The truth makes us holy. The truth sets us apart—from sin, ourselves, and everything besides God. The truth sets us free.

Actually, God does these things. He does these things in us and for us. But he uses truth.

All truth is God's truth, but the embodiment of truth is found in God's holy Word. God's Word contains truth and truth only. It is the only book that contains truth and nothing but the truth.

So God takes his holy Word of truth and uses it to transform human life. God liberates us to be the people we're destined to be. God sets us free by the truth of his powerful Word.

There are a lot of words out there. Too many words. Give full attention to those words that are the embodiment of truth.

John 20:28

Thomas answered him, "My Lord and my God!"

There's a bit of Thomas in all of us, a bit of doubt and unbelief. Maybe that's why we appreciate him. There's hope for Doubting Thomases.

The crucial event in his life is unforgettable. Jesus appears to the disciples on the evening of his resurrection, but Thomas isn't there.

When the disciples exclaim to Thomas about seeing the risen Jesus, Thomas doesn't buy it. No way. "Unless I see in his hands the mark of the nails, and place my finger into the mark of the nails, and place my hand into his side, I will never believe" (John 20:25).

Thomas is afraid to believe. He's afraid that he will get his hopes up and then be devastated with disappointment. There's a bit of Thomas in all of us.

But Jesus does not give up on Thomases. A week later, Jesus appears to the disciples again, and Thomas is there. "Then he said to Thomas, 'Put your finger here, and see my hands; and put out your hand, and place it in my side. Do not disbelieve, but believe.' Thomas answered him, 'My Lord and my God!'" (John 20:27-28).

What a response. Thomas no longer needs to touch Jesus. "Not necessary, Lord!" He is lost in love, wonder, and worship. "My Lord and my God!"

Jesus's response to Thomas is telling. If Jesus were not Lord and God, how would he respond? "Thomas, please. Yes, I'm the Messiah. Yes, I'm the prophet. Yes, I'm a great teacher. But I'm not the Lord. I'm not God."

Does Jesus respond that way? Hardly. He affirms Thomas and receives his declaration of faith. "Jesus said to him, 'Have you believed because you have seen me? Blessed are those who have not seen and yet have believed'" (John 20:29).

Jesus loves it when we see who Jesus really is and worship him as, "My Lord and my God."

"Blessed are those who have not seen and yet have believed" (John 20:29).

Acts 1:8

But you will receive power when the Holy Spirit has
come upon you, and you will be my witnesses in
Jerusalem and in all Judea and Samaria,
and to the end of the earth.

From the time of Abraham in Genesis 12 through the resurrection of Jesus, all of God's focus has been on the Jewish people. But no more. With the Great Commission, at the end of each of the four gospels and in Acts 1:8, Christ sends us to all the peoples of the earth. Now we are called to Jerusalem, to Judea and Samaria, and to the end of the earth.

We are called across the street and around the world. We are called everywhere and anywhere.

Our calling is simple: be witnesses for Christ.

You are not called to be an evangelist. You are not called to be a preacher. You are not called to be a glib speaker. No, you are called to be a witness—someone pointing to Christ. You're like a signpost pointing to Jesus. Just tell what you know. Tell what you've seen. Tell what he means to you.

But you're not on your own, mind you. God will be with you, in you, beside you. He will empower you with the Spirit. So lean on his power, not yours. Depend upon the Spirit to guide you, strengthen you, and empower you.

When a big storm comes and you lose power in the house, it's no fun at all. You need the power.

That's exactly the way our spiritual life is. Do we have power yet? Yes. We do have power. The power of the Spirit. Plug in!

Acts 1:14a

All these with one accord were devoting
themselves to prayer.

The early church in Jerusalem was devoted to prayer right from the very start. After the ascension of Jesus, the first 120 believers gathered together in an upper room and poured out their hearts to God. They were devoted to prayer because they were dedicated to and desperate for God.

What does God do? He pours out his Holy Spirit upon them and births the church. He gathers a large crowd, anoints a now-transformed Peter to preach, and saves 3,000 people. And the church was off and running, transforming the Roman Empire.

This continues throughout the book of Acts. The church moves from a small group of Jewish believers to sweep through the Roman Empire and become a large, international, multilingual, and multiethnic body of believers empowered by the Holy Spirit. And behind it all was one fact: the church was devoted to prayer.

At every critical juncture, all through the remarkable record of the early church, there is the power of prayer. United, passionate, believing prayer.

When God's people band together and devote themselves to prayer, things happen. God shows up. The Spirit comes in power. Christ is exalted. The lost get saved. The sick get healed. Lives become transformed. Breakthroughs happen.

All because of prayer.

When we are devoted to God and desperate for God, we will become committed to prayer.

God uses people who pray. God uses churches that pray. Prayer is the real work of ministry.

Acts 2:42

*And they devoted themselves to the apostles' teaching
and the fellowship, to the breaking of bread and the
prayers.*

There is no better summary of the church than Acts 2:42-47.
Acts 2 begins with the creation of the church and ends with the
character of the church.

Acts 2:42-47 is God's portrait of the church. This is what God
wants every church to look like, not so much in details, but in
values and focus.

The passage begins in verse 42 with the essential characteristics
of a good church: teaching, community, worship, and prayer. The
church in Jerusalem was devoted to these four things.

First, they were devoted to biblical teaching. It is impossible
to be a healthy, God-pleasing church with any other foundation
than biblical teaching. If you are looking for a church, find a
church where the pastor and the leaders believe the Bible is God's
word, not man's word. Find a church that preaches biblically
rooted messages, not motivational speeches with a few Bible
verses. Find a church that is focused not on knowing the Bible,
but obeying the Bible.

Second, the Jerusalem church was devoted to fellowship and
community. They shared their lives, their hearts, their struggles,
and their joys. They loved together, they served together, and
they suffered together. They did life together, not as lone rangers.
They met in large group celebrations at the temple and in small
group communities in homes. Find a church that deeply believes
in authentic community.

Third, they were devoted to the breaking of bread, or worship.
Breaking bread refers here to communion, which in many ways
is the high point of worship, when we joyfully celebrate Christ's
sacrifice for our sins. From Acts 2:42-47, one gets the strong
impression that the early believers, having fallen in love with
Jesus, were now caught up with love, wonder, and praise. Find a
church that is full of worshippers of God and not just workers for
God. Find lovers of Jesus.

Finally, the early church was devoted to prayer. That was their
power source. That was the engine that drove everything else.

All through the book of Acts, you see that the early church was devoted to prayer. No wonder God showed up and did remarkable things. Find a church that is devoted to prayer because they are desperate for God.

This is what God wants every church to look like. This is what God wants your church to look like.

Acts 4:13

*Now when they saw the boldness of Peter and John,
and perceived that they were uneducated, common
men, they were astonished. And they recognized
that they had been with Jesus.*

They were uneducated, common, ordinary men. They were everyday fishermen.

When Jesus Christ came to our planet, he did not choose the wealthy, the powerful, the scholarly, or the famous for his closest disciples. He chose ordinary men.

All through the Bible, this is God's way, isn't it? God uses ordinary men and women who recognize their inadequacy and thus their desperate need to depend upon Christ.

You can be too big for God to use, but you can never be too small.

But here's the key: they had been with Jesus, and that made all the difference. They were transformed forever.

Think about the people God used in the Bible. In *The Purpose Driven Life*, Rick Warren said:

> Abraham was old, Jacob was insecure, Leah was unattractive, Joseph was abused, Moses stuttered, Gideon was poor, Samson was codependent, Rahab was immoral, David had an affair and all kinds of family problems, Elijah was suicidal, Jeremiah was depressed, Jonah was reluctant, Naomi was a widow, John the Baptist was eccentric, Peter was impulsive and hot-tempered, Martha worried, the Samaritan woman had several failed marriages, Zacchaeus was unpopular, Thomas had doubts, Paul had poor health, and Timothy was timid. That is quite a variety of misfits, but God used each of them in his service. He will use you too if you stop making excuses.

Brother Yun, in *The Heavenly Man,* told his wife Deling:

> We are absolutely nothing. We have nothing to be proud about. We have no abilities and nothing to offer

God. The fact that he chooses to use us is only due to his grace. It has nothing to do with us. If God should choose to raise up others for his purpose and never to use us again we would have nothing to complain about.

God is looking for ordinary people who have been with Jesus. Are you one of those people? Will you be one of these ordinary people?

Acts 4:23-24a

When they were released, they went to their
friends and reported what the chief priests and
the elders had said to them. And when they heard it,
they lifted their voices together to God.

These are the early days of the church. Exciting things are happening. God has shown up in power. Thousands have come to faith in Jesus. Miracles have happened.

But now, Peter and John, two of the main leaders of the fledgling church, have been arrested, threatened, and now released. The situation is volatile. If the church doesn't toe the line, perhaps more executions could take place. After all, the people in power did not hesitate to execute Jesus. Would his followers be next?

In this dire situation, Peter and John report back to the church. What did the church do? "And when they heard it, they lifted their voices together to God."

This is what the people of God do in dire circumstances. They pray. They pray together. They lift their voices in prayer to God.

They don't plan, brainstorm, network, or make calls. At least, they don't immediately respond in these ways. How do they respond? They pray. They access omnipotence. They go right to the top. That's the first response, the immediate response, and the instinctive response.

God uses churches that pray. God uses churches that pray together. God uses churches that pray together as their first response.

A.C. Dixon wrote: "When we rely upon organization, we get what organization can do; when we rely upon education, we get what education can do; when we rely upon eloquence, we get what eloquence can do, and so on. Nor am I disposed to undervalue any of these things in their proper place. But when we rely upon prayer, we get what God can do."

What kind of people give themselves to prayer like the early church did?

1. The kind of people who are desperate for God.
2. The kind of people who are hungry for God.

3. The kind of people who want more of God.
4. The kind of people who long to be intimates of God.
5. The kind of people who recognize how much they need God.
6. The kind of people who understand that prayer is the real work for God.
7. The kind of people who understand that prayer is the greatest privilege in life.
8. The kind of people who see the unseen spiritual battle that is raging.
9. The kind of people who long to see God do a mighty work.

Are you one of those people?

Acts 4:24b

*Sovereign Lord, who made the heaven and the earth
and the sea and everything in them.*

How did they see God? How did they approach God? How did they view God?

The first Christians, that is. That band of spirit-infused, blood-bought believers who saw God work miracles in their midst and who would not be intimidated by the threats of the political and religious leaders. How did they see God?

Here's a clue: Peter and John are threatened and released. They go back to their church family, and naturally, they go to God in prayer. Hear their prayer, or at least the start of it: "Sovereign Lord, who made the heaven and the earth and the sea and everything in them."

Sovereign Lord. Absolute ruler. King of all kings. You are in charge. Not these self-important religious leaders. Not the mighty Roman army. Not the Roman governor Pilate. Not the emperor of all Rome. No. You alone are Lord and God.

That's who we talk with. The one who created the massive Rockies, El Capitan and Half-Dome, the Grand Canyon, the vast and powerful Pacific Ocean. The one, yes, who made the galaxies and the untold billions of stars, some of which are bigger than the orbit of the Earth around the sun.

That is whom we come to in prayer. That is the One we have access to. That is the One who hears our prayer. That is the One who delights in our prayer.

I am completely undone, dazzled by the sheer grandeur and greatness of our God.

How do you see God?

Acts 4:29

And now, Lord, look upon their threats and
grant to your servants to continue to
speak your word with all boldness.

It had not been long since their leader had been executed. Jerusalem, filled with hostile officials under the auspices of a ruthless Roman army, was dangerous soil for the fledgling group of Christ's followers. After all, if they did not hesitate to kill Jesus, would they be shy about killing his followers? Danger lurked everywhere.

And now the young church had just heard the news: Peter and John had been arrested and threatened. What would happen next?

Naturally, the Christians gather to pray. They begin their prayer by acknowledging God's greatness, by quoting Psalm 2, and by confessing God's sovereignty. Now they come to petition. What will they ask?

Most of us would be asking for protection, for life, for safety, for deliverance. And those are good and acceptable things to ask for. There are many examples in Scripture.

But the focus of the young church is elsewhere. Their request? "And now, Lord, look upon their threats and grant to your servants to continue to speak your word with all boldness."

Not a word about their safety, at least not recorded in Scripture. They were so intent on the gospel. They were so focused on the kingdom. They were so preoccupied with reaching lost people.

There is nothing wrong with asking for safety, nothing at all. Indeed, many times this is the proper expression of reliance on God. David does it all through the Psalms.

But what an example in Acts 4 of God-centered prayer. These Jesus-intoxicated, Spirit-empowered believers were so preoccupied with the kingdom of Jesus that this was the natural way they prayed: "Lord, advance the kingdom. Lord, give us boldness. Lord, save these dear people."

I imagine that the closer I get to God, the more my prayers will be focused on Jesus, not me.

Acts 4:30

While you stretch out your hand to heal,
and signs and wonders are performed through
the name of your holy servant Jesus.

When you are praying to a big God, you make your prayers big, God-sized, bold, impossible. Ask the sort of things that only God can do. When I am praying with people and I hear a big, bold ASK, I smile inside. I love it. I can only imagine what God thinks.

In Acts 4, we have a big ask. "While you stretch out your hand to heal, and signs and wonders are performed through the name of your holy servant Jesus." Heal. Do the miraculous. Do the impossible.

The request is not about self. Not about a person's ego, a person's pocketbook, or a person's comfort. It's about Jesus and his kingdom, so there's no need to hold back.

What God has done anywhere, God can do here. What God has done at any time, God can do now. What God has done with any other people, God can do with us.

God did it in Jerusalem. God did it in the first century. God did it with the early Christians. So why not ask? James 4:2 says, "You do not have, because you do not ask."

What are you trusting God for that only God can do?

What are we, as a church, trusting God for that only God can do? "While you stretch out your hand to heal, and signs and wonders are performed through the name of your holy servant Jesus."

After these Christians prayed, there was a most interesting result. It was as if God expressed his deep pleasure with this united, faith-filled prayer. "And when they had prayed, the place in which they were gathered together was shaken, and they were all filled with the Holy Spirit and continued to speak the word of God with boldness" (Acts 4:31).

O Lord, may it happen here. May it happen now. May it happen with us.

Acts 6:4

But we will devote ourselves to prayer and to the
ministry of the word.

It is an occupational hazard of pastors, missionaries, and Christian leaders to neglect God. We are constantly doing work for God, and we may think that translates automatically into greater love for God. That's not true. God has called us primarily to be lovers of God, not workers for God. We can get so busy doing the work of ministry that we neglect our own relationship with God.

The apostles in the early church did not make that mistake. They recognized that their calling was not to solve all the problems and do all the work, but to empower the entire body to do the work of ministry. Meanwhile, they would focus on their calling—prayer and the Word of God.

We have too many pastors, missionaries, and Christian leaders who are marvelously gifted, but their souls are only six inches deep because they fail to prioritize time alone with the Lord above all other things.

If pastors neglect God, then their ministries will lack depth and authenticity. There will be the unmistakable aroma of phoniness about them, and those pastors will eventually burn out or crash.

The first duty for the pastor is to love Jesus and seek his face. Not his hand, his face. This is true for every believer.

Jesus did this. Paul did this. The early church did this. Why would we think we don't need this time alone with the Lord?

Oswald Chambers hit the bull's-eye: "It is impossible for a believer, no matter what his experience, to keep right with God if he will not take the trouble to spend time with God. Spend plenty of time with God; let other things go, but don't neglect him."

Acts 7:59

And as they were stoning Stephen, he called out,
"Lord Jesus, receive my spirit."

Stephen was the first Christian martyr, and what a godly man he was. When he is introduced in Acts 6, he is described emphatically as "a man full of faith and of the Holy Spirit" (Acts 6:5) and "full of grace and power" (Acts 6:8). High praise indeed.

And then we see the way he dies: he's brutally stoned to death. "And as they were stoning Stephen, he called out, 'Lord Jesus, receive my spirit.' And falling to his knees he cried out with a loud voice, 'Lord, do not hold this sin against them.' And when he had said this, he fell asleep" (Acts 7:59-60).

When I read these words, I feel like bowing in hushed awe in the presence of such faith and love.

That's the way I want to die. Full of faith, peace, joy, and love. To be honest, I don't feel I've had this faith-filled perspective on death in the past, but I want it.

Paul, who watched Stephen die and even helped kill him, had this same perspective on death. "For to me to live is Christ, and to die is gain" (Phil. 1:21). In other words: "I'm not afraid of death because death means being with Christ."

John Owen, a great Puritan writer from the 1600s, lay on his deathbed, dictating a letter. He stated, "I am still in the land of the living," but quickly added, "Stop. Change that and say, 'I am yet in the land of the dying, but I hope soon to be in the land of the living.'"

Adoniram Judson, the American missionary who died in India in 1850, said on his deathbed: "Come, Holy Spirit, Dove Divine, I go with the gladness of a boy bounding away from school, I feel so strong in Christ."

What a statement. "I go with the gladness of a boy bounding away from school, I feel so strong in Christ."

Acts 13:2

*While they were worshiping the Lord and fasting, the
Holy Spirit said, "Set apart for me Barnabas and Saul
for the work to which I have called them."*

The church at Antioch, like the first church in Jerusalem, was
devoted to prayer. They worshiped, they prayed, they fasted.
No wonder God's hand was upon them. No wonder they were led
by the Holy Spirit. No wonder they were a great missions church.
They were fueled by prayer, the lifeblood of any church.

We learn from the church at Antioch the importance of prayer
and worship. It's no surprise that it was during a time of worship
that the Holy Spirit spoke to them about Barnabas and Saul being
sent out. God loves it when we worship together. God shows up
when we worship together. God speaks to us when we worship
together. God is looking for worshippers.

Thus, we learn from Antioch that the Holy Spirit must lead us.
Yes, a church must talk, plan, organize, and even strategize. But
we must be led by the Holy Spirit, not by our collective wisdom.
The church is no democracy. "Holy Spirit, lead us!" must be our
continual cry. If we are desperate, if we are obedient, if we are
surrendered, the Spirit will lead us.

We also learn about missions and how they are based in the
church. The church at Antioch, together, sent out Barnabas and
Saul. They prayed for them, financially supported them, and then
received them when they returned. They did missions together
as a church, not as individuals. This is God's ideal way to do
missions, for the church is God's chosen instrument for this age.

This is the way God wants his church—fueled by worship, led
by the Spirit, resulting in mission.

Acts 16:31

And they said, "Believe in the Lord Jesus, and you will be saved, you and your household."

The Philippian jailer, filled by the Spirit's conviction after his escape from death, puts the question straight: "What must I do to be saved?" (Acts 16:30).

Paul doesn't stutter. His succinct reply is, "Believe in the Lord Jesus" (Acts 16:30).

That's it? That's so simple. Too simple, it seems.

It's not too simple for God. It's the gospel truth. To be saved from our sin, we believe in the Lord Jesus. We put our faith in the Lord Jesus. We trust the Lord Jesus.

That's it. Just believe. Believe in Jesus. Believe in Jesus as Savior. Believe plus nothing.

Faith alone, in Christ alone, by grace alone.

How can you explain to a non-Christian friend how to become a Christian? Simply turn to Acts 16:31 and read it. There is no more straightforward verse on how to be saved. "Believe in the Lord Jesus."

Short and sweet. Oh, so sweet.

Acts 20:24

But I do not account my life of any value nor as precious to myself, if only I may finish my course and the ministry that I received from the Lord Jesus, to testify to the gospel of the grace of God.

Paul knew that trouble and trial awaited him in Jerusalem; God had made that clear. But God had also called him to go to Jerusalem, and he was resolved to make that trip no matter the cost. Paul was undeterred by the fear of danger because he was unreservedly surrendered to Jesus Christ.

Every believer must decide a basic question: Does my life belong to me, to do with as I choose, or does my life belong to another, to Jesus Christ?

In every generation, there have been followers of Jesus who were fully devoted to Christ. These believers could not be intimidated.

Polycarp was the bishop of the church in Smyrna (the city of Izmir in modern-day Turkey). The Apostle John mentored him in the church at Ephesus. Joseph Stowell tells Polycarp's story:

> In order to be a loyal member of the Roman Empire, you had to say, "Caesar is Lord." Most early Christians, rightly so, refused to say that. By the time Polycarp was 86, the empire had begun to persecute Christians who wouldn't say that. Polycarp heard this was in the works and fled to a little village miles away from Smyrna, but he was found. A captain knocked on the door with the troops behind him. Polycarp opened the door. He was so well respected that the captain pled with him, "Just say, 'Caesar is Lord.' You don't even have to mean it. Just say it. We don't want to do this to you."
>
> Polycarp said, "He's been my God 86 years, and he has never betrayed me yet. How can I now betray my Lord and my Savior Jesus Christ?"
>
> They led him back to Smyrna, tied him to a stake, and set it on fire. Unwaveringly he gave his life, because he would not deny his Lord.

Oswald Chambers puts it succinctly: "There is only one thing God wants of us, and that is our unconditional surrender."

Is that true for you—unconditional surrender to Jesus Christ?

Romans 1:7a

*To all those in Rome who are loved by God and
called to be saints.*

At the outset of Romans, Paul identifies his readers as having
two fundamental traits: they are loved by God, and they are
called to be saints.

They are loved by God. The infinite, sovereign, eternal God
of the universe loves them. Despite their sin, their failures, and
their flaws, he loves them. He loves them tenderly. He loves them
personally, fiercely, stubbornly, and emotionally. He loves them.

What if you saw yourself this way, as deeply loved by God?
Not because of who you are, but because of who he is, you are
tenderly loved by God.

Brennan Manning tells this story in his book, the *Lion and
Lamb*:

> Several years ago, Edward Farrell, a priest from De-
> troit, went on a two-week summer vacation to Ireland
> to visit relatives. His one living uncle was about to
> celebrate his eightieth birthday. On the great day, Ed
> and his uncle got up early. It was before dawn. They
> took a walk along the shores of Lake Killarney and
> stopped to watch the sunrise. They stood side-by-side
> for a full twenty minutes and then resumed walking.
> Ed glanced at his uncle and saw that his face had bro-
> ken into a broad smile. Ed said, "Uncle Seamus, you
> look very happy." "I am." Ed asked, "How come?" And
> his uncle replied, "The Father of Jesus is very fond of
> me."

When you see yourself this way, you can smile a big smile.

The believers in Rome are saints. This word in the Greek language means "holy ones" or "holy people." Not perfect, but forgiven. All of your sins have been charged to Jesus Christ, so they
are gone from you. Paid for. Done.

You are a holy one, forgiven, right with God. As blameless as
Christ because you are in Christ.

What if you saw yourself this way—completely holy and
blameless before God, rather than guilty and unworthy?

261

What could be more important than these two things: being loved by God and being holy before him? Loved by God in a deeply personal way. Holy before God in a fully righteous way.

Perhaps you would do well to confess who you are and your essence: "I am loved by God. I am holy before God. I am loved and holy."

Romans 1:9-10a

*For God is my witness, whom I serve with my spirit in
the gospel of his Son, that without ceasing I
mention you always in my prayers.*

Paul prays for the believers in Rome. Not only does Paul pray
for them, he prays for them constantly, without ceasing. And
not only does he pray for them constantly, but he tells them that
he prays for them constantly. Paul must have known that these
believers, whom he had never met, would be encouraged from
the depths of their hearts, knowing that the Apostle Paul was
regularly praying for them.

In the fall of 1972, I met John Lodwick, a fellow freshman at
Rice University. Little did I know that John and I would become
fast friends and room together for the next eight years, through
college and graduate school.

Sometime after meeting John, I began praying for him every
day. Perhaps it was in the first weeks or months after meeting
him—I no longer remember. But I began praying for him every
day. I have done that now for more than forty years, and I will
continue to pray for John for the rest of my years on this planet.

John is a close friend, and praying for him is the single most
important thing I could do for my friend.

Moreover, not only do I pray for John daily, but John prays
for me. I know he does, and from time to time, he tells me that
he prays for me daily. I already know it, but it is still good to hear
afresh, "I'm praying for you daily."

Just as Paul prayed continually for the Christians at Rome and
told them he did, and just as John Lodwick prays continually for
me and tells me he does, let's pray continually for the people God
puts in our hearts and tell them we are. They will be encouraged
from the depths of their hearts.

Romans 1:16

For I am not ashamed of the gospel, for it is the power
of God for salvation to everyone who believes,
to the Jew first and also to the Greek.

Have you ever been ashamed of the gospel? That is, have you ever shrunk back from telling others about Christ's death and resurrection because you were afraid you'd be rejected? Perhaps even ridiculed or talked about behind your back?

If so, you're in good company. Paul, the seemingly fearless Apostle Paul, faced this same temptation. Some say that Paul cannot mean he was ever ashamed of the gospel, but that's precisely his point. As Scottish theologian James Stewart pointed out, "There's no sense in declaring that you're not ashamed of something unless you've been tempted to be ashamed of it."

But Paul overcame his fear of embarrassment, and so can we. We must do what Paul did and remind ourselves that this gospel is powerful. It transforms lives for all eternity. It is the power of God for the salvation of anyone who will believe it.

When we are tempted to shrink back from the gospel, let's remind ourselves that this is the powerful, life-rescuing truth of God, the gospel of Christ. Over and over remind yourself: this is God's power to save.

Jim Elliot, who would later be martyred in the Amazon jungle, penned these lines as a young man, which his late wife, Elisabeth Elliot, cites in her book *Shadow of the Almighty*:

> We are so utterly ordinary, so commonplace, while we profess to know a Power the Twentieth Century does not reckon with. But we are "harmless," and therefore unharmed. We are spiritual pacifists, non-militants, conscientious objectors in this battle-to-the-death with principalities and powers in high places. Meekness must be had for contact with men, but brass, outspoken boldness is required to take part in the comradeship of the Cross. We are "sideliners" – coaching and criticizing the real wrestlers while content to sit by and leave the enemies of God unchallenged. The world cannot hate us, we are too much like its own. Oh that God would make us dangerous!

Romans 1:17

For in it the righteousness of God is revealed
from faith for faith, as it is written,
"The righteous shall live by faith."

The term *righteous* or *righteousness* can have negative connotations. For some, it may suggest images of long-faced priests in darkened cathedrals that smell of mildew and incense. Or it may suggest pharisaical, holier-than-thou Christians who have lips pursed with disapproval and condemnation, and who feel it's a sin to have fun.

I hope the term "righteousness" carries none of these connotations for you, because this word is extremely important in the book of Romans for a number of reasons.

First, the "righteousness of God" can refer to an attribute of God—God is upright and good in all he does. He is a righteous God.

Second, the "righteousness of God" is often used in the Old Testament to refer to God's deliverance of his people. It can almost be a synonym of "the salvation of God."

Third, the "righteousness of God" can refer to a gift of righteousness from God, a righteous status or right standing with God that he gives to all who trust in Christ. This righteousness or right standing is a gift of God.

The first two meanings may be invoked in the term "righteousness" in Romans, but Paul primarily uses the word with the third meaning. This is God's gift of right standing with himself. Paul is telling us at the outset of Romans that in the gospel, a right standing, which is God's gift, is being revealed.

Moreover, this gift of righteous status is "from faith for faith." That is, it's completely based on faith, from first to last. It is by faith in Christ, and nothing but faith in Christ. Faith plus nothing.

And to further clarify, Paul cites Habakkuk 2:4. Even the Old Testament taught us that we become righteous people by faith. We have life and we live by faith.

So this term "righteousness," far from being a religious, pharisaical, or morose word, is actually a wonderful word, referring to the incredible gift of God whereby he gives us right standing with him.

God removes our sins and puts them on Christ. Then he takes the righteousness of Christ and puts it on us, and it's all done through the cross. And that's the gospel: how sinners become right and righteous with a holy God. It's the best news ever.

From the point that you trust Christ as Savior, forever after, God will not see you in your sin, but only in the blood-bought righteousness of Christ.

That's exactly how you must see yourself.

Romans 3:23

For all have sinned and fall short of the glory of God.

Warren Wiersbe, in his book *Be Daring*, wrote, "In 1973, Dr. Karl Menninger, one of the world's leading psychiatrists, published a startling book, *Whatever Became of Sin?* He pointed out that the very word sin has gradually dropped out of our vocabulary, as he puts it, 'the word, along with the notion.' We talk about mistakes, weaknesses, inherited tendencies, faults, and even errors; but we do not face up to the fact of sin."

The Bible teaches us that our fundamental problem is sin. Our fundamental human problem is not education, poverty, drugs, politics, pollution, or war. The problem is deeper. The problem is in us. The problem is our bent towards sin.

That's why God did not send an educator, scientist, businessman, or statesman to the planet. God sent a savior because our greatest need is for a savior. Unless we realize and acknowledge our sin, we will never look to a savior.

There is no more succinct statement of sin in the Bible than Romans 3:23. God is clear: "For all have sinned and fall short of the glory of God."

The problem is universal—all have sinned. We are inclined to compare ourselves with others who seem to be worse sinners. We can always compare ourselves to drug lords, murderers, and human traffickers, but they're not the standard. Jesus Christ is the standard, and we all fall short of that high standard.

John Stott, in his book *The Message of Romans*, quotes Bishop Handley Moule: "The harlot, the liar, the murderer, are short of it [God's glory], but so are you. Perhaps they stand at the bottom of a mine, and you on the crest of an Alp; but you are as little able to touch the stars as they."

Not one of us attains the glory of God. Not one of us reflects the perfect character of Christ. Not one of us can touch the stars.

"All have sinned and fall short of the glory of God."

Romans 3:24

*And are justified by his grace as a gift, through the
redemption that is in Christ Jesus.*

Four parts in this verse emphasize that salvation is not the work of man for God, but the work of God for man.

The first part is, "and are justified." The verb is passive. You don't do it, you don't justify yourself; you are justified by God. You are given right standing with God. This is done for you, not by you.

Secondly, you are justified "by his grace." Grace is God's favor to those who don't deserve it and cannot earn it. Grace is absolutely free.

The third part, "as a gift," reiterates the same point. You don't deserve this. You can't earn it, pay for it, or work for it. It's a gift. Like all gifts, you can only receive it.

The final part reads, "through the redemption that is in Christ Jesus." Christ redeemed us from our sin. He bought us with his own blood.

So Christ did it all. We did nothing. Salvation goes to those who are justified by his grace as a gift because Christ redeemed us.

It's not the work of man for God. It's the work of God for man.

Every religion in the world is spelled D-O, focusing on what we do to earn salvation, but not the gospel. The gospel is spelled D-O-N-E. It's about what Christ has done to save us.

Craig Brian Larson, an author, notes that one ad for the US Marines Corps pictures a sword, and beneath it, the words "Earned, not given." If you want to become a Marine, be prepared to earn that name through sacrifice, hardship, and training. If you get it, you deserve it.

But if you want to become a Christian, you must have the exact opposite attitude, for the message of the gospel is given, not earned.

You cannot save your own soul, and God will not save anyone who tries to earn salvation; only those who will humbly receive it as a gift through faith in Jesus Christ will be saved.

Romans 3:26

*It was to show his righteousness at the present time,
so that he might be just and the justifier of the
one who has faith in Jesus.*

At the cross of Christ, we see the full glory and beauty of God revealed. We see his love, his grace, his mercy, his kindness, and his forgiveness. We see his justice, his righteousness, his holiness, his wisdom, and his sovereignty. The cross displays the glory of Christ.

In Romans 3:26, Paul underscores that the cross demonstrates God's righteousness, his upright and blameless character, because it reveals that God is both just and the justifier of believers.

First, God is just. He is just because he has been forgiving sinners since Adam, and now their sin is paid for. The blood of all those animal sacrifices from Adam to Christ could not really remove sin, but all those sacrifices would lead to the death of Christ, and his blood could remove sin. At the cross, sin was finally paid for, and therefore the justice of God was upheld. God is just.

But secondly, God is merciful. He is merciful because he extends grace to forgive rebel sinners. He is the justifier of rebel sinners, if they will only put their faith in Christ.

So God is just and justifier. God is the God of justice and mercy. Perfect justice and endless mercy meet in the cross of Christ.

And God is glorified.

Romans 4:5

And to the one who does not work but believes in him
who justifies the ungodly, his faith is
counted as righteousness.

This is startling. God justifies the ungodly? What do you mean? That makes no sense.

Yes, God justifies the ungodly. Not the godly—the ungodly. Why doesn't God justify the godly? Because there are no godly. We've all sinned. But because he is full of grace and a merciful God, he will justify the ungodly person who:

- Does not work. That is, does not rely on God's works.
- Believes in him who justifies the ungodly. That is, believes in a God who gives grace to sinners.

If we do that—not rely on our good works, but rely on a merciful Savior—God will justify us and make us right with him.

But how can God do this? How can he declare ungodly people forgiven and justified? There is only one basis—the cross. Romans 5:6 says, "Christ died for the ungodly." He paid for our sins and satisfied the justice of God.

I love this verse. Just love it.

This is so contrary to the human mindset of earning it, of performance, of being good enough, of religion. We are all affected by this mindset. It's inherent in us from the time we are born. Earn it. Be good enough. Measure up.

Do you remember the end of the movie *Saving Private Ryan*? "I only hope I earned what you did for me."

That's the human mindset, and it's embraced by every religion on the planet, including much of organized Christianity.

But it's not the gospel. The gospel does not say "earn it." The gospel is the message of grace.

God justifies the ungodly.

Romans 5:1

Therefore, since we have been justified by faith, we have peace with God through our Lord Jesus Christ.

Faith alone.

This was one of the rallying cries of the Reformation in sixteenth-century Europe. We are saved by grace alone, through faith alone, in Christ alone.

It is amazing how strongly the book of Romans emphasizes that we are saved by faith, not works. The Greek word for *faith* (and its cognates) is found four times in Romans 1:16-17, nine times in Romans 3:21-31, nine times in Romans 4:1-15, and eight times in Romans 4:16-25. It reappears often, including in this verse, which begins Romans 5.

Why this incredible emphasis that we are justified (made right with God) by faith and therefore have peace with God? Why is God so emphatic on this matter? I can think of five reasons why God is so emphatic that we are justified by grace.

First, the "earn this" mindset is so rooted in the human heart, and we need the continual reminder that we are saved by faith, not by our efforts or merit.

Second, the stakes are so high. We are talking about eternity—forever and ever. We must be crystal clear on how we receive salvation: by faith, not works.

Third, because there are difficult passages in the New Testament which seem to suggest that we are saved by works, or baptism, or obedience, or something else, rather than simply receiving the gift of salvation through faith or trust in Christ. Faith is receiving something, not doing something. Why does God include difficult passages? I don't know. I can guess, but I don't know. But I do know there are many clear passages that teach salvation by faith, not works. A sound rule of Bible study: the clear passages interpret the unclear passages.

Fourth, the gospel of grace alone, faith alone, Christ alone counters all human pride. If we are saved by anything we do, then we can take some of the credit. But if Christ did it all and we just receive it, then all glory goes to Christ.

Fifth, God is so emphatic because we need to hear the gospel over and over again. We need the continuous reminder that we get in by grace, not by performance. Jesus paid it all. We simply receive it by faith.

Faith plus nothing.

Romans 5:3

Not only that, but we rejoice in our sufferings.

God is saying to you: "Rejoice when you suffer." That may sound crazy, but that's what God calls you to do. Rejoice when you experience a setback, a disappointment, a heartache. Rejoice when you have car trouble or the refrigerator goes out. Rejoice when you have back pain, when you hear the diagnosis of cancer, when you lose a family member.

Rejoice, not because of those things, but in those things. Take joy. Choose to rejoice, to give praise, to give thanks. Don't complain or grumble or whine. Don't cry out, "How could God do this to me?" Rather, choose joy.

Let me ask you: Do you do this? What is your biggest burden right now? Are you rejoicing in that suffering?

It's what people of faith do. In Acts 16, when Paul and Silas were beaten and thrown in jail, they were singing songs and praising God. That's rejoicing in suffering.

When Aleksandr Solzhenitsyn was in a Soviet gulag prison for eight years, he lost his parents and his wife divorced him. Yet, in the ordeal of prison, God touched his heart and drew Solzhenitsyn to himself. Solzhenitsyn later wrote, "So bless you, prison, for having been in my life." He chose to rejoice.

But why? Why do we rejoice? Basically, because God says to, and because he's God. But we can say more. Romans 5:3 continues with, "Not only that, but we rejoice in our sufferings, knowing that suffering produces endurance, and endurance produces character, and character produces hope" (Rom. 5:3-4).

God uses these sufferings, painful though they may be, to build our faith, to shape our souls, and to grow our hearts. We need them.

Here is a classic quote from C.S. Lewis: "God whispers to us in our pleasures, speaks in our conscience, but shouts in our pain. It is his megaphone to rouse a deaf world."

So rejoice when you suffer.

Romans 5:5

And hope does not put us to shame, because God's love has been poured into our hearts through the Holy Spirit who has been given to us.

The Holy Spirit does many things for us. He seals us, dwells in us, baptizes us, fills us, teaches us, comforts us, convicts us, guides us, empowers us, and more. But one of the most important of all the ministries of the Holy Spirit is found in Romans 5:5: He pours God's love into our hearts.

How absolutely vital is this ministry? If we do not feel loved by God, then we won't fully love God back, nor will we fully trust him, enjoy him, worship him, obey him, or rest in him.

Our entire spiritual life hinges on whether we experience God's love for us. This is what the Spirit does for us: He reveals to us how much the Father loves us.

He does not pour out God's love when we've been good, dutiful, devout, disciplined, or because we've had our quiet time. We don't earn God's love.

Rather, the Spirit pours out the Father's love simply because this is the Spirit's nature—to pour the Father's love into our hearts.

Paul chooses a strong word: pour.

"It has the sense of an initial outpouring that remains a permanent flood," says John Stott.

"It is like a cloudburst on a parched countryside," states James Dunn.

But this is a cloudburst that leaves the ground permanently soaked in God's love.

Receive the Father's love afresh. Drink it in.

"O Spirit, pour out the Father's love afresh in my heart!"

Romans 5:8

But God shows his love for us in that while we were
still sinners, Christ died for us.

I love this verse. I have loved it for more than forty years. It is one of the mightiest verses in the Bible.

It tells me so much. It tells me that God loves me, and that God does not just love me but proves his love for me. God does not just prove his love for me, he proves his love while I'm still in my sin, while I'm a sinner.

Moreover, God proves his love for me primarily in the person of Christ. I best see God's love for me in Jesus. Not in Christ's teachings, his life, his healings, his miracles, or his example. No, I see God's love primarily in the death of Christ, because when he died, he died for me and my sin, to redeem me and rescue me.

In the universe, the heart of God's love is best seen on a bloody cross, where Christ lay dying for sinners. Sinners like me.

This means that God's love is undeserved. Christ died while we were sinners.

It also means that God's love is sacrificial. It was the greatest sacrifice imaginable—God dying in the place of rebels.

If you ever feel that you don't matter to God, look at the cross. If you ever feel that God doesn't care about your hurts, look at the cross. If you ever feel that God's not wild about you, look at the cross.

Take a long look at the cross of Christ and know how very loved you are, loved by the God who made you.

Romans 5:12

Therefore, just as sin came into the world through one man, and death through sin, and so death spread to all men because all sinned.

The Bible teaches that all of life needs to be viewed through two men (Adam and Christ), through two acts (an act of disobedience and an act of obedience), and through two destinies for all people: death and life.

The brilliant physician and pastor, Dr. Martyn Lloyd-Jones, wrote, "God has always dealt with mankind through a head and representative. The whole story of the human race can be summed up in terms of what has happened because of Adam, and what has happened and will yet happen because of Christ."

This is the key biblical passage about the truth of original sin: That all of us sinned in Adam because he was our representative.

The natural human response is: "Wait a minute! That's not fair. Adam sinned and his sin was charged to me?"

The idea of original sin is especially difficult for those of us in the West because of our pervasive individualism. I understand original sin is less foreign to Africans and Asians because they intuit the solidarity of a tribe or a village. In Africa, if the chief converts, the whole village converts.

But the idea is not completely foreign to us. For example, when one player on a football team jumps offside, the whole team is penalized, and no one has any trouble with that.

This is the teaching of original sin: Adam was our representative. When he sinned, we sinned, so we were born in sin.

I may not like this teaching. I may not like it that when Adam sinned, that sin was charged to me. But I love that Christ could be my representative and, when he paid for my sin, that forgiveness was given to me.

Original sin paves the way for the cross of Christ. It paves the way for the gospel, in which Christ died in my place.

We don't like Adam representing us. But we love Christ representing us.

Winston Churchill famously described the British pilots of World War II thus: "Never in the field of human conflict have so many owed so much to so few."

But this is even more true of the gospel: Never in human history have so many owed so much to just one.

Romans 5:19

*For as by the one man's disobedience the many were
made sinners, so by the one man's obedience
the many will be made righteous.*

Romans 5:12-21 is important theology, teaching us that all of life must be viewed through two representatives: Adam and Christ.

In verse 19, for the fifth verse in a row, two truths are taught: Because of Adam's disobedience, we died, but because of Christ's obedience, we have life.

Five times in a row. Look at it:

> But the free gift is not like the trespass. For if many died through one man's trespass, much more have the grace of God and the free gift by the grace of that one man Jesus Christ abounded for many. And the free gift is not like the result of that one man's sin. For the judgment following one trespass brought condemnation, but the free gift following many trespasses brought justification. For if, because of one man's trespass, death reigned through that one man, much more will those who receive the abundance of grace and the free gift of righteousness reign in life through the one man Jesus Christ.
>
> Therefore, as one trespass led to condemnation for all men, so one act of righteousness leads to justification and life for all men. For as by the one man's disobedience the many were made sinners, so by the one man's obedience the many will be made righteous.
>
> (Rom. 5:15-19)

Perhaps God is so emphatic because we are so slow to grasp that we cannot earn our salvation, but can only get right with God because of what Christ did on the cross.

I am not condemned because of my bad deeds but because of my representative, Adam. Similarly, I am not saved because of my good deeds but because of my representative, Christ.

I am not saved because of what I do. I am saved because of what Christ has done. That's the gospel.

Romans 5:20

Where sin increased, grace abounded all the more.

Don't you love this verse? "Where sin increased, grace abounded all the more." Or, we could translate it as, "Where sin abounds, grace *super* abounds."

At times, we may feel overwhelmed by our sin, and that can be a good thing. There are times when we should feel our profound brokenness over sin. But we must never stay overwhelmed by our sin because the grace of God is always bigger. However great our sin, God's grace is greater. Always.

Perhaps there is a particular sin in your past that is especially egregious to you. Perhaps Satan keeps throwing this sin in your face: "Look what you did. That was so horrible! God will never use you again. God will always be upset at you. You're done, finished!"

But Satan is an accuser and a liar.

Remind yourself of Romans 5:20: When sin abounds, grace *super* abounds.

It is not noble to wallow in your guilt in some sort of penitential self-flagellation, as if you could pay for your sin by your guilt. That's unbelief in God's love and grace. Unbelief is the fountainhead of all sin.

What *is* noble and pleasing to God is when we come to God in childlike trust and believe that God is a God of grace, that God's grace is greater than our sin.

The greats of the Bible, men like Moses, David, and Paul, were guilty of grievous sins, even murder. But they believed in God's grace, and God loved that.

Where sin abounds, grace *super* abounds.

Romans 6:11

*So you also must consider yourselves dead to sin
and alive to God in Christ Jesus.*

One of my favorite movie characters is the Catholic priest in the *Les Misérables* film with Liam Neeson. This priest is so Christlike. He forgives the criminal Jean Valjean in a startling and costly act of grace, and then he tells Valjean, "You are a new man."

I love this scene. It's what Christ does for us. He stuns us with an act of grace that cost him his blood. He forgives us and tells us, "You are a new man, a new woman."

Because Christ has forgiven us and made us new, because we died with Christ and rose with Christ, we are now dead to sin and alive to God.

It is vital, absolutely vital, to our spiritual life that we see ourselves as dead to sin and alive to God.

We must consider this to be true. See yourself this way: dead to sin—dead to the guilt, power, and penalty of sin—and alive to God, with a heart that longs to please God and serve him.

Every time you are tempted, remind yourself, "I am dead to that sin. I'm alive to God." Don't just listen to yourself, talk to yourself.

What sins are you struggling with? Envy? Jealousy? Anger? Bitterness? A quick temper? Worry? Fear? Self-centeredness? Not telling the truth? Lust? Greed? Self-reliance? Cowardice? Prayerlessness? Coveting what others have? An inability to forgive? Sexual sin? Not loving your spouse? Gossip? Impatience?

Is Satan telling you that you've got to do this sin, that it's just the way you are?

That's not true. God says you are dead to sin and alive to God. A new man. A new woman.

Believe it!

Romans 6:23

*For the wages of sin is death, but the free gift of God
is eternal life in Christ Jesus our Lord.*

Some of the most important verses in the Bible are found in
Romans, in verses 3:23, 5:8, 6:11, and 8:28. One of those highly
significant verses is right here in 6:23.

Romans 6:23 is the gospel in a nutshell. Here we see the
essential problem (sin), the result of the problem (death), God's
solution (Christ), the outcome Christ gives (eternal life), and the
way to get this life (as a free gift).

The poignancy of the verse is brought out by three contrasts:
sin and God, death and life, wages and a free gift.

If there is just one verse to share with a friend on how one
gets into heaven, this might be the best one.

The wages, or penalty, of sin is death. This is spiritual death
or separation from God. Because of our sin, we were spiritually
dead, separated from God, life, heaven, and all that is good. We
were without God, without hope, without life.

But God intervened and sent his Son to rescue us. God gives
us the most incredible offer imaginable: the free gift of life in
Christ Jesus.

How do we get eternal life, the life of God? We receive a gift.
We don't earn it. We don't work for it. We don't pay back the gift.
We just receive it. We come with empty hands and receive a gift.
Incredible! It's incredible but true.

Here's the gospel in a nutshell.

Romans 8:1

*There is therefore now no condemnation for those
who are in Christ Jesus.*

"When the message of Romans gets into a man's heart, there's no telling what may happen!" James Packer's comment on Romans is certainly true of Romans 8:1.

"No" is such a short word, but it carries complete and absolute finality here. No condemnation. None. Zero. You are completely and eternally set free from condemnation.

When is this true? When you get to heaven? No. It's true right now. "There is therefore now no condemnation."

Who is this true for? Is it true of good people? People who never fail? People who are superstar Christians? People who try hard to please God? People who measure up?

No. It's true for people who are in Christ Jesus. That's it. They are joined, by faith, to Christ. The blood of Jesus cleanses them from all sin, past, present, and future.

The famed psychiatrist Karl Menninger once said that if he could convince the patients in psychiatric hospitals that their sins were forgiven, 75 percent of them could walk out the next day.

If you have failed in your marriage, there's no condemnation for those in Christ Jesus. If you have fallen into sexual sin, there's no condemnation for those in Christ Jesus. If you have struggled with alcoholism or drug addiction, there's no condemnation for those in Christ Jesus. If you have committed some horrible sin, there's no condemnation for those in Christ Jesus. If you are a self-centered jerk, there's no condemnation for those in Christ Jesus. The blood of Jesus cleanses you of all your sin.

There is an ocean of love, grace, and peace in this one verse. Stand on it. Cling to it. Believe it.

Romans 8:5

For those who live according to the flesh set their minds on the things of the flesh, but those who live according to the Spirit set their minds on the things of the Spirit.

In his book *The Forgotten God*, Francis Chan quotes A.W. Tozer as having once remarked:

> We may as well face it: the whole level of spirituality among us is low. We have measured ourselves by ourselves until the incentive to seek higher plateaus in the things of the Spirit is all but gone....[We] have imitated the world, sought popular favor, manufactured delights to substitute for the joy of the Lord and produced a cheap and synthetic power to substitute for the power of the Holy Ghost.

The spiritual life is life in the Spirit, by the Spirit, through the Spirit.

Romans 8:1-17 is one of the great passages on life in the Spirit, and by way of contrast, the word *flesh* occurs eight times in verses 3-8. Here, the term refers to the sinful, self-focused, self-dependent tendencies that we all have. These tendencies are innate to the human condition and inherently opposed to the Spirit. Living by the flesh means living for one's self rather than living for Christ.

God tells us to set our minds not on the flesh, but on the Spirit. What does this look like? You are preoccupied with Christ, not yourself. You seek Christ's agenda, not your own. You see your life as belonging to Christ, not yourself. You see yourself as steward, not owner, of all you possess. You are focused on others, not yourself. You live for the next world, not this world. You don't love money and use people, but you love people and use money. You don't try hard to live right, but you trust the Spirit's power to live right. You don't rely on your strength but on the Spirit's power. Your whole life is surrendered to Jesus. That's life in the Spirit.

But how? How can we live this way?

To set your mind on the flesh, do this: Seldom read the Bible. Focus on knowing the Bible, not obeying the Bible. Don't live in community with all-out Christians. Don't reach out to people around you. Gather with God's people only once or twice a month, whenever it's convenient. Spend tons of time with the TV and little time alone with God. Chase after the things of the world.

However, to set your mind on the Spirit, do this: Fill your mind with God's Word. Meet with God daily. Memorize God's Word and obey it. Live in community with all-out believers. Gather with God's people weekly. Pray through the day. Be alert to and love the people around you. Live continually in God's presence.

If the Spirit of the living God dwells in us, we should be very different than our neighbors. How different are you? How different am I?

Romans 8:9

*You, however, are not in the flesh but in the Spirit, if
in fact the Spirit of God dwells in you. Anyone
who does not have the Spirit of Christ
does not belong to him.*

One of the great passages in the Bible on the Holy Spirit is Romans 8. In Romans 8, we learn about life in the Spirit, contrasted with life in the flesh.

The Holy Spirit is God. He is fully God, and he is in every believer. We are to live surrendered to him and dependent upon him.

The flesh is the selfish, sinful tendencies that we all have as humans. The flesh is not me but it is with me. Romans 8:9 teaches us that we are to live in the Spirit, characterized and governed by the Spirit, and not in the flesh, characterized and governed by the flesh.

Moreover, verse 9 teaches us that every Christian has the Holy Spirit inside him. "Anyone who does not have the Spirit of Christ does not belong to him." From the moment we trust Christ as Savior, the Holy Spirit comes into us.

Verse 9 says we are in the Spirit. Verse 4 calls us to walk according to the Spirit. Verse 5 says to live according to the Spirit. Verse 6 says set your mind on the Spirit. Verse 14 says we are led by the Spirit.

What does all this mean? What is life in the Spirit?

Two things—dependence and surrender. We depend upon the Spirit and not upon ourselves. We depend upon the Spirit to guide us, strengthen us, protect us, transform us, and lead us.

And because we are dependent, we surrender. The Spirit is in control, not me. I give up control. Spirit, lead on.

This is life in the Spirit, by the Spirit, from the Spirit. Dependence. Surrender.

Is this true of your life?

Romans 8:13

*For if you live according to the flesh you will die, but
if by the Spirit you put to death the deeds of
the body, you will live.*

"Put to death the deeds of the body." There is a theological term for this: mortification. Mortification is important. What is it?

We are familiar with words like mortician, mortuary, and mortality. They involve death. Mortification is putting to death sinful deeds. It means to put to death the deeds of the body (eyes, tongue, hands, feet, ears, etc.) that serve sin and not Christ.

Mortification is not masochism, which is inflicting pain on yourself. Mortification is not asceticism, which means to deny yourself physical pleasures. Mortification is rejecting sin. In fact, the only term strong enough to describe this is mortification—put that sin to death. Kill it!

John Stott remarked, "There is a kind of life which leads to death, and there is a kind of death which leads to life." Mortification of sin leads to life.

Examples of sins that we must slay: unkindness in our voice, lying, gossip, lust, self-centeredness, laziness, overeating, drunkenness, losing our temper, sexual sin, pornography, reckless driving, stealing, addictions, and more.

Deeds of the body. Kill 'em!

"But I can't," you say. That's right. You can't. That's why God says, "By the Spirit put them to death."

Lord, I cannot stop this sin, but you can. Please do it.

Romans 8:15

For you did not receive the spirit of slavery to fall back into fear, but you have received the Spirit of adoption as sons, by whom we cry, "Abba! Father!"

If the fundamental blessing of the gospel is justification, being declared legally right with God, then the highest blessing of the gospel is adoption, being adopted as God's own dear children.

God reveals his love for us when he tenderly adopts us as his own. God reached down to us when we were rebel sinners and his enemies. That he would reach down, rescue us, forgive us, and adopt us as his own kids is the most amazing act of love that we can imagine. Adoption reveals God's heart as Father. The perfect, tender, loving Father.

He sets us free from a spirit of slavery and fear. Yes, fear assails us, but we can say "no" to fear. We are no longer fear's slave because we are now God's sons and daughters. We are sons and daughters of the King.

So we call him Papa, Daddy, *Abba*. We bask in his love. We revel in his mercy. We dance in his grace.

Believer, see God as Papa. See yourself as adopted, as loved and safe. Rest in the Father's love.

Romans 8:18

For I consider that the sufferings of this present time
are not worth comparing with the glory that
is to be revealed to us.

The sufferings of this present time can be formidable. Unrelenting back pain; deep, dark, hopeless depression; a spouse betraying you and abandoning you; abuse by a parent who is supposed to protect you; or the death of a child.

These things are overwhelming, and yet Paul says, "For I consider that the sufferings of this present time are not worth comparing with the glory that is to be revealed to us." Was Paul naïve? Did he live in a protective bubble?

Hardly! When Paul came to faith, God said, "For I will show him how much he must suffer for the sake of my name" (Acts 9:16).

In 2 Corinthians 11:24-27, Paul wrote:

> Five times I received at the hands of the Jews the forty lashes less one. Three times I was beaten with rods. Once I was stoned. Three times I was shipwrecked; a night and a day I was adrift at sea; on frequent journeys, in danger from rivers, danger from robbers, danger from my own people, danger from Gentiles, danger in the city, danger in the wilderness, danger at sea, danger from false brothers; in toil and hardship, through many a sleepless night, in hunger and thirst, often without food, in cold and exposure.

No, there was no protective bubble for Paul, and yet Paul makes this astounding statement, "For I consider that the sufferings of this present time are not worth comparing with the glory that is to be revealed to us."

Glory? The immediate presence of God. Unbounded joy, peace, and love. Transformed body. Sinless heart. No pain, disease, or death. Incredibly rich relationships with people. Glory!

The sufferings of the present age, however great they are, cannot be compared to the glory of the next age. As S. Lewis Johnson summarized Paul's response, "[S]uffering is a drop. Glory is the ocean."

Paul said he considered this to be true. He adopted this perspective on suffering. He stood on this truth when the pain was overwhelming.

We must do the same thing. Cling to this truth. Cling to it and don't let go. The sufferings of the present day cannot be compared with the glory that awaits us.

Romans 8:26

*Likewise the Spirit helps us in our weaknesses. For we
do not know what to pray for as we ought,
but the Spirit himself intercedes for us with
groanings too deep for words.*

One of the great truths about the Holy Spirit is that he prays for us. In this one verse, we have five truths about the Spirit's ministry of intercession.

First, the Spirit helps us. "Likewise the Spirit helps us in our weaknesses." We have weakness and frailties—physically, mentally, emotionally, and spiritually. The Spirit knows our weaknesses and he helps us.

Second, the Spirit intercedes for us. "The Spirit himself intercedes for us." God the Spirit prays to God the Father for you. There is much mystery here, but it's true. It's so encouraging to remember that the Spirit is ever praying for you.

Third, the Spirit prays for us because we do not know what to pray for. "For we do not know what to pray for as we ought." We lack wisdom, we don't see the big picture, and we don't know the future, so we don't always know what to pray for. You might pray that you could marry a certain person. God says no. Later, you realize marriage to that person would have been a disaster. Thank God that the Spirit prays for us, because we do not know what to pray for.

Fourth, the Spirit prays for us with groans. "The Spirit himself intercedes for us with groanings too deep for words." Fascinating! Groanings! The point is not that the Spirit's requests cannot be put into words, but that they are not put into words. Perhaps this is deeper, more powerful prayer.

Fifth, the Spirit prays for us according to the will of God. Don't you know God hears and answers those prayers, prayers according to the will of God?

Richard Foster reminds us:

> When we stumble over our words, the Spirit straightens out the syntax. When we pray with muddy motives, the Spirit purifies the stream. When we see through a glass darkly, the Spirit adjusts and focuses

what we are asking until it corresponds to the will of God.

The point is that we do not have to have everything perfect when we pray. The Spirit reshapes, refines, and reinterprets our feeble, ego-driven prayers. We can rest in this work of the Spirit on our behalf.

Romans 8:28

*And we know that for those who love God all things
work together for good, for those who are called
according to his purpose.*

This is one of the most well-known verses in the Bible and one of
its most life-giving promises, a sure foundation to stand upon
in the storms of life, and an ever-flowing source of comfort. It
contains four unshakeable convictions.

First, God is at work in your life. He is always at work—
personally, uniquely, and continually. He is shaping you, healing
you, drawing you, and transforming you. He is always at work in
your life because you matter so much to him. What is God doing
right now? Pay attention.

Second, God is at work in your life for good. Not necessarily for
your success, comfort, or happiness, but for your good. In the Old
Testament, Joseph's own brothers betrayed him and sold him into
slavery in a foreign land. What pain and anguish he endured for
years! But God meant it for good and eventually elevated Joseph to
Prime Minister of all Egypt. Genesis 50:20 states, "As for you, you
meant evil against me, but God meant it for good, to bring it about
that many people should be kept alive, as they are today."

Third, God is at work in your life for good in all things. This is
the incredible part. Not some things or many things or most things,
but all things, even things that are bad, tragic, or evil. God will take
them and bring good out of it. Somehow, some way, someday, God
will redeem it, whatever it is.

Fourth, this is true for believers. This is true for those who love
God and are called according to his purpose.

We don't simply hope all of this is true. We know it. "We know
that God causes all things to work together for good." Every single
thing. Nothing will touch us that God will not use for good. Nothing.

Joseph in the Old Testament is a superb example of this truth,
but the best example is Jesus himself on the cross. When evil men
nailed Jesus to a cross, it was the worst sin, the greatest crime in all
history. But from God's standpoint, it was the greatest act of love,
and it did more good than anything else in history.

What man meant for evil, God meant for good.

Whatever happens to you, God will redeem it for good. "God
will have the final word and it will be good."

Romans 8:29-30

For those whom he foreknew he also predestined to be conformed to the image of his Son, in order that he might be the firstborn among many brothers. And those whom he predestined he also called, and those whom he called he also justified, and those whom he justified he also glorified.

This is the Golden Chain of Salvation, made of five unbreakable links. All those foreknown are predestined, all predestined are called, all called are justified, all justified are glorified.

No one falls out of the chain because God secures us. Salvation is not the work of man for God, but the work of God for man. It's all of grace. If God chose you, he can keep you and protect you. You are safe and secure. You are loved and chosen.

The first link, "foreknew," does not mean that God looks ahead and sees what we will do. Rather, it means he loves and knows us in advance. One scholar writes: "'Know'...is used in a sense practically synonymous with 'love'...'Whom he foreknew' is therefore virtually equivalent to 'whom he foreloved.'"

This fits in with Moses's great statement, "The Lord did not set his affection on you and choose you because you were more numerous than other peoples...But it was because the Lord loved you" (Deut. 7:7).

God is sovereign in salvation, so all credit goes to God and no credit goes to me. "What do you have that you did not receive?" (1 Cor. 4:7).

Yes, there are questions about these matters. Yes, the Bible teaches human responsibility. Yes, we cannot fully reconcile God's sovereignty and human free will. But the Bible teaches both, and so we gladly hold to both.

J.I. Packer points out that all Christian people believe in God's sovereignty in salvation, even if they deny it:

> Two facts show this. In the first place, you give God thanks for your conversion. Now why do you do that? Because you know in your heart that God was entirely responsible for it. You did not save yourself; he saved you...

There is a second way in which you acknowledge that God is sovereign in salvation. You pray for the conversion of others...You ask God to work in them everything necessary for their salvation. So our thanksgivings and our intercessions prove that we believe in divine sovereignty. On our feet we may have arguments about it, but on our knees we are all agreed.

Romans 8:31b

If God is for us, who can be against us?

If Romans is the greatest book in the Bible, and chapter 8 is the greatest chapter in Romans, then Romans 8:31-39 is the high point of Romans 8. In some ways, this passage is the "Mount Everest" of the Bible.

At the outset, there are four powerful words: "God is for us." There is an ocean of love and grace in this brief sentence. It is a power-packed summary of God's heart toward us. God is for us. God the Almighty, the Sovereign, the infinite and eternal God. He is for us.

He is for us. He adores us. He wants the best for us. He is on our team. He is your biggest fan. He is for you in the same way you are for your children or grandchildren or favorite person in the world. He is for you big time.

Since God is for us, who can be against us? This doesn't mean that no one is against us, because the demons of hell are against us, and perhaps some humans too. The point is simply that it doesn't matter who is against us, because God is for us.

We all know the pain of rejection. A parent who didn't have time for us. A spouse who betrayed us. A friend who turned from us. A boss who fired us. Rejection is so painful that the human heart can barely survive.

But God will never reject us. Never. You may reject him, but he will never reject you. He is for you in a way that no one else is.

David understood this truth. That's why he could write, "The Lord is my shepherd, I shall not want" (Ps. 23:1).

That's why he could write, "I will fear no evil for you are with me" (Ps. 23:4).

That's why he could write, "Surely goodness and mercy will follow me all the days of my life and I will dwell in the house of the Lord forever" (Ps. 23:6).

Dear friend, let these words sink deeply into your soul. God is for us.

Romans 8:32

*He who did not spare his own Son but gave him up
for us all, how will he not also with him
graciously give us all things?*

Romans 8:32 has to rank as one of the strongest verses in the Bible about God's love for us—his relentless, tender, and life-giving love for us.

Not only did the Father give us his Son, but with his Son, he will give us everything else we need.

And he will give us all these things graciously. Not reluctantly or begrudgingly, but graciously, freely, and joyfully. Such is the love of God for you. His own Son and everything else you need.

Do you know in your deepest heart of God's tender affection for you?

As a young pastor, I talked about and preached on God's love, but deep down, I didn't feel loved by God. I wouldn't admit this to myself, this unbelief in God's love—that would have been too painful to my spiritual pride. But it was so.

When God, in his mercy, showed me that I didn't feel loved by him, I was at least aware of the problem—always a vital first step to healing.

So I began a journey to know God's love, not a journey of the head, but a journey of the heart.

I prayed that God would show me his love, and change my heart. These were not sweet, gentle prayers, but desperate, urgent prayers. This was vital.

When I would read the Bible, I would look for passages on God's love, kindness, patience, and forgiveness.

God also used worship. As I sang to him, especially with God's people, God transformed the way I saw him. Worship is powerful and soul-transforming

Slowly, over years, not months, I began to feel more and more loved by God. I began to see God differently—more as he really is, as the tenderhearted, gracious, and merciful God he always was. The God who is easy to live with and who is for me.

I'm still on the journey, of course, but I feel loved by God now. And it has made all the difference.

Romans 8:38-39

For I am sure that neither death nor life, nor angels nor rulers, nor things present nor things to come, nor powers, nor height nor depth, nor anything else in all creation, will be able to separate us from the love of God in Christ Jesus our Lord.

Romans is the summit of the Bible. Romans 8 is the summit of Romans. Romans 8:31-39 is the summit of Romans 8, and the summit of Romans 8:31-39 are these final two verses.

Words fail to convey God's heart. Nothing can separate you from his love—nothing. Ten things are listed:

"Neither death nor life." Nothing in death and nothing in life. Death holds no threat to us.

"Nor angels nor rulers." Neither Satan nor all the demonic hordes can rob us of God's love.

"Nor things present nor things to come." Nothing in time— the present or the future. We need not fear the future.

"Nor powers." There is no power, human or demonic, that can keep us from God.

"Nor height nor depth." Nothing in space—from the highest heights to the deepest depths.

"Nor anything else in all creation." He has already included everything—Satan, demons, people, you, everything. But just in case your mind tries to find wiggle room around this, God adds, "Nor anything else in all creation." That includes everything in the universe—except God.

Romans 8 begins with no condemnation and it ends with no separation. Such is the love of God that will not let you go. Never!

In *The Knowledge of the Holy*, A.W. Tozer wrote:

> The love of God is one of the great realities of the universe, a pillar upon which the hope of the world rests. But it is a personal, intimate thing, too. God does not love populations, he loves people. He loves not masses, but men. He loves us all with a mighty love that has no beginning and can have no end.... To know that love is God and to enter into that secret place leaning upon the arm of the Beloved—this

and only this can cast out fear. Let a man become convinced that nothing can harm him and instantly for him all fear goes out of the universe. God is love and God is sovereign. His love disposes him to desire our everlasting welfare and his sovereignty enables him to secure it.

Rest in that love. Relax in that love. Revel in that love.

Romans 9:3

*For I could wish that I myself were accursed and cut
off from Christ for the sake of my brothers,
my kinsmen according to the flesh.*

This is one of the most incredible statements in the Bible. Paul says that he'd rather die in hell if it would mean the salvation of his fellow Jews.

In context, this is his heart cry: "I am speaking the truth in Christ—I am not lying; my conscience bears me witness in the Holy Spirit—that I have great sorrow and unceasing anguish in my heart. For I could wish that I myself were accursed and cut off from Christ for the sake of my brothers, my kinsmen according to the flesh" (Rom. 9:1-3).

Great sorrow. Unceasing anguish. Cut off from Christ. Forever doomed in hell.

Amazing. I take off my shoes and tremble before God. Such love for lost people. Such Christ-like love. I've never gotten close to that kind of love.

Martin Luther commented, "It seems incredible that a man would desire to be damned, in order that the damned might be saved."

A few years ago, Penn Jillette, noted atheist and member of the comedy/magic act *Penn and Teller*, filmed a video describing his encounter with a Christian fan. Penn recounts how after a show one night, the man walked up to him and told him how much he liked the show.

Penn points out several times how complimentary the man was and that the man looked him right in the eye. The man handed Penn a Gideon's New Testament with the book of Psalms and said, "I wrote in the front of it and I wanted you to have this. I'm kind of proselytizing. I'm a businessman. I'm sane. I'm not crazy."

Penn then went on about how he, an atheist, respects those who share their faith:

> I've always said that I don't respect people who don't proselytize. I don't respect that at all. If you believe that there's a heaven and hell. And people could be

going to hell, or not getting eternal life or whatever. And that you think that, well, it's not really worth telling 'em this cause it would make it socially awkward…How much do you have to hate somebody to not proselytize? How much do you have to hate somebody to believe that everlasting life is possible and not tell them that. If I believed beyond a shadow of a doubt that a truck was coming at you and you didn't believe it and that truck was bearing down on you…there's a certain point where I tackle you. And this (heaven and hell) is more important than (getting run over).

But the man who approached Penn did care enough:

This guy was a really good guy. He was polite and honest and sane and he cared enough about me to proselytize and give me a Bible, which had written in it a little note to me…and like five phone numbers and an email address if I wanted to get in touch.

"O God, break my heart with the things that break your heart!"

Romans 10:1

*Brothers, my heart's desire and prayer to God for
them is that they may be saved.*

Most likely you have friends who are not Christians. I hope so.
Perhaps they are family members, friends from work, people on
your street, or people you've met through your kids' sports teams.

And you care about them. As you get to know them better,
you become concerned for their salvation. You understand
eternity is at stake. You realize that salvation is the greatest gift
we can receive. You know that God cares about your friends. You
want your friends to experience the outrageous love and grace of
God just as you have.

You begin to experience what Paul gives voice to in Romans
10: a burden for your friends to know Jesus. You can almost sense
Paul's emotion as he writes, "My heart's desire and prayer to God
for them is that they may be saved."

You must do what Paul did. You must pray for your non-
Christian friends. You might do other things as well—love, serve,
listen, talk. But the first and most important thing you can do
for your friends is to pray for them, because only God can save a
person. Only God grants eternal life. Only God opens blind eyes.
Only God can change a stubborn heart. Only God can rescue a
lost person.

Let me encourage you to pray for your non-Christian friends.
Pray daily, fervently, persistently. You might ask God to give you
five friends to pray for daily. Pray for them until they come to
know Christ. If God puts someone in your heart, most likely God
is at work in his or her life and he wants to use you.

At some point in your friend's spiritual journey, you will
probably need to talk to your friend about God, but even more
important is that you talk to God about your friend.

George Müller, a native Prussian, immigrated to England in
the 1800s and pastored a church there for more than sixty years.

He believed in the power of prayer. His attitude towards
praying for the lost is evidenced by his commitment to five people
he knew. Müller wrote in his journal:

> In November of 1844, I began to pray for the conversion
> of five individuals. I prayed every day without a

single intermission, whether sick or in health, on the land, on the sea, and whatever the pressure of my engagements might be. Eighteen months elapsed before the first of the five was converted. I thanked God and prayed on for the others. Five years lapsed, and then the second was converted. I thanked God for the second, and prayed on for the other three. Day by day, I continued to pray for them, and six years passed before the third was converted. I thanked God for the three, and went on praying for the other two.

After thirty-six years, those two people still remained unconverted, but Müller was undeterred and wrote:

I pray on, and look yet for the answer. They are not converted yet, but they will be. I have not a doubt that I shall meet them both in heaven; for my Heavenly Father would not lay upon my heart a burden of prayer for them for over threescore years, if He had not concerning them purposes of mercy.

Müller would continue to pray for these two men. One of the men became a Christian shortly before Müller's death, and the other converted after Müller's death. He had been faithful in praying for those two men for over fifty-two years. He believed that God would save every person he puts in your heart.

If all of us prayed daily for five non-Christian friends, at some point in the future, we would see a whole host of people coming to faith in Jesus, including people we've been praying for. So join me in the adventure. Don't miss out. Pray regularly and fervently for the non-Christian friends that God puts on your heart.

Romans 10:17

*So faith comes from hearing, and hearing
through the word of Christ.*

The Word of God is critical to faith in God. If you want to grow in faith, then live in God's Word.

Paul exemplified this truth. He was a man of extraordinary faith who was all-out for Jesus. Not surprisingly, he was steeped in Scripture.

We see this in the book of Romans as Paul continually refers to the Old Testament scriptures. In fact, in the six verses around 10:17, Paul refers to the Old Testament scriptures six times. In six verses. Now, it is possible that Paul could have had a bunch of hefty scrolls out before him and he was searching through them for just the right verse. But more likely, Paul quoted these verses from memory. He had soaked and marinated in Scripture. He *knew* the Scripture and had memorized large parts of it. No wonder he was a man of faith.

Jim Tour is a chemistry professor at Rice University and a renowned leader in the field of nanotechnology. From 2000 to 2010, he was one of the ten most-cited science writers by other scientists. Yet his devotion is primarily to God's Word. An article in the *Houston Chronicle* testified:

> He wakes up each morning at 3:30 a.m. to spend his first two hours with his Bible. "I read the Bible from Genesis Chapter 1 to Revelation Chapter 22, and when I'm done I start again," Tour said. "I've been doing this for over thirty years. There is this amazing richness. I take a passage and I say, 'Lord, speak to me.' And then it just comes alive." (*Houston Chronicle*, January 3, 2010)

Charles Spurgeon wrote, "It is blessed, to eat into the very soul of the Bible until, at last, you come to talk in Scriptural language, and your spirit is flavored with the words of the Lord, so that your blood is 'Bibline' and the very essence of the Bible flows from you."

Or, more succinctly, someone wrote, "The Bible is as necessary to our safe passage through this life as oxygen to a dying man."

Romans 11:33

*Oh, the depth of the riches and wisdom and
knowledge of God! How unsearchable are his
judgments and how inscrutable his ways!*

In Romans 1-11, we have the most intense theological section in all of Scripture. Then there's a pivot, and Romans 12-16 is intensely practical. Knowledge about God should result in obedience to God.

Between these two parts of Romans, before Paul turns practical, there is an outburst of praise. Paul cannot constrain himself. He marvels at the greatness of God. "Oh, the depth of the riches and wisdom and knowledge of God! How unsearchable are his judgments and how inscrutable his ways! 'For who has known the mind of the Lord, or who has been his counselor? Or who has given a gift to him that he might be repaid?' For from him and through him and to him are all things. To him be glory forever. Amen" (Rom. 11:33-36). To rephrase my earlier point: the knowledge about God should lead to the worship of God, resulting in obedience to God.

In verse 33, Paul feels overwhelmed by God's wisdom and glory. "Oh, the depth of the riches and wisdom and knowledge of God! How unsearchable are his judgments and how inscrutable his ways!"

The word for this is *incomprehensible*. Finite man cannot fully comprehend the infinite God. We understand much about God and that which he has revealed to us, but we don't begin to fully fathom our boundless God. He is inscrutable. For example, we don't understand how God is one God and yet three persons, how Jesus is fully God and fully man, how God is fully sovereign in salvation and yet we are fully responsible to believe. We don't understand the reality of suffering and evil and hell. There is so much we don't understand.

If we could fully fathom God, then our God would be too small. But we know enough about God to trust him. We see God in the face of Christ and choose to trust our great, incomprehensible God. And because we trust him, we respond as Paul does, with wholehearted, exuberant worship.

Romans 12:1

*I appeal to you therefore, brothers, by the mercies of
God, to present your bodies as a living sacrifice,
holy and acceptable to God, which is
your spiritual worship.*

With Romans 12:1, Paul moves from the theological (verses 1-11) to the practical (verses 12-16). He moves from God's love for us (verses 1-11) to our love for others (verses 12-16).

He first looks back at eleven chapters on God's mercies, God's love, and God's grace, and on that basis, appeals to them to give their lives to Christ. The whole foundation and basis of the spiritual life is found in God's tender mercies and relentless love for us.

This is where the spiritual life begins. Without experiencing God's love for us personally, we have no power source for the spiritual life. We have no water well to drink from, we have no fire and music in our soul. Begin with God's tender, deep, and riveting love for you.

He charges you to present your body to God. Present your body—your whole self, including your physical body. Present your life, all that you have and all that you are, as a sacrifice to God. Make the irrevocable decision to say, "Lord, I'm yours. Have all of me. Whatever, whenever, wherever, however—I'm yours."

Have you done that? Have you decided on full surrender? Are you all in?

Oswald Chambers wrote, "There is only one thing God wants of us, and that is our unconditional surrender."

Nelson Mandela was arrested and tried for opposing apartheid. Everyone knew he would be convicted and sentenced, and perhaps tortured and killed. In fact, he would spend twenty-two years in prison on Robben Island. During his trial, he made this statement: "Ending apartheid is a cause for which I will gladly invest every day of the rest of my life and a cause for which I am fully prepared to die." Mandela was all in.

Our cause is even greater, for our cause is the eternal gospel of Christ, the gospel that gives people freedom both in this life and in the life to come. Can you say of the gospel what Mandela said of ending apartheid? "This is a cause for which I will gladly invest every day of the rest of my life and a cause for which I am fully prepared to die."

Romans 12:2

Do not be conformed to this world, but be transformed by the renewal of your mind, that by testing you may discern what is the will of God, what is good and acceptable and perfect.

J.B. Phillips has a famous translation: "Do not let the world squeeze you into its mold." This command is ever relevant because it is easy to be squeezed into a worldly mold. It is a challenge to be in the world but not of the world, to be godly and not worldly, to be like God and not like the world.

God has called us to live countercultural lives. He has called us to be different. Is that true of you? Are you significantly different than your neighbors or work colleagues who are not disciples of Christ? Do you have different values, different attitudes, and different actions?

The church in the United States, by all measures, is woefully similar to the world when it comes to divorce, sexual purity, materialism, gossip, greed, anger, withholding forgiveness, giving, temper, dreams, addictions, and more. As a whole, the church in the US is conformed to the world.

What can we do about this problem? The antidote to being conformed is to be transformed by the renewal of our minds. "Do not be conformed to this world, but be transformed by the renewal of your mind."

Note: we do not transform ourselves. We are transformed by God. We surrender to God and present ourselves as living sacrifices; then God transforms us and makes us more and more like Christ. We become godly, not worldly.

How does this transformation occur? God renews our minds by the Spirit of God, the Word of God, and the people of God.

As we are filled with the Spirit of God, as we study, read, and obey the Word of God, as we live in genuine community with the people of God, God changes us. It may occur slowly, but over time, we become different people.

Refuse to let the world squeeze you into its mold. We are not the people we once were, and we cannot live like we once lived.

Romans 12:21

*Do not be overcome by evil, but overcome
evil with good.*

When you are wronged, it can be so painful. A colleague at
work betrays you. A friend talks about you behind your back.
A business partner cheats you. Your father never had time for
you. A relative abused you. Your spouse had an affair and then
left you.

These betrayals hurt. It's like you were stabbed in the back, and
every time you remember the wrong, it's like you are turning the
knife in your back and you bleed a little more. Pretty soon you can
become enslaved to bitterness and resentment. All joy and peace
vanish. Your relationships with people around you turn sour.

What do you do? The human instinct is to retaliate, to get
even. Movie after movie glorifies the instinct for revenge: *Glad-
iator, Braveheart, The Count of Monte Cristo, The Avengers,* and
many more. There is even a television show called *Revenge.*

But God's way is different. God's way is to overcome evil with
good. Instead of retaliating, do good to the person. Forgive the
person who wronged you. Bless them in some way.

Forgiveness is so hard for us humans. It's the hardest work of
love. But the refusal to forgive destroys you. Frederick Buechner
writes, "Of all the deadly sins, resentment appears to be the most
fun. To lick your wounds and savor the pain you will give back is
in many ways a feast fit for a king. But then it turns out that what
you are eating at the banquet of bitterness is your own heart. The
skeleton at the feast is you. You start out holding a grudge, but in
the end the grudge holds you."

Lewis Smedes tells a remarkable example of forgiveness in his
book *Forgive and Forget:*

> A South African woman stood in an emotionally
> charged courtroom, listening to white police officers
> acknowledge the atrocities they had perpetrated in
> the name of apartheid.
>
> Officer van de Broek acknowledged his responsibil-
> ity in the death of her son. Along with others, he had
> shot her 18-year-old son at point-blank range. He and
> the others partied while they burned his body, turn-

ing it over and over on the fire until it was reduced to ashes.

Eight years later, van de Broek and others arrived to seize her husband. A few [hours] later, shortly after midnight, van de Broek came to fetch the woman. He took her to a woodpile where her husband lay bound. She was forced to watch as they poured gasoline over his body and ignited the flames that consumed his body. The last words she heard her husband say were "Forgive them."

Now, van de Broek stood before her awaiting judgment. South Africa's Truth and Reconciliation Commission asked her what she wanted.

"I want three things," she said calmly. "I want Mr. van de Broek to take me to the place where they burned my husband's body. I would like to gather up the dust and give him a decent burial."

"Second, Mr. van de Broek took all my family away from me, and I still have a lot of love to give. Twice a month, I would like for him to come to the ghetto and spend a day with me so I can be a mother to him."

"Third, I would like Mr. van de Broek to know that he is forgiven by God, and that I forgive him, too. I would like someone to lead me to where he is seated, so I can embrace him and he can know my forgiveness is real."

As the elderly woman was led across the courtroom, van de Broek fainted, overwhelmed. Someone began singing "Amazing Grace." Gradually everyone joined in.

If this mother can forgive her son and husband's killer, then we can forgive the person who wrongs us. By God's grace, we can choose to overcome evil with good.

Romans 13:8

*Owe no one anything, except to love each other, for
the one who loves another has fulfilled the law.*

You have an obligation to love people. Why? Because people
have loved you and you must pay them back? No. All people
haven't loved you. You have an obligation to love people, not because people have loved you perfectly (they haven't), but because
God has loved you perfectly.

"Beloved, if God so loved us, we also ought to love one another" (1 John 4:11). "We love because he first loved us" (1 John
4:19). In both of these verses, it is clear that we have an obligation
to love others because God loves us.

The whole motivation and wellspring behind you loving others must be God's prior love for you, God's perfect, relentless,
sacrificial, tender, and unconditional love.

Without this wellspring, your love for people will run dry.
You might love people who love you back, who are easy to love.
Everyone loves that way. But will you also love the person who
hurt you, wronged you, snubbed you, or annoyed you? Will you
love the spouse who betrayed you? The parent who neglected
you? The friend who talked about you behind your back?

Not a chance, unless you drink in God's overwhelming love
for you. Unless you drink it in daily and soak it in so much that it
oozes out of you to every single person you encounter.

Filled to the brim with God's love for you, you will see people
as God sees them: as people who matter, as people who are holy
objects of God's love. C.S. Lewis reminded us:

> There are no ordinary people. You have never talk-
> ed to a mere mortal. Nations, cultures, arts, civili-
> zation—these are mortal, and their life is to ours as
> the life of a gnat. But it is immortals whom we joke
> with, work with, marry, snub, and exploit—immortal
> horrors or everlasting splendors…Next to the Blessed
> Sacrament itself, your neighbor is the holiest object
> presented to your senses.

Yes, you have an obligation to love these immortals. Love fervently. As God has loved you, love others.

Romans 14:23

But whoever has doubts is condemned if he eats, because the eating is not from faith. For whatever does not proceed from faith is sin.

Faith is absolutely essential to pleasing God. In any situation, if we live by faith and trust God with our lives, then God is pleased. But if we lack faith and trust ourselves rather than trusting God, then we sin against God. Faith is the *sine qua non*, the indispensable and essential characteristic of everything we do.

But why is faith so all-important? Well, consider what faith is. Faith means we trust God, believe in God, depend upon God, and have confidence in God.

Conversely, if we don't act from faith, then we declare by our actions that God cannot be trusted, that God is not worthy of our trust, that God is not good enough and powerful enough to take care of us, that God is not worthy of our love and obedience. If we don't act from faith, we are declaring, by our lives, that we don't need God. We declare our independence from God. We, in essence, act as if we were God, and we can take care of ourselves just fine, thank you.

All through the Bible, we see how important faith is to God. Think of Abraham, Moses, David, Elijah, Gideon, and Samson. All were flawed men, but God so loved it when they trusted him, just as God loves it when you trust him today.

When the Roman centurion in Matthew 8 showed his complete confidence in Jesus, Jesus loved it and commended him exuberantly. "Truly I tell you, with no one in Israel have I found such faith" (Matt. 8:10). The main thing Jesus rebuked the disciples for was their lack of faith. Then in Hebrews 11, the great hall of faith chapter, we see example after example of men and women who delighted God because they lived by faith.

Indeed, Hebrews 11:6 makes the same point as Romans 14:23: "And without faith it is impossible to please him, for whoever would draw near to God must believe that he exists and that he rewards those who seek him" (Rom. 11:6).

Yes, God loves it when you trust him. He loves it when you declare, not with your words, but with your actions. Declare that God is good, God is great, and God is worthy of our trust.

So, dear friend, decide to trust your God. In heaven you won't need faith, for you will have sight. You will be right there with the Lord. That means that this is your only opportunity in all eternity to trust your God.

Don't focus on your faith. Rather, focus on your God, the object of your faith. Rivet your gaze firmly on the Lord Jesus Christ and choose to live by faith.

Today, God is still looking for people who will dare to live by faith. Be one of those people.

1 Corinthians 2:2

*For I decided to know nothing among you except
Jesus Christ and him crucified.*

When Paul fell for Jesus, he fell hard. He fell in love and never recovered from that fall. In one fell swoop, he went from hating Jesus to loving him. He went from vicious opponent to devoted follower.

For the rest of Paul's time on earth, life was pretty simple: Jesus was everything. He expressed his heartbeat in Philippians 1:21: "For to me to live is Christ." Christ was everything to Paul.

So it's no surprise that early in Paul's letter to the Corinthians, he emphatically states that he has made the decision, firm and irrevocable, to know nothing except Jesus Christ and him crucified. That is, Paul has resolved to live for Jesus, surrender to Jesus, glorify Jesus, obey Jesus, and love Jesus.

More specifically, Paul focused on Christ crucified. That is, he focused on the fact that Christ had died on a cross because on that cross Christ paid for our sin, won our salvation, demonstrated the Father's love, conquered Satan and all the enemies in hell, dealt a death blow to death, and shattered the barrier separating us from our God.

Yes, Christ crucified. Worthy is the Lamb who was slain.

Paul never felt he needed to advance beyond the simple message of Christ and him crucified. Paul didn't need some esoteric wisdom, deeper teaching, or special knowledge known only by the spiritual elite. Oh no! Not Paul. For Paul it was simple: Just give me Jesus. Jesus Christ and him crucified. He's my life. My love. My Lord.

What about you, dear friend? Are you intoxicated with Jesus Christ?

1 Corinthians 2:14

The natural person does not accept the things of the
Spirit of God, for they are folly to him, and he is
not able to understand them because they
are spiritually discerned.

What is a natural person? A natural person is simply an unbeliever in Christ, a non-Christian. This natural person, in contrast to a spiritual person, lacks the Spirit of God dwelling in him. Indeed, the natural person does not accept the things of the Spirit.

Why not? Why doesn't the natural person, the non-Christian, accept the things of God? It's not just that he does not accept them or that he will not accept them, but that he cannot accept them. "They are folly to him, and he is not able to understand them." The unbeliever lacks the capacity to grasp spiritual things. It's not mental capacity, but spiritual capacity. He lacks the spiritual capacity to grasp God's truths.

The Bible says that a natural person is spiritually blind and spiritually dead. Until God's Spirit opens a person's eyes and gives life to a person's soul, he is spiritually blind and spiritually dead. Just as a deaf man cannot hear a piano concert, just as a blind man cannot see a beautiful painting, just as human ears cannot hear high-frequency radio waves, so the unbeliever cannot accept God's truth.

Decades ago, as an enthusiastic young follower of Christ, I shared Christ with an unbelieving friend. No matter how cogent and persuasive my arguments, they didn't penetrate his heart. I was frustrated and probably a bit surprised, because I felt my reasoning was sound.

But I should not have been surprised. Blind people don't see, dead people don't move, and natural people don't grasp spiritual truth. Until God opens their eyes by his grace, they just don't get it.

God may use our reasoning and our speech, but never forget: only God can save people.

1 Corinthians 4:7b

What do you have that you did not receive?

This simple question challenges us to stop and reflect a moment: What do you have that you did not receive? What good thing in your life is not a gift from God? Can you take credit for even one thing in your life, even one small thing? No! Every single good thing in your life that you have ever experienced is a gift from a gracious God. Every single one.

Do you have enough food to eat? Water to drink? Shelter that keeps you warm and dry? Perhaps even a beautiful home? A car that takes you places? Do you have meaningful work, or at least a job that pays?

Are there some people in your life who care about you? A spouse? A child? A friend? A parent? A sibling? A teacher? A colleague?

The air you breathe. The health you have. The life you live.

What about the extra things—delicious meals, tasty restaurants, pleasing music, beautiful arts, good bookstores, a gorgeous sunset, a clear night full of stars, movies, sports, hikes, and so much more? These are all a gift.

And then, the greatest gift of all: a Savior. A Savior who loves you. A Savior who died for you. A Savior who rose in power. A Savior who forgave all your sin and gave you life eternal. A Savior who will never leave you. Never.

The Spirit of God inside you. The power to live a new life. The mind of Christ. Citizenship in heaven. Adoption as God's own loved child. The scriptures, living and active and sharper than a two-edged sword. The privilege of prayer. The power of prayer. The body of Christ. The opportunity to be used by God. The assurance of heaven. Peace, joy, and love poured out from God. A Father in heaven who is good and wise and powerful. The faith to trust God.

All this and more. So much more.

Every single good thing in your life, every good thing that you've ever experienced or ever will experience, whether in this life or in eternity, is a gift of a gracious God.

God has been good to you. So good to you.

What do you have that you did not receive?

1 Corinthians 6:18

Flee from sexual immorality. Every other sin a person commits is outside the body, but the sexually immoral person sins against his own body.

Sexual immorality is pervasive in our culture. It is pervasive not only outside the church but also inside. How we need to hear and obey the simple yet urgent command: "Flee immorality."

Flee it! Don't mess with it. Don't tolerate it. Don't play with it. Don't flirt with it. Flee it! Run from it. In fact, the verb flee is a present imperative, as if God had said, "Keep running from sexual immorality." Run and keep running.

Our example is Joseph. When Potiphar's wife approached Joseph for sex, Joseph ran and kept running. "But one day, when he went into the house to do his work and none of the men of the house was there in the house, she caught him by his garment, saying, 'Lie with me.' But he left his garment in her hand and fled and got out of the house" (Gen. 39:11-12).

What can you do to obey Christ's call for sexual purity? Nine principles:

1. Pursue the Lord. Passionately pursue a love relationship with Jesus. Guard your daily time alone with Jesus. If Jesus is your deep well, then you won't go looking for broken cisterns.
2. Pursue your spouse. If you are married, cherish your spouse. Give your marriage priority, attention, and energy. Never take your spouse for granted. If you are single, have clear boundaries and guidelines for dating and relationships.
3. See people as God does. In 1 Timothy 5, God tells us to treat younger women as sisters and younger men as brothers. Treat all people as if they belonged to your biological family. Treat them with love, dignity, and respect.
4. Live in community. If you are isolated from people, you are so much more vulnerable to sin of all kinds. Get in a small group, a healthy small group, and get real.

5. Have healthy boundaries. Don't have private meetings with members of the opposite sex. Dress appropriately, despite what our culture may say. Avoid all flirting. Don't be foolish—if you are a man, don't talk to another woman about your marriage problems.
6. Understand consequences. Do not be naïve and minimize the painful and life-wrecking consequences of sexual sin. Sin always hurts us, and often it also hurts the people we love most. Think in advance about all the pain sexual sin can bring.
7. Fight the battle. We are not ignorant of the devil's schemes. We know he is a deceiver and a liar who promises pleasure but gives pain, misery, and disaster. Do not listen. Resist the enemy by claiming Scripture and obeying it.
8. Never think you are immune. If you think, "It could never happen to me," then you are more vulnerable to sexual sin. "Therefore let anyone who thinks that he stands take heed lest he fall" (1 Cor.10:12).
9. God will hold you accountable. "Do not be deceived: God is not mocked, for whatever one sows, that will he also reap" (Gal. 6:7).

1 Corinthians 10:12

Therefore let anyone who thinks that he stands take heed lest he fall.

When the *Titanic* set sail on its first voyage in 1912, the ship's builders and officers believed that the *Titanic* was unsinkable. They believed their great ocean liner was invincible. In fact, the captain arrogantly remarked, "Even God himself couldn't sink her." Whenever we feel invincible, we are ripe for disaster.

This principle is also true of our spiritual lives. Whenever we feel invincible, we are ripe for disaster.

1 Corinthians 10:12 warns us against this feeling of being invincible. If, deep down, we feel immune to sexual sin, divorce, alcoholism, or any other sin: watch out. You are vulnerable to a fall. If we subconsciously think to ourselves, or worse, say to someone, "I could never fall into that sin," look out. "Therefore let anyone who thinks he stands take heed lest he fall."

This attitude of invincibility reflects spiritual pride, along with condescension and a lack of compassion towards those who have fallen. This attitude reflects a dangerous lack of dependence on and desperation for God. It reflects a superficial underestimation of the power of sin, the power of the flesh, and the power of demonic deception.

This is not to say that we will sin or that we have to sin. Of course not. But it is to say that we could sin and that we must be vigilant, for we are most vulnerable whenever we think we are invincible.

"Therefore let anyone who thinks that he stands take heed lest he fall."

1 Corinthians 10:13

No temptation has overtaken you that is not common
to man. God is faithful, and he will not let you be
tempted beyond your ability, but with the temptation
he will also provide the way of escape,
that you may be able to endure it.

I imagine I have pulled this arrow out of my quiver hundreds of times over the years. This verse is invaluable.

God is telling us three things about temptation. Three vital truths.

First, "No temptation has overtaken you that is not common to man." In other words, you are not the only one to wrestle with this sin. You are not alone. You are not an exception. In fact, this temptation is common. Lots of people have faced this temptation and defeated it.

Second, "God is faithful, and he will not let you be tempted beyond your ability." That is, your ability to say no. God is faithful to protect us, strengthen us, and give us what we need, and he will not let us be tempted beyond our ability to say no.

This is big. I can never think to myself, *I just cannot help myself. I have to give in to this sin. It's just the way I am.* That's a lie. If we believe this lie—"I've just got to succumb"—then we're defeated already.

And then, finally, "But with the temptation he will also provide the way of escape, that you may be able to endure it." What a splendid promise! You don't have to say yes to sin. You never have to say yes. Do you think you have to lose your temper? Do you think you have to cheat on your expense report? Do you think that you have to go to that pornography site on your computer? Do you think you have to take that drink (if you're an alcoholic)? Do you think that you have to give way to sexual sin? Do you think that you have to lose your patience with your kids? No, you don't. God will provide the way of escape. You can say no.

Verses 12 and 13 in 1 Corinthians 10 are back-to-back verses, giving complementary and vital truths:

Verse 12: You are not immune from sin.
Verse 13: You do not have to sin.
Verse 12: Never think that you are immune from that sin.
Verse 13: Never think that you have to do that sin.

1 Corinthians 10:31

So, whether you eat or drink, or whatever you do,
do all to the glory of God.

This charge, to do all for God's glory, embraces all of life. Every single thing you do, do it for God's honor, for God's glory, for the sake of the name.

In fact, if you cannot do it for God's glory, then don't do it.

It is, perhaps, easy to worship, preach, give, or serve for God's glory. But this command is not relegated to the spiritual things. In fact, it teaches us that everything is spiritual, even everyday things like eating and drinking.

Wash dishes for God's glory. Vacuum floors for God's glory. Take care of children for God's glory. Park cars at church for God's glory.

This principle has enormous implications for our work. In fact, this truth transforms work into worship.

Brother Lawrence, the seventeenth-century Catholic monk, felt he could worship God in the kitchen as well as in the cathedral. "I turn my little omelet in the pan for the love of God. When I can do nothing else, it is enough to have picked up a straw for the love of God."

And what about students? 1 Corinthians 10:31 is your deliverance from drudgery. In *The Flight*, John White discovered the relevance of this truth while he was a medical student:

> "For you Lord," became my motivation....The drudgery melted away and a sense of satisfaction and gratitude took its place. Exams or no exams I would study for God. And I took time off to play tennis with a carefree spirit.
>
> I don't mean that I forgot I had a certain number of months to complete a course. But my sense of responsibility had changed. I was no longer responsible to pass the examination. Rather I was responsible to use my study time in a way that pleased God. I covered the same ground but was carefree and enjoyed what I was doing. I certainly learned a lot more, though how this affected my marks I do not know. Nor do I care. I was no longer working for grades but for Christ.

The simplest task, the most routine duty at work; everything becomes a sacred act of worship when it is done for God.

1 Corinthians 11:24

And when he had given thanks, he broke it, and said,
"This is my body which is for you. Do this in
remembrance of me."

Schindler's List is a 1993 film by Steven Spielberg that won the Oscar for Best Picture. It is a black-and-white movie about the Holocaust, based on a true story. The story involves Oskar Schindler, a member of the Nazi party, who was a womanizer and war profiteer. But he saw what was happening to the Polish Jews, and he began spending his own money to rescue them. He ended up saving the lives of 1,100 Jews. At the end of the movie, there is a famous scene where the 1,100 Jewish survivors are expressing their deep, heartfelt thanks to Schindler for his sacrifice. In a very emotional manner, they give him a ring with the inscription, "Whoever saves one life saves the world entire." When Schindler, played by Liam Neeson, receives this ring, he begins to weep. He had spent so much of his own money, but he knows that he could have saved so many others. But can you imagine the gratitude of those 1,100 people and the thousands of their descendants? How could you not be incredibly grateful to the person who rescued you?

That scene epitomizes communion in a nutshell. We are grateful to the one who has rescued us. We are grateful to the one who has rescued us from our sin and an eternity of hell. We are incredibly grateful to the one who sacrificed and died for us.

Jesus rescued us, not with his money but his own precious blood. How could we not be incredibly grateful? He rescued us, not so we could have another thirty or forty years of physical life, but so that we could have an eternity of life with God. The message of communion is simple: Never forget. Remember. With deep joy and gratitude, remember.

1 Corinthians 11:23-26 underscores that the key principle of communion is to remember Jesus. God never tells us what words to say, what liturgy to follow, or what frequency to celebrate communion. There is no ceremony, ritual, or timetable prescribed.

But what God does tell us is this: Do it in remembrance of Jesus. Remember Jesus. Celebrate Jesus. Worship Jesus. Be grateful to Jesus.

Never let communion become a mundane or mechanical ritual for you. Reflect on what your Savior, God in the flesh, did for you. He died so you could live. He died to forgive your sins. He died to rescue you for all eternity.

Remember with deep gratitude and joy. Remember from a place deep in your heart. Remember and worship.

That's the essence of communion.

1 Corinthians 12:7

To each is given the manifestation of the
Spirit for the common good.

Don McCullough, a minister in San Francisco, wrote this of Winston Churchill in his book *Waking From the American Dream:*

> During World War II, England needed to increase its production of coal. Winston Churchill called together labor leaders to enlist their support. At the end of his presentation he asked them to picture in their minds a parade which he knew would be held in Piccadilly Circus after the war. First, he said, would come the sailors who had kept the vital sea lanes open. Then would come the soldiers who had come home from Dunkirk and then gone on to defeat Rommel in Africa. Then would come the pilots who had driven the Luftwaffe from the sky.
>
> Last of all, he said, would come a long line of sweat-stained, soot-streaked men in miner's caps. Someone would cry from the crowd, "And where were you during the critical days of our struggle?" And from ten thousand throats would come the answer, "We were deep in the earth with our faces to the coal."

This describes the kingdom of God. Every believer has a role in the great battle. Every believer is gifted by God to serve in the common cause. Every believer has a battle station.

You are included in this. Satan may whisper to you, "Oh, not you. Maybe others, but not you. You don't know enough. You have failed too much. You are not gifted. Not you." Don't you believe it! God has gifted and called you, and we need you.

Are you using your gift? Do you know your gift (or gifts)? If not, find out. Ask God. Listen to God. Pray and talk with your small group. Try some things.

Find your place in the battle and get started. It will be so fun, and you will impact eternity.

Then, one day in heaven, there will be a great victory parade, and you will be in the parade. You won't be a bystander watching but one of the soldiers in the parade.

1 Corinthians 13:1

If I speak in the tongues of men and of angels,
but have not love, I am a noisy gong
or a clanging cymbal.

There aren't many passages in the Bible quite like 1 Corinthians 13, one that describes the power, glory, and beauty of love so magnificently. Indeed, there is no passage in all of literature quite like 1 Corinthians 13.

The first paragraph uses graphic imagery to underscore that there is nothing, absolutely nothing, more important to God than love:

> If I speak in the tongues of men and of angels, but have not love, I am a noisy gong or a clanging cymbal. And if I have prophetic powers, and understand all mysteries and all knowledge, and if I have all faith, so as to remove mountains, but have not love, I am nothing. If I give away all I have, and if I deliver up my body to be burned, but have not love, I gain nothing. (1 Cor. 13:1-3)

The point? Love is supreme. Love is first. Love is the top priority. Not eloquent speech, sublime prophecy, profound mystery, incredible knowledge, generous giving to the poor, sacrificing your life, or even amazing faith. No, you can have all of these, but if you don't have love, you have nothing that really matters to God.

Love is supreme. God's heart wants us to love one another, love our neighbor as ourselves, love people fervently, and actually care about the people around us.

God's call to you and me is to make love the top priority of our lives. Apart from loving God himself, nothing matters more than loving our neighbor.

People devote their lives to all kinds of things: a career, house, cars, fitness, hobbies, sports, retirement, knowledge, or education. These are not bad things, but they are not worthy of a human life made for eternity. They are not big enough.

Devote your life to loving people. Devote your life to becoming the most loving person you can be. What else is a human life worth?

1 Corinthians 13:4-6

Love is patient and kind; love does not envy or boast;
it is not arrogant or rude. It does not insist on its own
way; it is not irritable or resentful; it does not rejoice
at wrongdoing, but rejoices with the truth.

A re you a loving person? God tells us that if we don't have love, we have nothing. Love is supremely important.

Not love in theory, not the feeling of love, but love in real life. Concrete love. Active love. Sacrificial love.

Do you have that? Do you have love? Assess yourself before God. Ask God to show you your heart.

"Love is patient." I am not harsh or irritable. I don't yell or raise my voice. I'm easy to live with and easy to work with. I'm patient.

"Love is kind." I am thoughtful and considerate. I speak with a gentle voice, not a harsh or abrasive one. I smile at people. I build people up, not tear them down. I am kind.

"Love does not envy." I am not jealous of others. I am not in competition with others. I am content and secure with who I am. I want the best for others. I do not envy.

"Love does not boast." I don't seek attention. I don't practice name-dropping. I don't have to be the center of conversation. I don't tell others what I've accomplished. I do not boast.

"Love is not arrogant." I'm not proud or conceited. I don't think I'm better than others, including people who work menial jobs or people who are homeless. I understand that any good in me is a gift. I'm not arrogant.

"Love is not rude." I'm sensitive to the feelings of others. I treat people with respect and courtesy. I don't use a cutting, harsh tone of voice. I am not rude.

"Love does not insist on its own way." I don't insist on my way or my preferences. I easily defer and submit to others. I'm not a control freak. I look for opportunities to serve people and not control them. I don't insist on my way.

"Love is not irritable." I'm not touchy, defensive, overly sensitive, or easily offended. People don't walk on eggshells around me. It's hard to make me angry. I'm not irritable.

"Love is not resentful." I forgive quickly. I don't hang on to grudges and nurse resentments. I don't grow bitter at those who have hurt me. I am overwhelmed by God's forgiveness and so I gladly extend grace to others. I am not resentful.

"Love does not rejoice at wrongdoing, but rejoices with the truth." I am not secretly glad when people around me have setbacks or failures. I don't gossip about the problems of others. I genuinely want the best for people. I'm glad when my friends thrive. I don't rejoice in wrongdoing but I rejoice in the truth.

That's it. That's love. How did you do? Do you love people?

Does this matter? Oh yes, it matters. It matters more than anything else, for unless we love in this way, whatever else we have going for us will not matter. For love—active, concrete, real-life, sacrificial love—is the greatest thing in the world.

1 Corinthians 13:7-8a

Love bears all things, believes all things, hopes all things, endures all things. Love never ends.

Love never ends. It never gives up on a person. It never stops loving.

True love has lasting power. It has the tenacity of a bulldog. It keeps going until the end of time.

Love doesn't give up when the other person turns from you. It doesn't quit if the other person is unkind to you or insensitive to you. It doesn't even cease when the other person betrays you. The friend keeps loving the undependable friend. The mother keeps loving the wayward child. The husband keeps loving the unfaithful wife.

It is striking how much emphasis the Bible's classic chapter on love, 1 Corinthians 13, places on this characteristic. "Love bears all things, believes all things, hopes all things, endures all things. Love never ends" (1 Cor. 13:7-8a).

The remainder of 1 Corinthians 13 stresses how temporary other things are and then concludes, "So now faith, hope, and love abide, these three; but the greatest of these is love" (1 Cor. 13:13).

This kind of enduring love is seen in the love of the prodigal son's father in Luke 15. The son insults the father and leaves, but the father keeps right on loving the son. Each day he is found gazing down the road, hoping against hope that his son would one day return. And when that day finally comes, the ever-loving, grace-filled father is found running down the road toward his son, giving him a flurry of kisses, a tender embrace, and an unrestrained welcome home. Love never stops.

Jesus's story of the prodigal son's father is a picture of God's heart for us, the heart of God for you. And if we love the way God loves, then our love will not be dependent on the other person loving us back. It will not be contingent on the other person deserving our love. It will go to people who do not deserve to be loved. People like us, who are loved fiercely by God, even though we don't deserve it.

Love never ends.

1 Corinthians 13:13

So now faith, hope, and love abide, these three;
but the greatest of these is love.

1 Corinthians 13 is the great love chapter. God pulls back the curtain on love and tells us exactly how he feels about love for people: Without love, you have nothing. You may have a lot of great characteristics, but if you don't love people, you have nothing at all.

Love is not primarily a feeling, but an action. It is a verb. Love people in concrete, practical, everyday ways.

Love is radically focused on others. It is the most immense unselfishness.

Love never quits on people and never gives up. Love endures.

Love is the greatest thing of all. Faith is vital. Hope is essential. But love? Love is supreme.

Let me challenge you: Decide that you will devote the rest of your life to loving people. Love outlandishly, outrageously, lavishly. Love fiercely and relentlessly.

Decide that you will give your life to love—loving God first, but also loving people. Decide to prioritize love over all else because God prioritizes love over all else. Decide to give yourself to love because you were made to love. You were put on this planet to love.

Choose to love people. Dismiss any flimsy excuse like, "That's just not the way I am." Nonsense! You were made to love people, and God commands you to love people. Love with all you've got. Love like you've never loved before.

Devote the rest of your life to becoming a big-hearted lover of people.

Let God so fill you with his love that it spills over to other people. It spills over freely and lavishly so that other people can bask in the fountain of God's pure love.

Love! Love family and friends. Love neighbors and coworkers. Love strangers and enemies. Love one and all. Love somebody. You've got to love somebody.

Because if you don't have love, you have nothing at all.

1 Corinthians 15:3-5

For I delivered to you as of first importance what I also received: that Christ died for our sins in accordance with the Scriptures, that he was buried, that he was raised on the third day in accordance with the Scriptures, and that he appeared to Cephas, then to the twelve.

The gospel of Jesus Christ is our message to a lost world. Martin Luther once remarked that the gospel is "the principle article of all Christian doctrine...Most necessary it is, therefore, that we should know this article well, teach it unto others, and beat it into their heads continually." Strong language: "beat it into their heads." But his point is well taken: The gospel is our central message.

In 1 Corinthians 15, the great chapter on the resurrection, Paul mentions the gospel in verse 1. In verse 3, he says that the gospel is of first importance, then he summarizes the gospel. It has four basic points, four historical events:

1. Christ died for our sins.
2. Christ was buried.
3. Christ was raised.
4. Christ appeared to people.

That's the essence of the gospel, the good news. Christ died, Christ was buried, Christ arose, and Christ appeared to people.

Twice Paul adds the phrase "in accordance with the Scriptures." This good news is not new. It was foretold long ago in the Old Testament.

It is noteworthy that "in accordance with the Scriptures" is added twice, not four times. It is added to the two key elements: that Christ was buried and Christ arose. That Christ was buried underscores the reality of his death—he really died. That Christ appeared to people underscores the reality of his resurrection—he really rose.

This is the essence of the gospel: Christ died for our sins and was raised on the third day. God came to this earth and died on a cross for my sin, and then rose from the dead in triumph to win my salvation.

Friend, that is not just good news. It's the best news ever.

1 Corinthians 15:58

Therefore, my beloved brothers, be steadfast, immovable, always abounding in the work of the Lord, knowing that in the Lord your labor is not in vain.

Because Christ's resurrection is a reality, because Christ triumphed over death, because we have the sure hope of resurrection, Paul charges the much-loved brothers and sisters in Corinth to be steadfast, immovable, and always abound in God's work.

Things will get difficult. There will be persecution and hardship. Life will be full of tribulation. But we should endure, persevere, and refuse to throw in the towel, for the risen Christ has triumphed.

Be undeterred and unwavering, for Christ has triumphed over sin and death. Abound in the work of God always.

Decide that you will go all-out for the Savior for the rest of your days, no matter what.

In his August 23, 2006, *High Octane for the Mind* newsletter, pastor and writer Dwight Edwards talked about an example of relentless perseverance:

> William Carey translated the Bible into over 40 different Indian dialects from 1793 to 1834. Though he never graduated even High School, Carey became one of the greatest linguists the world has ever known. This Englishman overcame tremendous obstacles and setbacks during his years in India, including the destruction of his home and much of his translation work in a great fire. But he kept pressing on. Shortly before he died, he gave out his secret for success.
>
> "If, after my removal, anyone should think it worth his while to write my life, I will give you a criterion by which you may judge its correctness. If he will give me credit for being a plodder, he will describe me justly. Anything beyond this will be too much. I can plod. I can persevere in any definite pursuit. To this I owe everything."

William Carey exemplifies the spirit of Paul's charge: Be steadfast, be immovable, and always abound in God's work.

2 Corinthians 2:14

But thanks be to God, who in Christ always leads us in triumphal procession, and through us spreads the fragrance of the knowledge of him everywhere.

The imagery in Paul's mind was that of a Roman military parade. Mark Batterson describes this in his book *All In*:

After winning a great victory, the Roman army marched through the streets of Rome with captives in their train. The triumphal procession started at the Campus Martius and led through the Circus Maximus and around Palatine Hill. Immediately after the Arch of Constantine, the procession marched along the Via Sacra to the Forum Romanum and on to Capitoline Hill.

I've stood under the triumphal arch that spans the Via Triumphalis. It was erected by the Roman Senate to commemorate Constantine's victory over Maxentius at the Battle of Milvian Bridge on October 28, 312. It wasn't hard to imagine conquering armies returning to the pomp and circumstance of a military parade. More than five hundred triumphal processions passed under that arch during the reign of the Roman Empire.

Our triumphal procession begins at the foot of the cross. Christ is the Conquering King, and we are the captives in His train, set free from sin and death. But that is just the first step of faith. Going all in is following in the footsteps of Jesus wherever they may lead us, including down the Via Dolorosa, the "Way of Grief." But even on the way of suffering, God is leading us in triumphal procession.

Your life may not feel like a continual triumph. Mine doesn't, and I bet Paul's didn't either. In fact, in this same letter he describes what he's gone through:

Three times I was beaten with rods. Once I was stoned. Three times I was shipwrecked; a night and a day I was adrift at sea; on frequent journeys, in danger from rivers, danger from robbers, danger from my own people, danger from Gentiles, danger in the city, danger in the wilderness, danger at sea, danger from false brothers; in toil and hardship, through many a sleepless night, in hunger and thirst, often without food, in cold and exposure. (Rom. 11:25-27)

That doesn't sound like triumph, but it was. God redeemed those setbacks. God took them and worked them with other things for good in Romans 8:28. God had the final word in every case.

Apparent defeats. Actual triumphs.

That's the way God does it for his people. He always leads us in triumph in Christ. God will do it, not us. He will do it in Christ, never apart from Christ. He will do it always, not sometimes. And as he does it, the results spread the fragrance of Christ to a dying world.

As Paul says, thanks be to God. Thanks be to God that we are part of Christ's great triumphal procession.

2 Corinthians 3:18

And we all, with unveiled face, beholding the glory of
the Lord, are being transformed into the same image
from one degree of glory to another. For this
comes from the Lord who is the Spirit.

Behold the glory of the Lord. There is no one like him.

See Jesus turn the water into wine.
See Jesus touch the leper and heal him.
See Jesus walk on water and calm the storm.
See Jesus heal the sick, the lame, and the blind.
See Jesus raise the dead to life.
See Jesus, for there's no one like him.

See Jesus nailed to a cross.
See Jesus forgiving those who killed him.
See Jesus bearing your sin.
See Jesus bursting forth from the grave.
See Jesus triumph over sin, death, and Satan.
See Jesus, for there's no one like him.

See Jesus as the Lamb who takes away the sin of the world.
See Jesus as faithful and true.
See Jesus as the Alpha and the Omega.
See Jesus as head over all things.
See Jesus as King of kings and Lord of lords.
See Jesus, for there's no one like him.

See Jesus in his glory. Behold him, gaze upon him, sing to him, pray to him, read about him. Fix your eyes firmly on him.

And as you do, the Spirit will do something incredible. He will make you like Jesus. More and more each day, little by little, you will become like Jesus.

And that, dear friend, is not only your calling; it is also your privilege, your purpose, and your destiny.

2 Corinthians 4:7

*But we have this treasure in jars of clay, to show that
the surpassing power belongs to God and not to us.*

Jars of clay: That suggests frailty, vulnerability, weakness, brokenness, and humanness.

God does not use us in spite of our weakness; God uses us because of our weakness.

In our weakness, God gets all the glory. God gets all the glory because it's obvious that the power comes from God. The power doesn't come from the broken, dirty jars of clay.

In our weakness, we recognize our complete dependence on God. We are poor in spirit, desperate, humble, and dependent.

God can use people like this, people who recognize how much they need God.

Hudson Taylor, a man used so powerfully by God to bring the gospel to China, shares the story in *Hudson Taylor's Spiritual Secret* of a conversation he had with a church leader in Scotland. The leader says, "You must sometimes be tempted to be proud because of the wonderful way God has used you. I doubt if any man living has had greater honour."

"On the contrary," was Taylor's earnest reply, "I often think that God must have been looking for someone small enough and weak enough for him to use, and that he found me."

God does not use us in spite of our weakness, but because of our weakness.

2 Corinthians 4:17

For this light momentary affliction is preparing for us an eternal weight of glory beyond all comparison.

In this one verse, there are three implicit contrasts: light and weight, momentary and eternal, affliction and glory.

Our suffering in this world is light. It may not feel light to us. Indeed, it may be extremely painful, even overwhelming. But compared to the weight of glory that God has for us in heaven, all our suffering is light.

Paul spoke from painful experience. Later in 2 Corinthians, he recounts his experience:

> With far greater labors, far more imprisonments, with countless beatings, and often near death. Five times I received at the hands of the Jews the forty lashes less one. Three times I was beaten with rods. Once I was stoned. Three times I was shipwrecked; a night and a day I was adrift at sea; on frequent journeys, in danger from rivers, danger from robbers, danger from my own people, danger from Gentiles, danger in the city, danger in the wilderness, danger at sea, danger from false brothers, in toil and hardship, through many a sleepless night, in hunger and thirst, often without food, in cold and exposure. And, apart from other things, there is the daily pressure on me of my anxiety for all the churches. (2 Cor. 11:23b-28)

That's an incredible list.

And yet Paul says that our affliction is light? Yes, light, compared to the glory that awaits us.

It is light because it is momentary. However painful our troubles are, they won't last. They won't—they will end. But the glory of heaven, the glory of life with God in heaven, that will never end, for it is eternal.

In *If God Is Good: Faith in the Midst of Suffering and Evil*, Randy Alcorn retells the story of Howard Hendricks, longtime professor at Dallas Theological Seminary, when he visited a leprosy center in India. He met a woman with leprosy who was

330

remarkable. Even though she was partially blind and badly disfigured, Hendricks called her one of the most beautiful women he had ever seen. Raising nearly fingerless hands to heaven, she exclaimed, "I want to praise God that I am a leper because it was through my leprosy that I came to know Jesus Christ as my Savior. And I would rather be a leper who knows Christ than be completely whole and a stranger to His grace."

This woman got it. She understood suffering from God's perspective. She understood that even extensive suffering here is light and momentary compared to the eternal weight of glory that awaits us in heaven. That glory is beyond all comparison.

Heaven must be far richer than we can even begin to imagine.

2 Corinthians 4:18

*As we look not to the things that are seen but to the
things that are unseen. For the things that are
seen are transient, but the things that
are unseen are eternal.*

We must distinguish between the transient and the eternal, between the perishing and the permanent.

Though the things of this world preoccupy everyone around us, we must continually hear the voice of God, which tells us to live for the eternal, not the transient. Live for the next world, not this world.

It is the wise man or woman who lives with the perspective of eternity. There is a cathedral in Milan, Italy, with a remarkable entryway. To enter, you must pass three doors in succession, each one with an elaborate inscription.

The first door, stone etched and wreathed in roses, reads, "All which pleases is but for a moment." The second door features a cross with the engraving, "All which troubles is but for a moment." The third door, the largest doorway into the sanctuary, has the inscription, "That only is important which is eternal."

Live for the eternal, not the transient. Live for the things of God.

If you live with this eternal perspective, does that mean you will miss out on a full, happy life in this world? Not at all—quite the opposite. Living for the next world is essential to a full life in this world. In *Mere Christianity*, C.S. Lewis points out, "Aim at heaven and you will get earth thrown in: aim at earth and you will get neither."

2 Corinthians 5:7

For we walk by faith, not by sight.

In the seminary newsletter *Connection*, Dr. Douglas Cecil, a professor of pastoral ministries at Dallas Theological Seminary, shared this insight on the Civil War:

> When Robert E. Lee took command of the Army of Northern Virginia, the situation looked pretty bleak for the Confederacy. General McClellan's Union force of approximately 100,000 was only five miles from Richmond. Lee was defending Richmond with a holding force of about 25,000 men out of the total Confederate strength of roughly 70,000 soldiers.
>
> However, Lee intended to "change the character of the war." He led his smaller force on an offensive—known as the Seven Day campaign—until McClellan was driven back a full 25 miles from Richmond. McClellan's retreat became affectionately known in the South as "the great skedaddle."
>
> After driving McClellan back from the outskirts of Richmond, Lee's task, as he saw it, was to continue his offensive and push Union General John Pope out of northern Virginia. But that would be no easy task. McClellan, still at Lee's front, outnumbered the Confederates even more than he had before the Seven Day campaign. Pope also had greater numbers than Lee, which could be increased if McClellan joined forces with Pope. Lee would have to "defend Richmond with one hand and strike Pope with the other."
>
> The odds on paper were bleak, but Lee was determined. "If you go on ciphering," he said, "we are whipped beforehand." Lee attacked, and three months later Washington, D.C., was being threatened as he drove two Union armies across the Potomac.

Robert E. Lee's statement about war applies to the life of faith. "If you go on ciphering, we are whipped beforehand."

Faith always involves the unseen. It's the nature of faith. "Now faith is the assurance of things hoped for, the conviction of things not seen" (Heb. 11:1).

If we already saw the results, if we had guarantees, if we had it all figured out on our own, we would not need to trust God.

But faith involves the unseen, the unknown, and the uncertain. Faith does not always seem reasonable.

Is God calling you to do something that seems scary, something that seems too big for you? If so, trust God. Walk by faith, not sight, and remember Robert E. Lee's statement: "If you go on ciphering, we are whipped beforehand."

2 Corinthians 5:17

Therefore, if anyone is in Christ, he is a new creation.
The old has passed away; behold,
the new has come.

You are not the person you once were. When you placed your trust in Christ as Savior, radical things happened. Eternal, cosmic, permanent things:

> Christ invaded your life.
> Your sins were swept away forever.
> You became a child of God.
> You became spiritually alive with God's life.
> You became a citizen of heaven, a citizen of the kingdom.
> God the Spirit came to live in you.
> You were given a new heart.
> You now had the power to please God.
> You were justified—made right with God.
> You were adopted as God's own child.
> You were given the mind of Christ.
> You moved from the kingdom of darkness to the kingdom of light.
> Your name was permanently etched into the book of life.

Your deepest heart was now to please God.

All of this happened in you and to you. All this and much more.

This is who you are. This is your true identity. We must see ourselves the way God sees us, for this is the truth. This is who we are.

Do not listen to what Satan says about you. He is a liar, and he is out to devour you. Listen only to God's voice. You are a new creation. You are a much-loved, blood-bought child of God.

This is your true self—this is how God sees you. This is who you are.

2 Corinthians 5:21

For our sake he made him to be sin who knew no sin,
so that in him we might become the
righteousness of God.

What a strong and poignant statement of Christ's substitutive atonement. Is it ever stated more strongly in the Bible?

"For our sake." God did all this—take his eternal, sinless Son and make him sin, while taking sinful rebels and making us holy—for our sake. For you and me.

"He made him to be sin." Jesus, the Sovereign God of eternity, too holy to look upon sin, comes to earth and is made into sin on the cross. Bearing our sin, he becomes sin. And that leaves you speechless.

"So that in him we might become the righteousness of God." Jesus took our sin, while we took his righteousness. What a good deal for us. He's the best deal imaginable.

Martin Luther perhaps had this verse in mind when he wrote, "Learn to know Christ and him crucified. Learn to sing to him, and say, 'Lord Jesus, you are my righteousness, I am your sin. You have taken upon yourself what is mine and given me what is yours. You have become what you were not so that I might become what I was not.'"

2 Corinthians 9:7

*Each one must give as he has decided in his heart, not
reluctantly or under compulsion, for God
loves a cheerful giver.*

Imagine someone comes to your house to help you paint some bedrooms, but it becomes clear that he doesn't want to be there. He complains the whole time and doesn't give one smile or kind word. He clearly feels a sense of obligation and duty to be here. There's no love, no joy, and no warmth in his presence. Would you want that help? No way! You'd tell him to please stay home.

God has feelings too. He doesn't want us to give ourselves to him with a reluctant, begrudging attitude. If we give reluctantly, out of duty, it ruins the whole thing. After all, God wants our heart, not our money.

However, when we give to God out of sheer joy, when we have a blast giving to God, when it's so much fun for us—well, that's a different story. God loves that kind of giving.

After all, cheerful giving is evidence that we love and trust God. Why do you give cheerfully? Because you love him, delight to give to him, and trust him. You know he will take care of you and provide for you, so it's a pleasure to give. Cheerful giving always reveals a heart that loves and trusts God, but joyless giving reveals a heart full of religion and duty.

2 Corinthians 12:9

But he said to me, "My grace is sufficient for you, for my power is made perfect in weakness." Therefore I will boast all the more gladly of my weaknesses, so that the power of Christ may rest upon me.

God does not use me in spite of my weakness; he uses me because of my weakness. In fact, because of my weakness, Christ's power is seen.

What is your weakness? Is it a physical problem? A mental problem? Failure in your past? Some emotional or spiritual struggle? Don't simply be resigned to having this problem, but thank God that he uses you in your weakness. Yes, ask God to remove the problem, like Paul did. But meanwhile, glory in your weakness because Christ will be exalted.

The problem that you want to get rid of the most may actually be the thing you most need. Let your weakness drive you to God. The biggest enemy of your spiritual life is self-sufficiency. God uses weakness to cripple our self-sufficiency and pride, and lead us closer to Christ.

Hear the testimony of God's people:

According to Dr. and Mrs. Howard Taylor's *Hudson Taylor and the China Inland Mission*, Hudson Taylor said, "Many Christians estimate difficulties in light of their own resources, and thus attempt little and often fail in the little they attempt. All God's giants have been weak men who did great things for God because they reckoned on his power and presence being with them."

Jim Cymbala in *Fresh Wind, Fresh Fire*: "That evening, when I was at my lowest, confounded by obstacles, bewildered by the darkness that surrounded us, unable even to continue preaching, I discovered an astonishing truth: God is attracted to weakness. He can't resist those who humbly and honestly admit how desperately they need him. Our weakness, in fact, makes room for his power."

And as Dan Ortlund purportedly stated, "The pattern in God's work on earth is to channel his power through human weakness. God does not skim off the top ten percent–the most gifted, the most articulate, the smartest, the best educated–for significance in the kingdom. He picks the screw-ups. The nobodies. He picks people like you and me."

Galatians 1:10

For am I now seeking the approval of man, or of God?
Or am I trying to please man? If I were still trying to
please man, I would not be a servant of Christ.

So many of us are inveterate pleasers. Our desire to please people is so deep in our hearts that we are not even conscious of it. It's just the way we live life. It's as strong in our lives as the pull of gravity.

We want to please our parents, our spouse, our friends, our boss, our teacher, our coworkers, and strangers. We want to please anybody and everybody. We want people to like us.

Paul tears down this deep, subconscious, gravity-like tendency when he declares, "For am I now seeking the approval of man, or of God? Or am I trying to please man? If I were still trying to please man, I would not be a servant of Christ."

This is not a call to be mean to people, ignore them, or not care about them. Rather, it is a call to live for an audience of one, to live for the approval of Christ alone.

Ironically, it is when I am no longer seeking to please people that I am free to love people. If I am not a pleaser, I can focus on loving the person rather than pleasing them, which means I focus on their needs and not my comfort.

To live as a pleaser, trying to please anybody and everybody, is a recipe for failure and frustration. To live as a servant of Christ, pleasing him alone—that's a recipe for freedom.

There is great freedom in living for an audience of one.

Galatians 2:20

I have been crucified with Christ. It is no longer I who live, but Christ who lives in me. And the life I now live in the flesh I live by faith in the Son of God, who loved me and gave himself for me.

Is this the way you see yourself? Read these four statements as referring to you: I have been crucified with Christ. It is no longer I who live. Christ lives in me. Christ loved me and gave himself for me.

If you have trusted Christ as Savior, these four things are true of you.

You have been crucified with Christ. No, you did not physically hang on a cross. No, you did not experience the searing physical pain. But nonetheless, in a spiritual sense, you were crucified with Christ. The old you died and cleared the way for you becoming a new person. That's you: a new creation.

Moreover, you no longer live. It's not about you; you are not the point of your life. You're not the hero. It's not your strength or power that matters. Your life is not about your dreams, your wants, your fulfillment, your comfort, or your happiness. You no longer live.

Rather, your life is Christ. He lives in you and through you. He is your strength and power. He is the point of everything. He is the hero. You belong to him and he is closer than close. He is not distant; he is in you and lives in you. It is all about Jesus.

You live by faith in the Son of God, who loved you and gave himself for you. It's not just that Jesus is loving, loves people in general, and loves people like Paul, John, Mother Teresa, and Billy Graham. It's more than that. Jesus loves you. He loves you personally, intimately, emotionally, and intensely. You!

Do you see yourself this way?

Dear friend, it is so vital that you see yourself this way. This is who you are.

Galatians 5:1

For freedom Christ has set us free; stand firm there-
fore, and do not submit again to a yoke of slavery.

Christ has won your freedom. Christ came to earth, died, and rose from the dead to set you free. He is all about your freedom.

He liberates you from your sin. He liberates you from the penalty of sin forever, from the hell of eternal separation from God. He liberates you from the power of sin so that you no longer have to give way to it.

Christ frees you from the prison of your anger and inability to forgive, from fear and worry, from religion and rule-keeping.

However, we can forfeit our freedom. We can lapse back into slavery and bondage of all kinds. We can listen to the lies of our enemy who would enslave us.

But we must not. If Christ died to set us free, if he gave his own life to set us free, how vital it is that we stand firm and say no to slavery in all its forms.

Dwight Edwards, in *Revolution Within*, writes eloquently about the power of freedom in the New Testament world and what it can mean to us:

> We do well to remember that the word freedom meant much more to the original readers of the New Testament than it does to us. Over half the population in the Roman world was enslaved. Aristotle's view was widely held: "A slave is a living tool, just as a tool is an inanimate slave."
>
> Freedom in Christ is a spiritually intoxicating wine, a breathtaking flight into space, a soul-thrilling escape from enemy territory. It's the spiritual exhilaration of having one's soul set free for the high adventure of a God-enabled assault upon life.

Galatians 5:22-23

But the fruit of the Spirit is love, joy, peace, patience, kindness, goodness, faithfulness, gentleness, self-control; against such things there is no law.

The fruit of the Spirit is so compelling. Everyone wants these traits, and we especially want these traits in the people we live with or work with.

It is only fitting that love is at the top of the list, for love is the most important trait of all. This love includes love for God and love for people. It is a passionate, wholehearted, fully obedient love for God, and it is a selfless, sacrificial, and other-centered love for people.

Joy is the deep sense of well-being and inner contentment that exists no matter our circumstances.

Peace is the soul-resting freedom from worry and fear, from guilt and shame, from envy and jealousy, from all that troubles us.

Patience means that we are not quick-tempered, easily irritated, or difficult to live with.

Kindness is the encouraging word, the helping hand, or the warm smile we offer.

Goodness is love in action. It includes generosity of spirit and always wanting to help and bless people.

Faithfulness means we are reliable, dependable, and trustworthy. Our words are true. We keep our promises. We do what we say.

Gentleness means we are never arrogant or haughty, never harsh or abrasive, never demanding or curt. The gentle person is always patient and kind.

Self-control simply means that we have no area of our life that is out of control—not money, food, drink, sex, words, or work. There is no addiction crippling our soul.

This is the fruit of the Spirit: nine compelling traits that everyone wants and few have. No one has ever modeled these traits like Jesus did. In fact, we could put his name in the verse: Christ is love, joy, peace, patience, kindness, goodness, faithfulness, gentleness, and self-control.

A final thought: We cannot manufacture these in our lives. We cannot try hard to have these qualities. No, this is the fruit of the Spirit. Only the Spirit produces this Christ-like cluster of life in us. We surrender, depend upon, and obey the Spirit, and he transforms us. Slowly, steadily, and surely, the Spirit produces fruit.

Galatians 6:14

But far be it from me to boast except in the cross of
our Lord Jesus Christ, by which the world has
been crucified to me, and I to the world.

Our only boast is in the cross of Christ. Not in our goodness, devotion, efforts, determination, merits, cleverness, Biblical knowledge, obedience, or anything. Our only boast is the cross of Christ. For on that cross, our debt was paid, our sins were expunged, and our salvation was won.

Every single spiritual blessing in our lives was made possible because Christ our Lord died on a cross and bore our sin. Of course we boast only in the cross.

John Piper, in his book *Don't Waste Your Life,* passionately proclaims of the cross:

> Christ is the glory of God. His blood-soaked cross is the blazing center of that glory. By it he bought for us every blessing—temporal and eternal. And we don't deserve any. He bought them all. Because of Christ's cross, God's elect are destined to be sons of God. Because of his cross all guilt is removed, and sins are forgiven, and perfect righteousness is imputed to us, and the love of God is poured out in our hearts by the Spirit, and we are being conformed to the image of Christ.
>
> Therefore, every enjoyment in this life and the next that is not idolatry is a tribute to the infinite value of the cross of Christ—the burning center of the glory of God. And thus a cross-centered, cross-exalting, cross-saturated life is a God-glorifying life—the only God-glorifying life. All others are wasted.

Ephesians 1:3

*Blessed be the God and Father of our Lord Jesus
Christ, who has blessed us in Christ with every
spiritual blessing in the heavenly places.*

If you are a Christian, then God has given you every spiritual blessing in Christ Jesus. There is no spiritual blessing that some Christians have that you don't have. You have every single one.

At the moment you trusted Christ as Savior, God gave you these spiritual blessings. You have life eternal, complete forgiveness, all the righteousness of Jesus Christ, the empowering presence of the Holy Spirit, adoption as God's own child, the mind of Christ, a sure and secure destiny, and much more.

This means you are complete in Christ. You have everything you need to walk with God in joy and freedom. You have everything you need to live a life pleasing to the Father. You have everything you need to live the life you've always wanted to live.

You don't need some special experience, and you don't lack some secret knowledge. You are not missing anything you need. You already have all you need in Christ.

Think of a healthy newborn baby. That baby already has all the organs and limbs he will ever need. He needs to grow and develop, but he is already complete.

The same is true of every believer. We all need to grow and develop, but we already have every blessing and resource we need for that growth and development.

Be alert to the enemy's lies:

- You are a second-class Christian.
- God is done with you because of your sin.
- God will never use you.
- You can never change.
- You've just got to do this sin. You can't help it.
- You are not forgiven.

These are all lies, and you don't have to listen. Stand firm in Christ's strength against the enemy. Know that you are a much-loved child of God, fully forgiven, empowered by the Spirit, safe in God's arms, and alive with every spiritual blessing and resource that Christ has to offer.

344

See yourself this way. See yourself as God sees you. See yourself as you really are.

Ephesians 1:4-5a

*Even as he chose us in him before the foundation
of the world, that we should be holy and blameless
before him. In love he predestined us for
adoption as sons through Jesus Christ.*

This passage should make you feel special because it tells us that God chose you. God chose you before the creation of the world. Before God created anything else, in eternity past, you were in the mind of God. More importantly, you were in the heart of God.

With a heart bursting with tender compassion for you, God predestined you to be adopted as his own child. If this doesn't make you feel special, nothing will.

I know that there are lots of questions about God choosing us or predestining us. It is one of the great mysteries in the Bible. Let me clarify a few points:

- The Bible clearly teaches that God is sovereign in salvation. God chooses us or elects us to be saved.
- The Bible also clearly teaches that we have free will and that we must believe. We are not puppets or robots. We are responsible for responding to God and putting our faith in Jesus.
- There is mystery surrounding how the sovereignty of God and the free will of man fit together, but it is only a mystery to us, not to God. Why would we think that the infinite God would tidily fit inside our little theological boxes?

Embrace divine sovereignty and human responsibility. While a guest lecturer at Calvin Seminary, R.B. Kuiper compared this mystery to a pulley:

> I liken them to two ropes going through two holes in the ceiling and over a pulley above. If I wish to support myself by them, I must cling to them both. If I cling only to one and not the other, I go down.
>
> I read the many teachings of the Bible regarding God's election, predestination, his chosen, and so on.

I read also the many teachings regarding "whosoever will may come" and urging people to exercise their responsibility as human beings. These seeming contradictions cannot be reconciled by the puny human mind. With childlike faith, I cling to both ropes, fully confident that in eternity I will see that both strands of truth are, after all, of one piece.

Despite the mysteries, here is the main point: God chose you. He chose you because you are incredibly special to him.

Ephesians 1:5

*He predestined us for adoption as sons through Jesus
Christ, according to the purpose of his will.*

We are adopted by the God of the universe. He has become
Father to us. "Father" is the Christian name for God. For us,
God is Father, *Abba*, Daddy.

In his classic book, *Knowing God*, J.I. Packer writes:

> If you want to judge how well a person understands
> Christianity, find out how much he makes of the
> thought of being God's child, and having God as his
> Father. If this is not the thought that prompts and
> controls his worship and prayers and his whole out-
> look on life, it means that he does not understand
> Christianity very well at all. For everything that
> Christ taught, everything that makes the New Testa-
> ment new, and better than the Old, everything that is
> distinctively Christian as opposed to merely Jewish,
> is summed up in the knowledge of the Fatherhood of
> God. 'Father' is the Christian name for God.

But maybe you're thinking, *I did not have a good model of a
loving father.* Maybe you didn't. None of us had a perfect father,
but all of us have an idea of fatherhood, and our idea may be by
way of contrast, not comparison, with our human father. We all
know what a good father is all about.

God is your Father. He's the most loving and wise Father
imaginable. He's the perfect Father.

What does it mean to call God "Father"?

- You are deeply loved by Father, deeply loved. He is committed to your welfare.
- He is strong. He can protect you, provide for you, and
  strengthen you. There is no wiser parent anywhere. Father
  can take care of you.
- He understands you completely. He knows you and cares
  about you. He is the only one who completely understands
  all that is in your heart. You are not alone in a vast, cosmic
  universe.

- You never have to be confused about who you are. You are a child of God. You are the Father's adopted and much-loved child.

Adoption is the highest blessing of the gospel. Through it, you can call God "Father."

Ephesians 1:7

In him we have redemption through his blood.

The Roman Empire was full of slaves. In fact, one-third of the people in major cities were slaves. Whenever a slave was purchased, the Greek word for *redemption*, found in our verse, was used to describe the transaction.

The Bible says that God redeemed us in Jesus Christ and purchased us out of our slavery. We were all slaves to sin (we couldn't help but sin), and God purchased us and set us free.

And what was the purchase price of our redemption? The blood of Jesus. No amount of money could set an eternal soul free. No amount of religion, good works, or striving. Only the blood of Jesus.

Perhaps one hymn says it best: "What can wash away my sin? Nothing but the blood of Jesus."

But why? Why is the price so high for the blood of God's own Son—the blood of God?

It's simple: God is a holy God. Sin is not ignored or dismissed lightly. Sin must be paid for by death. The Bible says that "The wages of sin is death" (Rom. 6:23a), and "Without the shedding of blood there is no forgiveness of sins" (Heb. 9:22b).

Blood must be shed, either our blood or that of a substitute. Someone must die.

God says to us: "I will die. I will come to earth and become a human being so I can die. I will die for you."

That's the answer to our sin problem. A death.

The answer to our sin problem is not trying harder, feeling guilty, religious performance, or determination to do better. God's answer to sin is the death of a substitute.

In *The Body*, Charles Colson tells the story of Father Maximilian:

> In February 1941, Father Maximilian Kolbe was arrested by the Gestapo and sent to Auschwitz. He was a Polish monk who founded a Franciscan order near Warsaw called the Knights of the Immaculate.
>
> Eventually he was assigned to Barracks 14 where he continued to minister to his fellow prisoners. He would nod his understanding as men poured out their hearts. Then he would raise his emaciated arm and make the sign of the cross in the foul air of the packed barracks.

The cross, he thought. Christ's cross has triumphed over its enemies in every age. I believe, in the end, even in these darkest days in Poland, the cross will triumph over the swastika. I pray I can be faithful to that end.

Then one night a man escaped from Barracks 14. The next morning there was tension as the ranks of phantom-thin prisoners lined up for roll call in the square. Afterwards, Commandant Fritsch ordered the dismissal of all but Barracks 14, who were forced to stand still in the hot sun all day long. By evening the commandant would make a lesson out of the fate of this miserable barracks. "The fugitive has not been found. Ten of you will die for him in the starvation bunker!" he screamed.

Anything was better—death on the gallows or even the gas chambers; this method forced one to go without food and water until death. After the ten were chosen, the cry rang out from one of the men chosen, "My poor children! My wife! What will they do?"

Suddenly there was commotion in the ranks. A prisoner had broken out of ranks and volunteered to take this crying man's place. It was Father Kolbe. The frail priest spoke softly, even calmly, saying, "I would like to die in place of one of the men you condemned."

The commandant ordered it done, and the ten were marched to Barracks 11 where they would spend the last of their days.

As the hours and days passed, the camp became aware of something extraordinary happening in the death cell. Past prisoners had spent their dying days howling and attacking one another in a frenzy of despair. But now, those outside heard the faint sound of singing. For this time the prisoners had a shepherd to gently lead them through the shadows of the valley of death, pointing them to the great shepherd.

Franciszek Gajowniczek was the prisoner whose life was spared. He survived Auschwitz and for 53 years—until his death at age 95—he joyously told everyone about the man who had died in his place.

Jesus is the one who died in your place.

Ephesians 1:7-8a

In him we have redemption through his blood, the forgiveness of our trespasses, according to the riches of his grace, which he lavished upon us.

I once visited a man who was dying of cancer at MD Anderson Cancer Center. He was in his early fifties and had been an Olympic runner.

At one point, he said to me, "I'll shoot straight with you. I'm afraid to die."

I appreciated his honesty and vulnerability. I gently asked, "Bob, are you ready to meet God?"

He replied, "Yes. I've asked forgiveness from Jesus. But I'm worried whether I've been good enough."

Then I explained to him, "No one is good enough. That's why we need grace. Jesus Christ died on the cross for our sins, and we trust him to save us. It's all about grace, Bob."

The gospel is the message of grace. The Bible is the book of grace. God is the God of grace. Jesus Christ is all about grace.

Grace is the theme of the Bible. Our faith begins with grace, it is built on grace, it crescendos with grace.

Grace means God has forgiven you and given you eternal life. If it's eternal, then it can never end. You are secure and safe in God's grace.

Grace means the pressure is off. It's like the football kicker who kicks the last-second field goal. The pressure is now off. You can laugh, dance, and sing.

The writer and counselor David Seamands expressed in *Healing for Damaged Emotions* his deep conviction about grace:

> Many years ago I was driven to the conclusion that the two major causes of most emotional problems among evangelical Christians are these: the failure to understand, receive and live out God's unconditional grace and forgiveness; and the failure to give out that unconditional love, forgiveness, and grace to other people…We read, we hear, we believe a good theology of grace. But that's not the way we live. The good news of the gospel of grace has not penetrated the level of our emotions.

God has lavished his grace upon us. Enjoy it, revel in it, rest in it. It's all about grace.

Paul, the writer of Ephesians, was a champion of grace. Be a champion of grace in your world.

Ephesians 2:1

*And you were dead in the trespasses and sins in
which you once walked.*

Sin hurts us. It always hurts us. There is a story about a man who
had parked his RV at a campground near Seattle. One night,
someone was trying to steal gas. He put the hose in and sucked
hard. At this point, the RV owner heard a noise and went outside
to see a man throwing up. Turns out, the thief had put the hose in
the sewage tank instead of the fuel tank.

Yuck! Drinking sewage.

That's a good picture of sin. Sin is like drinking sewage. It
always hurts us.

In Ephesians 2, God describes what sin does to us:

> And you were dead in the trespasses and sins in
> which you once walked, following the course of this
> world, following the prince of the power of the air,
> the spirit that is now at work in the sons of disobedi-
> ence—among whom we all once lived in the passions
> of our flesh, carrying out the desires of the body and
> the mind, and were by nature children of wrath, like
> the rest of mankind. (Eph. 2:1-3)

What an indictment. Because of sin, we were spiritually dead,
separated from the life of God, conformed to the world around
us, influenced by the devil, given to self-centeredness and self-indulgence, and subject to God's holy wrath against sin.

This is the gravity of the human condition apart from Jesus
Christ. Clearly, we don't need a self-improvement plan, a motivational seminar, a bit of religion, or to try a little harder. No, the
disease—sin—is far too serious.

We need God to intervene and rescue us by his grace. We
need a Savior, desperately.

That's exactly what God gave us. He sent a Savior who would
die in our place, eradicate all our sin, guilt, shame, and death, and
give us eternal life.

"For the wages of sin is death, but the free gift of God is eternal life in Christ Jesus our Lord" (Romans 6:23).

What a Savior. Thank God for a Savior.

Ephesians 2:4-5

*But God, being rich in mercy, because of the great
love with which he loved us, even when we were dead
in our trespasses, made us alive together with
Christ – by grace you have been saved.*

It all starts with God's love. The entire spiritual life, all that God has done for you in Christ, starts with God's great love for you.

This is the wellspring and the fountainhead of the spiritual life.

It does not start with me. It does not begin with my goodness, my cleverness, my devotion, or my churchmanship.

God's love for us, for you, is pure, strong, and tender. Do you know his love? I do not mean if you know it mentally, I mean if you know it with your heart. Do you feel loved by God?

I hope so. Oh, I hope so.

God doesn't love you because you are so lovable, but because he is so loving:

> He is outrageous in his love for you.
> He is relentless in his love for you.
> He is unfettered in his love for you.
> He is gracious in his love for you.
> He is personal in his love for you.
> He is emotional in his love for you.

This is God's love for you. Receive it, believe it, embrace it, enjoy it.

In *Speechless*, Steven Curtis Chapman put it this way: "In the gospel, we discover we are far worse off than we thought, and far more loved than we ever dreamed."

Ephesians 2:6-7

*And raised us up with him and seated us with him
in the heavenly places in Christ Jesus, so that in the
coming ages he might show the immeasurable riches
of his grace in kindness toward us in Christ Jesus.*

In the coming ages, to human and angelic beings throughout the cosmos, you will forever be an example of God's grace.

Grace is God's lavish love to sinners. Grace is God's abundant forgiveness to the undeserving. Grace is God's outrageous mercy for the desperate.

Grace is God's free gift to sinners. Grace is God's outlandish love to rebels. Grace is God's forgiving tenderness to us.

There's nothing like it. It is incomparable.

The Bible begins with grace and ends with grace. Grace is the message of our lips and the song of our hearts. We rest in grace, we revel in grace, and we glory in grace.

It's the theme of the Bible. It was the song of Paul's heart. It is our only hope.

In *What's So Amazing About Grace,* Philip Yancey recounts an anecdote on grace:

> During a British conference on comparative religions, experts from around the world debated what, if any, belief was unique to the Christian faith. They began eliminating possibilities. Incarnation? Other religions had different versions of gods appearing in human form. Resurrection? Again, other religions had accounts of return from death. The debate went on for some time until C.S. Lewis wandered into the room.
>
> "What's the rumpus about?" he asked, and heard in reply that his colleagues were discussing Christianity's unique contribution among world religions. Lewis responded, "Oh, that's easy. It's grace."
>
> After some discussion, the conferees had to agree. The notion of God's love coming to us free of charge, no strings attached, seems to go against every instinct of humanity. The Buddhist eight-fold path, the

Hindu doctrine of karma, the Jewish covenant, and Muslim code of law—each of these offer a way to earn approval. Only Christianity dares to make God's love unconditional.

If you have received God's free gift of life, then you are completely accepted, you are eternally forgiven, you are totally secure in God's love.

That's grace.

Believe it. Enjoy it. Celebrate it.

Ephesians 2:8-9

*For by grace you have been saved through faith. And
this is not your own doing; it is the gift of God, not a
result of works, so that no one may boast.*

In a *Reader's Digest* interview, Muhammad Ali said, "One day
we're all going to die, and God is going to judge us—[our] good
deeds and bad deeds. If the bad outweighs the good, you go to
hell. If the good outweighs the bad, you go to heaven."

Ali's statement expresses the nearly universal belief of humans
all over the world that they must earn their way to heaven. In fact,
it is quite likely that you held this opinion before you came to
Christ.

Every religion in the world holds this view in one form or
another. Every religion except one: Christianity.

Jesus teaches us that we could never be good enough to earn
salvation. We need a Savior who will be a substitute for us, who
will die in our place and give us life. Jesus teaches grace, not
works.

Grace is countercultural. Grace is counterintuitive. Grace is
counter to all human pride.

The Bible teaches grace.

Perhaps the most emphatic passage on grace in the Bible is
Ephesians 2:8-9. In just two verses, one sentence, there is a sixfold
emphasis that we are saved by grace, not works:

1. "For by grace you have been saved." We are saved by
   God's grace, God's free gift of life to undeserving people.
2. "Through faith." We are saved through trust in Christ,
   not by our own efforts. We transfer trust from self to
   Jesus.
3. "And this is not your own doing." We do not save
   ourselves. God saves us. We can take no credit.
4. "It is the gift of God." Salvation is God's gift, not my
   work.
5. "Not a result of works." In case we are not crystal clear,
   God reiterates that we are not saved by our good works,
   our churchmanship, or our religious efforts.
6. "So that no one may boast." If we earned our salvation,

or if we even contributed to our salvation, then there would be some grounds to boast. But alas, there are no grounds for boasting. God did it all.

Could God be more emphatic? Yet human pride still resists the message of grace.

Don't resist the gospel message of grace.

God does it all. We are saved by grace alone through faith, and by faith alone in Christ. Christ alone.

Glory in God's grace. Glory!

Ephesians 2:10

For we are his workmanship, created in Christ Jesus
for good works, which God prepared beforehand,
that we should walk in them.

We are not saved by good works. We are saved for good works.
We are saved so that we can serve God.

Amazingly, God has prepared a lifetime of good works
in advance for each one of us. We simply need to be available,
willing, obedient, and alert to his promptings and leadings.

This is your destiny, your purpose, your calling. Don't miss
the journey of love and servanthood that God has for you.

There are prayers to pray, offerings to give, spiritual gifts to
leverage. Be all that God wants you to be, for you have a vital role
in the kingdom.

Each day varies. Perhaps today there is a friend who needs
encouraging, or a colleague who needs forgiving, or a stranger at
Wal-Mart who needs a smile and sincere greeting.

Perhaps your daughter needs to be affirmed, or your spouse
needs to be listened to and understood, or a friend needs to be
invited to church.

Each day becomes an adventure with God.

Every day, think to yourself, *Lord, I'm available to you today*
however you want to use me, for whoever you bring in my life. Lead
me, O Lord.

God uses people to show his love and compassion. God uses
ordinary people like you and me.

Are you ready? Are you available? Are you alert to his
leadings?

Ephesians 2:13

But now in Christ Jesus you who once were far off
have been brought near by the blood of Christ.

Normally when I study at work, I hibernate in my office with my door closed. If someone on our staff team needs to interrupt me, they knock first.

Some years ago, I was studying when I noticed my door was very slowly opening. I thought to myself, *This is odd. Someone is coming in and not even knocking, and they are opening that door ever so gingerly.*

Finally, I saw who was behind the door. It was my son John Paul, who, when he finally appeared, greeted me with a big smile and a warm, "Hi, Dad."

How do you think I responded?

Well, I was delighted. He's my son, and I was thrilled to see him. I was not annoyed in the least. I gave him a big hug.

If that's how I, a fairly human, self-centered dad, responded to my child, then how does your Father in heaven respond when you come into his presence?

That's right: He loves it. You never annoy him. He's thrilled that you come into his presence.

It is only because of Jesus that we can even come into the presence of God. It is because of his blood. Once we were far from God, enemies of God. But Christ's blood has covered our sin, and now we have nearness to God.

The central motif of the Old Testament was the distance between humans and a holy God. No one could come into God's presence in the Most Holy Place except the high priest once a year.

But now, because of Christ's shed blood, the temple curtain before the Most Holy Place has been torn, and access to God is thrown wide open. If distance marked Old Testament faith, then nearness marks New Testament faith. We are now near to the holy God. We have access at any time. At any moment, without knocking, we can walk right into our Father's presence and receive his smiling embrace.

Ephesians 3:17b-19a

*That you, being rooted and grounded in love, may
have strength to comprehend with all the saints what
is the breadth and length and height and depth, and
to know the love of Christ that surpasses knowledge.*

Paul's main prayer for the Christians at Ephesus is that they
would know Christ's love for them. He did not mean that they
should know Christ's love in their heads, but in their hearts.

Paul feels so strongly about this request that he gives it a
three-fold emphasis:

- "Being rooted and grounded in love"
- "To comprehend with all the saints what is the breadth
  and length and height and depth"
- "And to know the love of Christ that surpasses knowledge"

It seems like Paul does not have the words to express how
deeply he feels about this request. These believers simply must
know how much Christ loves them.

Why? Why is this so important?

Well, God's love for us is the most important thing in our
lives. If we do not feel loved by God, then we will not love God
back. At best, we will have religious duty, but we will not have a
love affair with Jesus. We will not fulfill the first commandment
to "Love the Lord your God with all your heart and with all your
soul and with all your mind" (Matt. 27:32).

If we do not feel loved by God, we will not trust him, not for
the big things. Will you trust God if you don't believe he loves you
and that he wants the best for you? Not a chance.

If we do not feel loved by God, we will not obey God. We'll
obey the easy commands, the ones we would do anyway, but not
the hard ones. We won't obey God because we don't believe that
he has our best interests at heart.

We could go on and on. Every aspect of the spiritual life
hinges on the love of God for us. If we do not know, in the deepest
places of our soul, that our God loves us so much, then we will
not love him, trust him, obey him, serve him, enjoy him, worship
him, rest in him, or seek him.

This is the foundation of the spiritual life. Nothing is more important.

No wonder Paul's greatest prayer focuses on Christ's love for us. No wonder Paul places such inordinate emphasis on this love that he wants others to know the "breadth and length and height and depth, and to know the love of Christ that surpasses knowledge."

No wonder.

If you pray only one prayer for your loved ones, if you pray only one prayer for your church, if you pray only one prayer for yourself, make it this prayer: "O Lord, may we know how much you love us."

Ephesians 3:20-21

Now to him who is able to do far more abundantly than all that we ask or think, according to the power at work within us, to him be glory in the church and in Christ Jesus throughout all generations, forever and ever. Amen.

Paul is praying about Christ's unknowable love, and he bursts out in a song of praise:

> God is able, for he has all power.
> God is able to do, for he is active and at work in our lives.
> God is able to do what we ask, for he hears and answers our prayers.
> God is able to do what we ask or think, for he knows what we dream of, even that which we are afraid to ask for.
> God is able to do all that we ask or think, for there are no limits to his power and goodness.
> God is able to do more than all we ask or think, for he is gracious and exceeds our biggest dreams.
> God is able to do far more than all we ask or imagine, for his power and goodness transcend all boundaries. This is the God we come to. This is the God who hears our every prayer.
> To him be the glory.

Ephesians 4:11-12a

And he gave the apostles, the prophets, the evange-
lists, the shepherds and teachers, to equip the
saints for the work of ministry.

The role of leaders in the church is not to do ministry but develop ministry. Leaders develop ministry when they equip, empower, coach, cheerlead, and encourage God's people.

When the church was started, everyone understood this. But at some point, there arose a group of professional clergy, a spiritual elite who took over the ministry. The attitude then developed that meaningful ministry was for the professionals and that the people were recipients and spectators of ministry.

This is not God's way of doing church.

In fact, this is a diabolical strategy to hamstring God's work and to stifle the spiritual growth of God's people.

Moreover, pastors and priests were also to blame for this tragedy, because they enjoyed their status as the spiritual elite and did not want to give up control.

Let me ask you: What is the most effective way of doing church? Should we put the ministry in the hands of a few seminary-educated, robe-wearing, jargon-talking professionals, or should we empower all of God's people to do the ministry?

I think it's a no-brainer. Let's go with God's way.

God says you are a minister—you. Moreover, you are a missionary, because you are on a mission for God wherever you are. You are a soldier of the gospel in the great battle.

And the church? It's not a cruise ship where you go to be served and entertained.

It is a battleship, and every soldier is needed to man their battle stations. What is your battle station?

Ephesians 4:26-27

Be angry and do not sin; do not let the sun go down on your anger, and give no opportunity to the devil.

A traveler, between flights at an airport, went to a lounge and bought a small package of cookies. Then she sat down and began reading a newspaper. Gradually, she became aware of a rustling noise. From behind her paper, she was flabbergasted to see a neatly dressed man helping himself to her cookies. Not wanting to make a scene, she leaned over and took a cookie herself.

A minute or two passed, and then came more rustling. He was helping himself to another cookie. After a while, they came to the end of the package with one cookie left, but she was so angry she didn't dare allow herself to say anything. Then, as if to add insult to injury, the man broke the remaining cookie in two, pushed half across to her, ate the other half, and left.

Still fuming some time later when her flight was announced, the woman opened her handbag to get her ticket. To her shock and embarrassment, there she found her package of unopened cookies.

I smile at that story because it reminds me that we all have been angry when there was no need.

Anger is a challenge. Aristotle observed, "Anyone can become angry. That is easy. But to be angry with the right person, to the right degree, at the right time and in the right way—that is not easy."

How do you respond when you are angry? For some people:

- They explode. They rant and rave. They spew venom at anyone who comes near.
- They withdraw. They pout and sulk. They are masters of the silent treatment.
- They are passive-aggressive. They get jabs at people with their actions rather than their words.
- They use sarcasm extensively to subtly express their anger.
- They go to a third party. They do not talk with the person they are angry with, but they talk about that person to a third party.

- They deny they are ever angry. They grew up in a household where it was not OK to be angry. Even though they are bursting with anger, they insist, "I'm not angry."

God says it is OK to be angry. The issue is: How do I respond to my anger?

By God's grace—and only by his grace—we can respond to anger in a godly way:

- Slowly. "Be slow to anger" (James 1:19). "A man of quick temper acts foolishly." (Prov. 14:17a)
- Calmly. "A soft answer turns away wrath, but a harsh word stirs up anger." (Prov. 15:1)
- Lovingly. "Love is patient and kind…it is not irritable or resentful." (1 Cor. 13:4-5)
- Gracefully. "Be kind to one another, tenderhearted, forgiving one another, as God in Christ forgave you." (Eph. 4:32)

Can you imagine what would happen if we followed God's practical advice on anger? Can you imagine how many marriages would be saved? How many parent-child relationships and friendships would be saved? Can you imagine the gift this would be to our children, our coworkers, and our friends? Can you imagine the difference in our own health?

What if we consistently responded to anger in God's way—slowly, calmly, lovingly, and gracefully?

O Father, give us grace to do this.

Ephesians 4:32

Be kind to one another, tenderhearted, forgiving one another, as God in Christ forgave you.

All of us have been hurt. It's a painful part of life. A parent neglects you or even abuses you. A friend disappoints you or betrays you. A spouse is unfaithful to you or abandons you. A stranger assaults your loved one.

It's as if you have been stabbed in the back, but the knife is still there. And every time you replay the hurt in your mind, you twist the knife a little more. The pain never leaves and the wound never heals.

What can we do? What can we do about this pain and poison that ruins our life and robs our joy?

God has a solution.

God's solution is simple, but it's not easy. God's solution is grace. Extend grace to the person who hurt you. Forgive.

Forgiveness does not mean that all of your hurt and pain are gone. That may take a very long while. Forgiveness means that you have made a choice to forgive, to let go of your anger, to let go of your resentment, to let go of your right to get even. You have said to God, "Lord, I forgive him. I choose to forgive him. I give you my anger and my resentment, my desire to get even. I give it all to you."

Take the knife out. Let the pain go. Let the wound heal.

Set a prisoner free. Set yourself free from a prison of pain and poison.

Forgiveness is a healing choice, a choice made by Christ's strength in us, a choice made because of Christ's grace to us.

Ephesians 5:1-2

*Therefore be imitators of God, as beloved children.
And walk in love, as Christ loved us and gave himself
up for us, a fragrant offering and sacrifice to God.*

Jesus calls us to make love the defining mark of our lives. Most of us do fine when it comes to loving people in the abstract, like loving all of humanity. But how do we do when it comes to loving people in the concrete and practical?

Just between you and God, assess yourself, on a scale of one to ten, on the following ten expressions of love. Ask God how you are doing when it comes to love:

1. Are you a great listener? Do you give people your undivided attention? Do you probe and ask follow-up questions? Do the people around you consider you a great listener? The first duty of love is to listen.

2. Do you serve people? Are you always looking to serve people in practical ways, from helping with the dishes and giving someone a call to helping a single parent? Do you find ways to serve at church? Do you exude servanthood? Are you more a giver than a taker?

3. Are you a big-hearted forgiver? Forgiveness may be the biggest test of love, and the hardest. Do you freely forgive people who hurt you? Or do you hold grudges, keep score, and give the silent treatment? Forgive people the way your dog forgives you.

4. Do you pray frequently and fervently for people? Prayer for someone, especially for someone with a big need, might be the most powerful way you can love them, yet it is unseen and often not done. When you tell someone you will pray for them, do you wholeheartedly pray and ask them later how the prayer was answered?

5. Do you accept people who are different? Do you enjoy the differences in people and readily accept others who are different in ethnic background, racial background, economic status, political affiliation, personality, and more? Do you revel in the glorious way that God has made us different?

6. Do you verbalize your love? Do you say the words "I love you"? Do you write the words "I love you"? These are the three most life-breathing words in your tool belt.
7. Do you touch people to express love? Touch, such as a hug or a hand on the shoulder, is powerful. Jesus touched the leper, which exploded his heart with tender compassion. Do you regularly utilize the power of touch?
8. Are you an encourager? Encouragers are lovers and lovers are encouragers. Are you always alert to encourage and affirm people? Do you speak to people's fears and give them hope and confidence?
9. Do you consistently speak well of people? Do people know that you will not slander them behind their backs, because when you are talking with these people you never slander others? Do you consistently say good things about people?
10. Do you weep with those who weep, and rejoice with those who rejoice? Romans 12:15 gives us this important test of love. Both are crucial, but the latter, rejoicing with someone, is much rarer. When someone has a broken heart, just show up and care. When someone has lots of success, then dance and sing.

When it comes to loving the way Christ loved, how are you doing?

You might be marvelously successful in some areas, but it won't matter if you fail when it comes to love. Trying is what matters most.

At the end of your life, will it be said that you, above all else, loved people?

Ephesians 5:18

*And do not get drunk with wine, for that is
debauchery, but be filled with the Spirit.*

In the classic movie *The African Queen,* Humphrey Bogart plays a
riverboat captain who rescues Katherine Hepburn, a missionary.
On their long voyage down a river, they encounter various problems: a pipe is severed, there are severe rapids, a propeller breaks,
and German soldiers fire at their boat.

However, the worst problem occurs when the river turns into
a muddy, marshy, grass-filled swamp. They become mired in the
muck and have no power to move. They push and pull but get
nowhere. They finally give up in exhaustion.

This scene is a parable of the Christian life. Too many Christians feel mired in the muck. They have no power to move. They
push and pull, but finally give up in exhaustion.

This is the inevitable result whenever we depend on our power to please God and our power to change. We cannot do it, because the spiritual life is a supernatural life, and supernatural life
requires supernatural power, the power of the Holy Spirit.

The Christian life should be lived in the power of the Spirit. Whenever we become Christians, God's Spirit comes inside
us. From that point on, he is our power source. Depend on his
power. Ask the Spirit to fill you, control you, empower you, and
transform you.

The spiritual life is life in, by, and from the Spirit.

At our conversion, the Holy Spirit comes and dwells in us.
He fills us. Unfortunately, most of us leak. At times, we resist the
Spirit, grieve the Spirit, and disobey the Spirit. At those times, we
need God to fill us afresh with his Spirit.

God fills us with his Spirit as we surrender to the Spirit's control in our lives. He fills us with the Spirit as we depend upon the
Spirit's power in our lives. He fills us with the Spirit as we obey
the Spirit's leadings in our lives.

This is the spiritual life in the age of the Spirit. God contrasts
being filled with the Spirit to being filled with spirits or alcohol.
Whereas too much alcohol will make you act unnaturally, the
Spirit will make you act supernaturally.

Right now, if you find yourself frustrated with your Christian
life—if you are struggling with some sin or addiction and you are

losing that struggle, if you feel like a failure, then it is quite likely you have no power. It's like you're vacuuming your floor, but the vacuum picks nothing up because it is not plugged in. Plug the vacuum in.

Depend on God's Spirit. "Not by might, nor by power, but by my Spirit" (Zech. 4:6).

O Lord, fill us afresh with your Spirit.

Ephesians 5:25

*Husbands, love your wives, as Christ loved the church
and gave himself up for her.*

One of the longest and most important passages on marriage in
the New Testament is found in Ephesians 5. The most striking
note in this passage is the emphatic call to husbands to love their
wives.

Three times the call goes out:

Love her. (Eph. 5:25)
Love her. (Eph. 5:28)
Love her. (Eph. 5:33)

Clearly, that husbands love their wives matters to God a great
deal. Every husband will be accountable to God for loving his
wife. In the eyes of God, it is a tragedy when a woman is married
to a man and is unloved by him. It should not be. When she was
a young girl, just about every wife dreamed of a knight sweeping
her off her feet and loving her devotedly for the rest of her life.
When a woman is married and yet largely unloved and lonely, it
is a sad and serious thing in the eyes of our God.

But why doesn't God tell wives to love their husbands?
Shouldn't wives love their husbands also? Of course they should,
but I suspect that most wives will naturally love their husbands.
Generally, a wife will naturally and enthusiastically love her
husband unless she has felt so unloved by him for so long that the
love inside her has withered away and died.

When God calls a husband to love his wife, he provides a
model in the way Christ loved his bride, the church. "Husbands,
love your wives, as Christ loved the church and gave himself up
for her, that he might sanctify her, having cleansed her by the
washing of water with the word, so that he might present the
church to himself in splendor, without spot or wrinkle or any
such thing, that she might be holy and without blemish" (Eph.
5:25-27).

Two things should be noted about a husband's love:

1. If Christ is the example for husbands (and he is),
    then a husband's love is a sacrificial love. A husband

373

must be willing to die for and live for his wife. He sacrifices for her. He puts her feelings, her needs, and her interests ahead of his own. This sort of love is as powerful as it is rare. Every wife will respond to it.

2. Just as Christ's love results in a radiant church, so a husband's love leads to a radiant bride. When a wife feels deeply loved by her husband, she will flourish and thrive. She will not be crushed or stifled, held back or frustrated. She will come alive and become the woman God designed her to be. To a large extent, you can look at the face of a wife and tell how her husband loves her. Is she radiant? Does she thrive? Is she more secure and confident because of her husband's love? Have her gifts flourished? Is she closer to God? Is she more the person God created her to be?

Husbands, God has placed within you all that you need to love your wives. Love your wife with everything you've got. Love her the way Christ loved us: sacrificially, selflessly, fervently, and devotedly.

You will not regret it.

Ephesians 5:28

In the same way husbands should love their wives as their own bodies. He who loves his wife loves himself.

A ndrew Jackson was a fierce warrior of a man. He fought in the Revolutionary War as a youngster, he fought Native Americans in Tennessee, he led soldiers into battle, and he was a military hero in a great battle at New Orleans. He would become a senator and the president of the United States. He was a tough, fierce, and formidable man.

And yet, Jackson had the most tender and loving relationship with his wife, Rachel. He was devoted to her. Whenever he was away from home, he would pine for her and miss her terribly. He wrote the most tender love letters to her.

One of Jackson's biographers, H.W. Brands, wrote in *The People's President* that they were soul mates: "Their affection for each other was of the tenderest kind...The General always treated her as if she were his pride and glory, and words can faintly describe her devotion to him."

When Rachel died, "A friend recalled that he held her so tightly after death that the body had to be pried from his arms to prepare it for burial. Another remembered that he looked 'twenty years older in a night.'"

Andrew Jackson was incredibly successful: a military hero, a US senator, the president, and one the most famous men in America. But I have no doubt that the highlight of his life was his tender, loving relationship with his wife. Andrew Jackson understood the priority, the urgency, and the beauty of a husband loving his wife.

This is God's call to every husband. Love her, love her, love her.

Ephesians 5:33

However, let each one of you love his wife as himself,
and let the wife see that she respects her husband.

Ephesians 5:33 summarizes and concludes one of the most important passages on marriage in the New Testament.

God's call is clear: Husband, love her. Wife, respect him.

God does not say to husbands to love her if she deserves loving, or to love her if she respects you.

Rather, the charge is unconditional: Love her!

Similarly, God does not say to wives to respect him if he deserves respect, or to respect him if he loves you.

Again, the call is unconditional: Respect him!

It may be difficult to love a wife who shows you little respect, and it may be difficult to respect a husband who demonstrates meager love. But God can give us grace to obey him.

The book *Love and Respect* by Dr. Emerson Eggerichs relates the results of an extensive marital study:

> Dr. John Gottman, professor in the Department of Psychology at the University of Washington, led a research team that spent twenty years studying two thousand couples who had been married twenty to forty years to the same partner. These people came from diverse backgrounds and had widely differing occupations and lifestyles. But one thing was similar—the tone of their conversations. As these couples talked together, almost always there was what Gottman calls "a strong undercurrent of two basic ingredients: Love and Respect. These are the direct opposite of—and antidote for—contempt, perhaps the most corrosive force in marriage."

Isn't it interesting that this extensive research, at a secular university no less, concludes that the two vital elements of marriage are the same two elements that God calls us to in the most significant New Testament passage on marriage?

And isn't it interesting that the key area of marriage, the acid test, was something so simple and mundane as the tone of conversations—a tone of love and respect? Love is more than the tone of our conversations, but apparently our tone is vital.

Husbands, what if you focused, for the next thirty days, on loving your wife with all your heart? What might God do in your marriage?

Wives, what if you focused, for the next thirty days, on respecting your husband with all your heart? What might God do in your marriage?

Ephesians 6:4

Fathers, do not provoke your children to anger, but bring them up in the discipline and instruction of the Lord.

How do fathers and mothers provoke their kids? How do parents provoke their children to anger?

We do it in numerous ways. Here are some of those ways:

1. We provoke our kids to anger when we don't express our love to them. Just about all parents love their kids, but not all parents express it so that their children will feel loved. Parents express love to their children with their words, with listening, with touch, with focused attention, and with discipline.

2. We provoke our kids to anger through too much discipline or through too little discipline.

3. Every child needs discipline. It is proof of love, as the proverbs teach us and God models for us. But too much discipline (too harsh, too stern, too rigid, too severe) or too little discipline (no boundaries, no rules, no consequences) causes a child to be frustrated.

4. We provoke our kids to anger if we smother them or neglect them. Parents who smother their kids, who are hovering, controlling, and overprotective, will drive them away. Every child needs increasing freedom and independence from their parents so that the child is ready to leave home as a young adult. On the other hand, parents who neglect their children, who are too busy for their children, or who even abandon their children also provoke great anguish in them.

5. We provoke our kids to anger if we don't listen to them. Every child longs to be heard and understood by mom and dad. If they do not feel heard, deeply heard, they will be frustrated and hurt. This means that parents must always be ready to listen, for they never know when their child is ready to talk.

6. We provoke our kids to anger when we use sarcasm or ridicule. Sarcasm and ridicule wound a child, especially when they come from a parent. Speak words that breathe life into your child.

Ephesians 6:7

*Rendering service with a good will as to the Lord
and not to man.*

Your work matters to God. All of us work. Not all of us are employed, but we all work. Work includes volunteer work, housework, schoolwork, yard work, and other forms of work.

God made us to work. He works, and because we are made in his image, we work. Work is a big part of our lives, and God wants it to be a source of fulfillment and satisfaction, not a source of frustration and drudgery.

In Ephesians 6, Paul addresses slaves in the Roman Empire who are followers of Christ. In verse 7, he gives them the guiding principle behind all of our work as Christians: "Rendering service with a good will as to the Lord and not to man." Here is the fundamental principle for every Christian in all of our work: Work for the Lord.

The principle is simple but profound, and it can transform our work. As followers of Jesus, we do not work for a human boss, customers, clients, or patients. Nor do we work for a paycheck or for retirement.

Rather, we work for the Lord. We work to please the Lord and to honor him. We work as an expression of worship to God. Indeed, because we do it for the Lord, our work is transformed into worship. Every little act of work becomes invested with meaning and dignity because we do it for Jesus.

Howard Hendricks, who was a mentor of mine in seminary school, once told me about his being on an American Airlines flight that was delayed for six hours. As you can imagine, the passengers became irate. One man was especially difficult with a flight attendant, and yet the flight attendant was a model of grace and kindness.

After a long while, Hendricks remarked to the flight attendant, "I have been extremely impressed with the way you handled that difficult passenger. Could I have your name so that I can write the company you work for?"

Her answer surprised him. "Sir, thank you very, very much. But you should know that I do not work for American Airlines. Sir, I work for Jesus Christ."

She went on to explain that she had been a Christian for six months, and three months ago, she had led her husband to the

Lord. Their lives had been completely transformed. Before every trip, they prayed together for her ministry on the flight.

She was a brand-new Christian who understood what work is all about.

Ultimately, work is an act of worship.

Whenever you work, whatever you do, do it for the Lord. For you, Lord, for you.

Transform your work into worship.

Ephesians 6:12

For we do not wrestle against flesh and blood, but against the rulers, against the authorities, against the cosmic powers over this present darkness, against the spiritual forces of evil in the heavenly places.

The enemy is not human, but demonic. There are spirit beings— evil, unseen spirit beings called demons—who follow Satan in opposing God and God's people in every possible way.

These beings are powerful. Look at the four terms in verse 12: rulers, authorities, cosmic powers over this present darkness, and spiritual forces of evil.

These beings are invisible, yet real. They are vicious, venomous, unscrupulous, and diabolical. They don't normally announce their presence and attack openly; they scheme and deceive, accuse and condemn. They come in disguise as something harmless and benign, and before we know it, they have us by the throat, ready to devour.

Now, make no mistake: We need not fear Satan. "He who is in you is greater than he who is in the world" (1 John 4:4). Jesus, who is in us, is greater than Satan, who is in the world. Satan and his demons are finite, limited beings who have been defeated by Jesus Christ. But they are not yet banished, and they still bluster and condemn, connive, and deceive. We take the battle seriously, but we are unafraid and not intimidated, for our strength is in Jesus Christ.

Understand who the enemy is; then do battle. Wrestle in Christ's strength.

Ephesians 6:18

*Praying at all times in the Spirit, with all prayer
and supplication. To that end keep alert with all
perseverance, making supplication for all the saints.*

Prayer is warfare. Prayer is not a nice, sweet, Sunday school
picnic. An invisible war rages across the galaxies. Angels and
demons do battle for the souls of people. Lives, families, and
marriages are at stake.

The context of this charge to pray is found in verse 12:
"For we do not wrestle against flesh and blood, but against the
rulers, against the authorities, against the cosmic powers over
this present darkness, against the spiritual forces of evil in the
heavenly places." Then God tells us to don our armor for the
battle. Finally, there's the call to prayer.

Because prayer is warfare; because an invisible war is being
waged everywhere; because our struggle is not against flesh and
blood, but against dark, invisible powers; because prayer is the
real work of ministry: for all of these reasons, it is vital that we
pray in the Spirit. Our prayer must flow out of a Spirit-led, Spirit-
filled, Spirit-empowered life. The Spirit prompts our prayer, fuels
our prayer, and directs our prayer. We pray in the Spirit.

Moreover, we must be alert in our prayer. There is urgency in
the air. Bullets are flying, bombs are exploding, and soldiers are
bleeding. Lives and souls are at stake. Be alert!

Thomas à Kempis once wrote: "The devil sleepeth not, neither
is the flesh as yet dead, therefore cease not to prepare thyself for
the battle, for on thy right hand and on thy left are enemies who
never rest."

Chip Ingram, in *The Invisible War,* relates one graphic
example of prayer and the battle:

> There was a missionary in Africa also serving as a
> medic. To get the medical supplies he needed he
> had to travel by bike to a neighboring city. The trip
> took two days so he had to sleep alone in the jungle
> overnight. On one particular occasion he came to the
> city to get the supplies and he helped a man that was
> badly injured in a fight. He also shared the gospel with

the man. The next time the missionary went to the city to get medicine, he saw the same man he helped previously. This man proceeded to tell the missionary of his plan to kill him and steal the supplies the last time he was there.

However when the man and some others followed him into the jungle they saw 26 armed soldiers surrounding the missionary. Being outnumbered they left the missionary alone. The missionary was puzzled by this as he was alone that night in the jungle. Several months later the missionary shared this story with his home church and a man in the congregation stood and told the missionary that he remembered that night well as he had received a strong urge to pray for the missionary that night. This same man gathered others to pray with him. As the men stood one by one they counted 26.

Never underestimate the power of prayer.
Prayer is the main work.

Philippians 1:21

For to me to live is Christ, and to die is gain.

This would be a good verse for your tombstone. Why did Paul say, "For to me to live is Christ"? Because Paul was consumed with, focused on, and intoxicated with Jesus. Paul, the man who once hated Jesus, had been ambushed by Christ's love on the road to Damascus, and he never got over it.

Paul is saying, "My life is not about me. It's not about my comforts, my security, my dreams, my rights. It's all about Jesus. Loving Jesus, following Jesus, trusting Jesus, obeying Jesus, enjoying Jesus. For to me to live is Christ."

But Paul goes on to say, "and to die is gain." Why did Paul say that death is even better than life? How could he say that?

It's simple. Death, for the believer, means you go immediately to the presence of Christ. You are with the Lord in a tangible, physical way. You are home.

For the believer, death simply means that you are more alive than ever, and that will be so good.

May God give us the heart and mind that Paul had here. May Paul's words characterize you and me. "For to me to live is Christ, and to die is gain."

Philippians 2:3-4

Do nothing from selfish ambition or conceit, but in humility count others more significant than your-selves. Let each of you look not only to his own interests, but also to the interests of others.

Vincent Van Gogh once remarked, "The more I think it over, the more I feel that there is nothing more truly artistic than to love people."

True love is unquestionably beautiful. If it is indeed an art, it is an art form worth all of our attention.

But what does this art involve? What does it include? What does it look like? These questions are relevant because the word *love* has lost most of its punch and much of its clarity.

Love is not self-centered, self-preoccupied, or selfish. It is un-failingly other-centered. All the focus rests upon the other per-son. God tells us in Philippians 2:3-4, "Do nothing from selfish ambition or conceit, but in humility count others more signifi-cant than yourselves. Let each of you look not only to his own interests, but also to the interests of others."

Verse 4 clarifies verse 3. What does it mean to "count others more significant than yourselves"? It does not mean we have to consider them more gifted, whether that is true or not. It simply means we are to focus on them and not on ourselves, to look to their interests and not just our own.

For example, let's say you run into someone you know at the grocery store and you are focused on that person. How can you en-courage her? You can ask how she is doing, and see if that problem with her child that she had asked you to pray about is resolved.

It means you will probably do more listening than talking. You will not be concerned with how you look or whether you seem clever or not. All the focus will be on the other person. This is extremely difficult for those of us who are mere humans. There is a deeply rutted streak of self-centeredness running right through most of our hearts.

There was a farmer who placed an ad in a newspaper that read, "Farmer, age 38, wants wife, about age 30, with a tractor. Please enclose picture of tractor." We chuckle at the farmer, but we tend to love that way, more interested in what we get than what we give.

But true love is unselfish and other-centered. In *Mission Legacies*, Florence Allshorn notes, "I used to think that being nice was loving people. Now I know it isn't. Love is the most immense unselfishness and it is so big I've never touched it."

I feel exactly the same way: Love is so big, I've never touched it.

Søren Kierkegaard, the Danish philosopher, caught the essence of love when he wrote in 1851, "Christianity did not come in order to develop the heroic virtues in the individual, but rather to remove self-centeredness and establish love."

Other-centeredness is not natural, but it is exceedingly Christ-like. All of Jesus's attention went to others because that's the way love is.

Philippians 2:5-6

Have this mind among yourselves, which is yours in
Christ Jesus, who, though he was in the form
of God, did not count equality with
God a thing to be grasped.

The supreme example of humility in the universe is Jesus Christ. The word translated into "form" is the Greek word *morphē*. Our English words *morph* or *metamorphosis* come from this Greek word, which means "essential nature." The Bible tells us that Jesus's essential nature is God. He did not become God, look like God, or appear as God—he is God. He is truly and fully God, and always has been.

But Jesus "did not count equality with God a thing to be grasped." That is, Jesus did not cling to his glory, his honor, or his privileges as God. He did not hang onto these things, but relinquished them. He was still God, make no mistake, but he gave up the glory, honor, and privileges of being a deity.

The humble God. The very phrase is almost jarring to the ears. It sounds like an oxymoron, but it is true. Jesus Christ, God incarnate, exemplifies humility.

The one who created the galaxies with his mere breath, the one who had received the worship and adoration of innumerable angels, the one who exuded a blinding holiness, became a wrinkled little baby who was completely dependent on his teenage mother. He needed his diaper changed. Talk about humility.

C.S. Lewis wrote in *Mere Christianity*:

> The Second Person in God, the Son, became human himself: was born into the world as an actual man—a real man of a particular height, with hair of a particular color, speaking a particular language, weighing so many stone. The Eternal Being, who knows everything and who created the whole universe, became not only a man but (before that) a baby, and before that a fetus inside a woman's body. If you want to get the hang of it, think how you would like to become a slug or a crab.

Philippians 2:7-8

But emptied himself, by taking the form of a servant,
being born in the likeness of men. And being found
in human form, he humbled himself by becoming
obedient to the point of death, even death on a cross.

Jesus, at the Incarnation, emptied himself. But what did Jesus empty himself of? Not his status as a deity, but his glory, his honor, and his privileges.

In 1936, the King of England, Edward VIII, abdicated the throne so that he could marry a divorced American named Wallis Simpson. British laws forbade the king to marry a divorced woman, and Edward chose love over royalty. He was still the same person, but he gave up his glory and all the trappings of royalty. The abdication of Edward VIII provides a human parallel to the Incarnation when Jesus emptied himself, choosing love for us over glory.

The word *form* in verse 7 is our word *morphē*, the exact same word we saw in verse 6. Remember, the word means "essential nature." Jesus's essential nature is not only that of God but also that of a servant. His nature has always been a servant nature, for it is an essential part of him, not peripheral, optional, or temporal. Jesus did not become a servant when he came to earth; he has always been a servant.

God is a servant by nature, a humble servant. Indeed, God is the biggest servant in the universe. He serves us and meets our needs because he loves us. Therefore, we must become humble servants if we are followers of Jesus.

Peggy Noonan, a biographer of Ronald Reagan, interviewed a friend of Reagan's for her book *When Character Was King*. "'What you have to understand,'" Mrs. Jorgensen says, "'the key about Ronnie is this: I knew him as a movie actor, as a Governor of the State of California, as President of the United States, and the thing about him is he never changed. He was humble. He had no sense of entitlement. It wasn't about him, ever.'"

Richard Halverson, on his appointment as chaplain to the United States Senate, recoiled at the idea of using the position as a platform to speak to the nation. "That would be an awful abuse of this position. I go there to be a servant to the senators, their families, and their staffs, not to find a platform to speak to the nation." He asked, "When you pray for me, pray that I'll stay invisible."

The late Dawson Trotman, founder of the Christian ministry The Navigators, was visiting Taiwan on one of his overseas trips. During the visit, he hiked with a Taiwanese pastor into one of the mountain villages to meet with some of the local Christians. The roads and trails were wet, and their shoes became very muddy. Later, someone asked this Taiwanese pastor what he remembered most about Dawson Trotman. Without hesitation, the man replied, "He cleaned my shoes." How surprised this humble pastor must have been to arise in the morning and realize that the Christian leader from America had risen before him and cleaned the mud from his shoes. A spirit of servanthood marked Dawson Trotman throughout his Christian life. He died as he lived, actually giving his life to rescue someone else from drowning. That's servanthood.

Am I a servant? Do I look for ways to serve people around me? Does someone at church or work need a listening ear, an encouraging word, a warm hug, or even a loving challenge? Does my spouse need more attention, affirmation, affection, or help at home? Do my children need my time, my hugs, or my discipline? Who is God calling me to serve today?

*Indeed, I count everything as loss because of the sur-
passing worth of knowing Christ Jesus my Lord. For
his sake I have suffered the loss of all things and count
them as rubbish, in order that I may gain Christ.*

The main reason you exist is to know God. Paul understood that. His life had been so transformed by the love and grace of Jesus Christ that he never recovered. For the rest of his life, his passion was to know Christ. Paul understood that this was the privilege of human life.

J.I. Packer, in his classic book *Knowing God,* wrote:

> What were we made for? To know God. What aim should we set ourselves in life? To know God. What is the "eternal life" that Jesus gives? Knowledge of God. "This is life eternal, that they might know thee, the only true God, and Jesus Christ, whom thou hast sent" (John 17:3). What is the best thing in life, bringing more joy, delight, and contentment, than anything else? Knowledge of God.

And Jim Elliot, who was martyred as a young man in the jungles of Ecuador, gave eloquent voice in his journal to the glory of knowing Christ, as seen in his wife Elisabeth's book *Shadow of the Almighty*:

> I walked out to the hill just now. It is exalting, delicious. To stand embraced by the shadows of a friendly tree with the wind tugging at your coattails and the heavens hailing your heart–to gaze and glory and to give oneself again to God, what more could a man ask? Oh the fullness, pleasure, sheer excitement of knowing God on earth. I care not if I ever raise my voice again for him, if only I may love him, please him. Mayhap in mercy he shall give me a host of children that I may lead through the vast star fields, to explore his delicacies, whose finger-ends set them to burning. But if not, if only I may see him, touch his garments, and smile into my Lover's eyes–ah, then, not stars, nor children shall matter–only himself.

Philippians 3:13

Brothers, I do not consider that I have made it my own. But one thing I do: forgetting what lies behind and straining forward to what lies ahead.

The ability to remember can be a good thing, but the ability to forget can be a great thing.

When it comes to the spiritual life, we must diligently forget many things. Forget your failures, your sins, your regrets, your hurts by other people. Forget what lies behind.

Of course, Paul realized we had to deal with these things in a healthy manner: confessing and repenting your sins, apologizing for your wrongdoings, grieving your losses, and forgiving those who hurt you. This is all clear in the Bible. But there comes a time when we forget the past, when we turn from the past to the future and pursue the prize of knowing Christ with single-minded abandon. There is no virtue in turning away from the prize of Christ and looking back at your failures. Fix your eyes on Christ.

In May 1954, Oxford University medical student Roger Bannister was the first man to break the four-minute mile. A month later, John Landy of Australia broke Bannister's world record by 1.4 seconds. This caused a spirited debate on who was the world's best miler: Landy or Bannister? A few months later, in August 1954, they raced each other in Vancouver, Canada. The race was close from start to finish. Coming down the final stretch, Landy and Bannister were neck and neck, with Landy slightly ahead. Landy looked back to see where Bannister was, and Bannister sprinted by on his other side to win the race. Later, Landy lamented, "If I hadn't looked around, I would have won."

Don't look back. Focus on the prize. Win the race.

Philippians 4:4

Rejoice in the Lord always; again I will say, rejoice.

Choose to rejoice. Choose to rejoice always. Choose to rejoice always in the Lord.

We know Paul feels this deeply because he gives the command twice, as if to say, "This is so important. Rejoice! Do it!"

This is not a recommendation but a command. Make a choice to rejoice in God. Choose to respond with joy regardless of the circumstances or the situation. Even when there's bad news. Even when there's heartbreaking news.

I don't imagine that God is telling us to have a feeling of happiness. I know he's not telling us to paste a plastic smile on our face (God is never for phoniness). Rather, God is telling us to take action. Rejoice, praise God, give thanks, worship God in song, cite a passage on God's goodness and faithfulness, express in prayer that God can be trusted: all of these are ways to rejoice.

If we obeyed this command, it would transform most of our lives. When you get criticized, rejoice. When your car breaks down, rejoice. When you experience physical pain, rejoice. When you lose your job, rejoice. No matter what happens, rejoice.

That's what God says, isn't it? Rejoice in the Lord always.

It seems crazy. But behind this countercultural, counterintuitive command is the conviction that God is good, can be trusted, will have the final word, is still on his throne, and will redeem this problem. God is God.

So do it. Rejoice in the Lord always.

Philippians 4:6-7

Do not be anxious about anything, but in everything by prayer and supplication with thanksgiving let your requests be made known to God. And the peace of God, which surpasses all understanding, will guard your hearts and your minds in Christ Jesus.

Just about all of us struggle at times with worry. I certainly do. We struggle with worry because life can be so unsettling and uncertain. At times, life is painful.

Philippians 4:6-7 is God's antidote to worry. So many times over the years, I have cited these words to myself or I have prayed them over someone.

"Do not be anxious about anything." Worry about nothing, absolutely nothing.

"But in everything." Everything. Every single worry. No worry is too big or too small for God.

"By prayer and supplication with thanksgiving." Include thanksgiving to God: Father, thank you that you have delivered me in the past and that you will deliver me in this problem too.

"Let your requests be made known to God." Ask God to take care of the problem. Bring your burdens to God and leave them there.

"And the peace of God, which surpasses all understanding." This peace does not come because I understand everything or because I have it all figured out. It is supernatural, suprarational peace from God.

"Will guard your hearts and your minds in Christ Jesus." Ah! That's what I need, Lord. That's what I need. Your peace, guarding my heart, filling my soul.

God's solution for worry: worry about nothing; pray about everything.

Philippians 4:13

I can do all things through him who strengthens me.

In Philippians 4, Paul is talking about contentment. He has learned to be content with very little and to be content with plenty. He then says that the key to this contentment is not in him, but in Christ: "I can do all things through him who strengthens me." The key to contentment is Christ's transforming power.

But this principle applies to all of life. "I can do all things." Where do you struggle? Worry? Fear? Jealousy? Guilt? Anger? Temper? Depression? Loneliness? Addiction?

The power to change is not in you. It's in Christ. Pray, "Lord, I cannot do this, but you can. Would you please change me? I can do all things through him who strengthens me."

When I was a young Christian at Rice University, learning to live in dependence on God, I heard a little saying that I wrote in the fly page of my Bible: "When I try, I fail. When I trust, I succeed."

That's the heart of Paul in Philippians 4:13.

"I can do all things through him who strengthens me."

Colossians 1:13

*He has delivered us from the domain of darkness and
transferred us to the kingdom of his beloved Son.*

Hardly anything in life is as exciting and thrilling for the soul as
a dramatic rescue. Think of a child who has been kidnapped,
a couple who is lost in the mountains, a crew lost at sea, a man
taken hostage by a guerilla army, or POWs in a World War II
concentration camp. The rescue is thrilling beyond words.

But of all rescues, there is no rescue quite like this one. God
rescued us from the kingdom of darkness, from an eternity away
from him, and brings us into the kingdom of his Son, the kingdom
of light and love.

The Bible tells us that all people were in the domain of darkness.
We were spiritually dead, slaves to sin, blinded by Satan, rebels
against God, immersed in a prison of self-centeredness, headed for
a Christ-less eternity, and we could do nothing about it. We were
helpless and hopeless, locked in the kingdom of darkness.

But then, in the most beautiful of rescues, Christ intervenes
decisively and rescues us out of death and darkness. He transfers
us to a place of life and light, a land of love and grace, a haven of
peace, rest, and every good thing. It is the rescue of all rescues.

Mother Teresa's incredible ministry of love and compassion
was located in a temple of a Hindu goddess in Calcutta. This
goddess, Kali, was the goddess of vengeance and destruction, and
she was depicted with an evil, horrible face.

David Bryant tells the story of visiting that temple and being
surrounded by dirt, blood, and noise. People were slitting the
throats of animals to sacrifice and throwing coins at the image of
Kali. It was a place filled with gloom and darkness.

But then he walked around the corner into a wing of the
temple that Mother Teresa had rented. When you entered their
space, everything was spotless, clean, white, and peaceful. There
was a bright atmosphere of love, tenderness, and joy as the nuns
cared for the poor and the dying. The difference between the two
places could hardly have been more dramatic. It was a picture of
what God did for you when he rescued you from the kingdom of
eternal darkness and transferred you to the kingdom of his own
much-loved Son.

Colossians 1:15

*He is the image of the invisible God, the firstborn
of all creation.*

In Colossians 1:15-23, we have one of the greatest passages in the Bible on the glory of Christ. The passage begins with the sublime statement: "He is the image of the invisible God."

This means that Christ is the very image of God. He is the exact representation of God, for he is God. The Son of God is indeed God the Son. In Christ, the invisible God takes visible form. When you see Jesus, you see God. Jesus once said to Philip, "Whoever has seen me has seen the Father" (John 14:9).

So many people have distorted ideas about who God is and have rejected a God who doesn't even exist. They have rejected a caricature of God.

If you want to know what God is like, then look at Jesus, for Jesus is the image of the invisible God.

The phrase "firstborn of all creation" has been abused and distorted by cults. The term does not mean that Jesus was created, as Jehovah's Witnesses suggest.

In the ancient Near East, to be a firstborn meant much more than it does in our culture. To be the firstborn son meant you had a position of privilege and honor. Over time, the term "firstborn" was used as a title of honor even when it was not talking about the oldest son.

For example, in Exodus 4:22, God calls Israel his firstborn. This simply means that Israel was specially chosen and loved by God, and has no reference to Israel being born or being an oldest son. It is simply a title of honor and privilege.

Even more clear is the reference to David in Psalm 89:27: "I will make him [David] the firstborn." David was not the oldest boy; indeed, he was the youngest. But he was the son of Jesse that God honored and exalted.

So what does this title mean in Colossians 1:15? To say that Christ is the firstborn of all creation is to say that he has priority over all, just as an oldest son has priority over other sons. Jesus Christ has the place of preeminence, honor, and glory in the universe. He has the place of supremacy above all. He is the King of kings and Lord of lords. There is no one like him.

No wonder Augustine once wrote of Christ, "In my wounded heart I saw your splendor, and it dazzled me."

Are you dazzled by the splendor of Christ?

Colossians 1:16

*For by him all things were created, in heaven and
on earth, visible and invisible, whether thrones or
dominions or rulers or authorities – all things were
created through him and for him.*

Ponder the immense size of our solar system, then the size of our
galaxy, then the size of the universe. Here is a picture painted
by Philip Yancey in *Prayer*:

> If the Milky Way galaxy were the size of the entire
> continent of North America, our solar system would fit
> in a coffee cup. Even now two Voyager spacecrafts are
> hurtling toward the edge of the solar system at a rate of
> 100,000 miles per hour. For almost three decades they
> have been speeding away from earth, approaching a
> distance of nine billion miles. When engineers beam a
> command to the spacecraft at the speed of light, it takes
> thirteen hours to arrive. Yet this vast neighborhood of
> our sun—in truth the size of a coffee cup—fits along
> with several hundred billion other stars and their
> minions in the Milky Way, one of perhaps 100 billion
> such galaxies in the universe. To send a light-speed
> message to the edge of that universe would take 15
> billion years.

The universe is so big. And just think, this stunningly vast
universe was created by Christ, by his mere word. Jesus of
Nazareth, who was born to a Jewish teenager, who walked the
dusty streets of Judea, and who was executed like a common
criminal. This Jesus created the galaxies.

Jesus was fully man, but he was no mere man. He was so much
more. He is the God who became man without ceasing to be God.

Colossians 1:16 gives emphasis to Jesus as Creator by these
three phrases: "in heaven and on earth, visible and invisible,
whether thrones or dominions or rulers or authorities." Jesus
created all things, including all angelic beings, in the universe.

And then, in case we have not fully grasped the point, Paul
says again, "all things were created through him and for him."
Jesus Christ is both the cause of creation and the goal of creation.
He is the starting point of creation and the end point of creation.
We live in a Christ-centered universe. Such is the greatness and
grandeur of the glory of Jesus Christ.

Colossians 1:18

And he is the head of the body, the church. He is the
beginning, the firstborn from the dead, that in
everything he might be preeminent.

We inhabit one planet belonging to a solar system in one small part of a vast galaxy of stars, and there are a hundred billion of these vast galaxies.

Jesus Christ is preeminent over all of this. Not just over our lives, our country, our planet, our solar system, or our galaxy, but over the entirety of creation. Out of all that there is or ever will be, one person is preeminent, and that person is Jesus Christ.

Some people say that Jesus was just a great teacher of morals, but they have no idea who he really is. The person who has preeminence and supremacy over the cosmos is no mere man. Oh no! He is so much more. He is the very God, Creator of all things everywhere, exalted and infinite, King of kings and Lord of lords, dazzling in the splendor of his glory

Christ not only has preeminence over the vast stretches of the cosmos, but he also must have preeminence in my life. This primacy of Christ means I depend upon him, worship him, serve him, love him, and follow him. It means a life lived for Christ: not my dreams, my wants, my desires, my comforts, or my security, but Christ's calling for me. As Paul succinctly put it in Philippians, "For to me to live is Christ."

There is a classic story of the renowned composer Arturo Toscanini:

> One evening he brilliantly conducted Beethoven's Ninth Symphony. The audience went mad; people clapped, whistled, and stomped their feet. Toscanini bowed and bowed and bowed. He signaled to the orchestra, and its members stood to acknowledge the wild applause. Eventually the applause began to subside. With the quieting applause in the background, Toscanini turned, looked intently at his musicians, and almost uncontrollably exclaimed, "Gentlemen! Gentlemen!" The gentlemen in the orchestra leaned forward to listen. Why was the maestro so disturbed? Was he angry? Had somebody missed a cue? Had the

orchestra flawed the performance? No. Toscanini was not angry. Toscanini was stirred to the very depths of his being by the sheer magnificence of Beethoven's music. Scarcely able to talk, he whispered fiercely, "Gentlemen, I am nothing." That was an extraordinary admission since Toscanini was blessed with an enormous ego. "Gentlemen," he added, "you are nothing." That was hardly news. The members of the orchestra had often heard the same message in rehearsal. "But Beethoven," said Toscanini in a tone of adoration, "is everything, everything, everything."

This must be our perspective about Christ. Christ is everything, everything, everything.

Colossians 2:13-14

And you, who were dead in your trespasses and the uncircumcision of your flesh, God made alive together with him, having forgiven us all our trespasses, by canceling the record of debt that stood against us with its legal demands. This he set aside, nailing it to the cross.

When God saves us, he gives us spiritual life. He takes a person who is spiritually dead and makes them alive with the life of God. At the heart of this life-giving salvation is forgiveness: "Having forgiven us all our trespasses."

"All our trespasses." That's strong language. Every thought, word, and deed that's displeasing to God, every single one. Past trespasses, present trespasses, and future trespasses. "All our trespasses."

What did Christ do with all those sins? He paid for them with his own death. He canceled the record of debt that stood against us by nailing it to the cross.

In the Roman Empire, when you had a financial debt and you paid it off, the record of your debt was canceled. That's what Jesus did for our debt of sin: he paid it in full and canceled the record of debt.

God tells us that Christ nailed that debt to the cross. All your sins are written in a large book, and Christ is nailing that book of sins to the cross, canceling the debt by paying for it with his blood.

If we wallow in guilt and self-flagellation for sins that Christ has already paid for, we despise Christ's sacrifice. We waste it.

A few years ago, on a rainy, cold February day, a limousine traveling down a New Jersey expressway got a flat tire. The limo driver got out to change the tire, only to discover that the spare was flat. Before he could call road service, a man in a pickup truck stopped and offered to help. Among the equipment on his truck was an air tank. As the man and the driver finished up, the car window slid down, and the man was shocked to see Donald Trump sitting inside.

"This was very nice of you to stop and help," Trump said. "What can I do to thank you?"

The man thought for a moment and said, "Tomorrow is Valentine's Day. My wife would really get a kick out of receiving a dozen roses from you." Trump agreed and drove off. The next day, a messenger arrived with a box. Inside were two dozen roses and a note:

> "Happy Valentine's Day from a friend of
> your husband.
> > Donald Trump
>
> P.S. Thanks for helping us out. By the way, I
> paid off your mortgage."

If the mortgage is paid for you, you are free of the debt. You don't do anything to earn it or pay it back. You simply say thank you.

If the debt of sin is paid for you, you are free of the debt. You do nothing to earn it or pay it back. You simply say thank you.

Colossians 3:12-13

Put on then, as God's chosen ones, holy and beloved,
compassionate hearts, kindness, humility, meekness,
and patience, bearing with one another and, if one
has a complaint against another, forgiving each other;
as the Lord has forgiven you,
so you also must forgive.

If we are in Christ, we are new creatures, and we must live like it. We cannot live like we once lived because we are not the people we once were.

In Colossians 3, God gives us eight traits that characterize this new life, but first he reminds us of our new identity. We are God's chosen ones, adopted by the Father. That God chose us reminds us that God loves us and that we are special to God. Moreover, we are holy. We are saints. We are blameless before God because we are in Christ. We are beloved by God. We are the objects of the Father's tender affection.

With this assurance of our new identity, we are ready to adopt these eight traits, to firmly and decisively live this way:

First, live with a compassionate heart. Care about people, about suffering, about hurts. See people as God sees them.

Second, put on kindness. Kindness in your voice, your smile, your eyes, your touch, your actions.

Third, take on humility. Humble yourself. Focus on Christ and others, not yourself. Lie low and exalt Jesus.

Fourth, live with meekness. Be gentle, not harsh or demanding. Be tender with people.

Fifth, take on patience. Choose to be easy to live with, not irritable, difficult, or quick-tempered.

Sixth, bear with one another. Be patient with people. Don't fly off the handle. Choose to let some things go.

Seventh, forgive one another. Choose to forgive the person who has wronged you. Make the choice because God has forgiven you. Let them off the hook.

Eighth, put on love. All seven of the previous traits are about love. Love is the bottom line. "And above all these put on love which binds everything together in perfect harmony." (Col. 3:14)

You can live this way, characterized by all eight of these traits. You can live this way and you must live this way. Brook no excuse. Depend on Christ's power to obey the Lord, and live out these eight traits.

Colossians 3:23

Whatever you do, work heartily, as for the
Lord and not for men.

Whatever your work is, give it your best, give one hundred percent. Be the best teacher, engineer, businessman, pilot, homemaker, nursery worker, musician, athlete, or student you can be. Don't be half-hearted. This honors Christ.

One month before he was assassinated, Dr. Martin Luther King Jr. said this to sanitation workers in Memphis: "All labor has value. If you're a street sweeper, sweep streets the way Michelangelo painted pictures. Sweep streets the way Beethoven composed music. Sweep streets the way Shakespeare wrote poetry. Sweep streets in such a profound way that the Host of Heaven will say, 'There goes a great street sweeper.'"

Moreover, not only do your best, but do it for the Lord. When it comes to work, this is *the* principle behind every other. You don't work for the boss, your supervisor, the CEO, your coworkers, your customers, the shareholders, for a paycheck, or for retirement. No, you work for the Lord.

In the classic movie *Chariots of Fire*, which is based on a true story, there is a great contrast between two 100-meter runners. Harold Abrahams reflected before the Olympic 100-meter finals, "I've got ten seconds to justify my entire existence." Clearly, Abrahams felt enormous pressure to prove that he was a somebody.

By contrast, when Eric Liddell, a devoted follower of Christ, was discussing his running with his sister Jenny, he remarks to her in a lighthearted way, "God made me fast. When I run, I feel his pleasure." Liddell understood what it meant to do his work, including the work of running, for the Lord.

Whatever our work is, whether it is the work of an athlete or the work of an engineer, whether it is yard work or homework, in every form of work, do it for the Lord. When you work for the Lord, it transforms your work into worship.

Colossians 4:12

Epaphras, who is one of you, a servant of Christ Jesus,
greets you, always struggling on your behalf in his
prayers, that you may stand mature and fully
assured in all the will of God.

You've got to love Epaphras. He is from the city of Colossae, but now he is in Rome with Paul. Yet his heart is still in Colossae with his people, so he prays for them, and how he does pray.

He struggles in prayer. What does it mean to struggle in prayer? I'm not completely sure, but I am sure what it is to not struggle: to pray a tepid, lifeless, soulless, or mechanical prayer. No, Epaphras struggles in prayer for his people. He goes to battle, storms the gates, attacks the hill. The prayer has heart, life, passion.

"O God! Please intervene. You've just got to protect them, deliver them, rescue them."

Moreover, not only does Epaphras struggle in prayer for them, he is always struggling in prayer for them. Not just on rare occasions but continually, day in and day out.

And what does he pray? That the Colossians would stand mature with God, right in the middle of God's will, mature and fully assured of where they stand with God. Epaphras is praying for a healthy and strong spiritual life so that they would be all God wanted them to be.

Let me ask: Wouldn't it be something to have an Epaphras or two praying for you?

Wouldn't it be something to have a whole church full of Epaphrases going to battle for each other and for the kingdom?

Wouldn't it be something?

1 Thessalonians 5:17

Pray without ceasing.

This three-word command seems impossible at first glance, yet we know that our Father doesn't give us commands to defeat and frustrate us. He gives us commands for our good. What is God telling us here? Be in an attitude of prayer all the time. Live your life in the presence of God. Realize that God is right there with you throughout the day and night. Sense, remember, and enjoy his presence. Talk with him throughout the day.

The idea is to have an ongoing conversation with God: talking, listening, singing, thanking, asking, interceding, praising, confessing, laughing, and weeping. It is a life lived in God's presence, enjoying God throughout the day.

Maybe it's a bit like a persistent cough. That cough is in your throat throughout the day, ready to erupt into an actual cough at any moment. Similarly, we are in an attitude of prayer throughout the day, ready to erupt into actual prayer at any moment.

We're driving to work, talking with God about our day: about a project, about a conflict, about an important meeting. We're playing with our preschooler on the living room floor and we breathe a prayer of thanksgiving. We're at our desk, working away, and we pray for wisdom at various points. We're walking to our car and remember a friend who needs a job, and we lift our friend to God. We're driving to the grocery store with a worship CD in the stereo, and we're singing to God.

It's life lived before God. It's not a burden or a discipline to practice, but an attitude to adopt. "God is here with me, right now and all the time."

Lord, teach us to pray. Teach me to pray. Teach us what it means to live life in your presence, praying without ceasing.

1 Thessalonians 5:18 (NASB)

In everything give thanks; for this is God's will for you
in Christ Jesus.

I imagine that this is one of the most disobeyed commands in the New Testament.

Do you find yourself giving thanks to God in all circumstances, both in good times and in bad? This is God's will and God's call to you.

Thank him when you get a promotion, and thank him when you get fired. Thank him when you are healthy, and thank him when you get sick. Thank him when you succeed, and thank him when you fail. Thank him when you make money, and thank him when you lose money. Thank him when your car runs, and thank him when your car won't start.

In everything, give thanks.

Do you do that?

To be clear: this verse does not tell us to thank God for everything, but to thank God *in* everything, in every situation and circumstance.

Say someone you love gets involved in adultery. You don't thank God for the sin of adultery, but you can still give thanks. "Lord, as bad as this is, I thank you for still caring about my friend. Lord, thank you that you can bring good out of this horrible situation. Thank you that your grace is bigger than our sin. Thank you."

Giving thanks shows faith that God is bigger than your problem. Giving thanks shows faith that we can trust God no matter what.

Giving thanks has always been the surefire mark of the people who trust their God.

1 Timothy 6:17

As for the rich in this present age, charge them not to be haughty, nor to set their hopes on the uncertainty of riches, but on God, who richly provides us with everything to enjoy.

Who are the rich? Does that word apply to Bill Gates, Warren Buffett, and the others who make a gazillion dollars? Is it the people in your community who live in mansions? Is it anyone who makes a lot more money than you?

There's nothing wrong with being rich, nothing at all. But there is a danger. If you are rich, your tendency is to put your hope in your wealth. Your tendency is to trust your assets, your resources, your income, your investments, and your 401(k). Your tendency is to trust your wealth, saying, "I just want security for my family," rather than to trust your God.

There are two problems, noted in 1 Timothy 6:17, with trusting wealth. First of all, it is haughty. It is haughty to put your hope in wealth because that means you are not trusting God, dependent on God, or desperate before God. In fact, you are only trusting yourself. In effect, you are saying to God, "I can do it myself. I don't need you." That, my friends, is haughtiness.

There's a second problem with trusting wealth: wealth is uncertain, and you can't depend on it. You have $100,000 in the stock market, and then suddenly it's only $50,000. What happened to the $50,000? It sprouted wings and flew with the wind. Houses, jobs, income, savings, and the stock market—they're all so uncertain. So many people today know this from first-hand experience.

The problem is not money; the problem is trusting money. The problem is depending upon money, loving money, thinking that money will make you happy.

You can enjoy the things God gives you, for he "richly provides us with everything to enjoy." He is a good and generous God. Enjoy his gifts, but put your hope only in the giver.

2 Timothy 1:7

*For God gave us a spirit not of fear but of power
and love and self-control.*

Whenever we are tempted to give way to fear or timidity, we must remember Paul's words to Timothy: God has not given us a spirit of fear. That's not who we are. That's not the Spirit of Christ Jesus in us.

Instead, God has given us a spirit of power, love, and self-control. That's who we are, because of the risen, all-powerful, all-loving, all-disciplined Christ within us. His presence changes everything.

In *Seeing With Our Souls*, Joan Chittister recounts a story about a man who had this kind of courage. The story, perhaps legendary, comes from the literature of the monastics and tells of a time when a great army invaded a country and left a path of destruction. Their greatest wrath was reserved for the monks:

> When the invaders arrived in one of the villages... the leader of the village reported to the commander, "All the monks, hearing of your approach, fled to the mountains."
>
> The commander smiled a broad, cold smile, for he was proud of having a reputation for being a very fearsome person.
>
> But then the leader added, "All, that is, but one."
>
> The commander became enraged. He marched to the monastery and kicked in the gate. There in the courtyard stood the one remaining monastic. The commander glowered at the figure. "Do you know who I am?" the commander demanded. "I am he who can run you through with a sword without batting an eyelash."
>
> And the monastic fixed the commander with a serene and patient look and said, "And do you know who I am? I am one who can let you run me through with a sword without batting an eyelash."

That's the fearless spirit of the risen Christ within us.

2 Timothy 2:2

And what you have heard from me in the presence of
many witnesses entrust to faithful men who
will be able to teach others also.

Paul knew he was near death. At any time, the Roman Emperor Nero could execute him. Paul was passing the baton of ministry to his protégé, Timothy. Timothy was to take that baton and pass it on to faithful men, who in turn were to pass it on to others. That makes four runners in the relay of discipleship: Paul, to Timothy, to faithful men, to others.

We stand in this legacy today, the legacy of discipleship. Now it is our turn. We too must disciple others, who in turn will disciple others. This is God's way: life-on-life discipleship.

If you traveled to Montreal, Canada, and you visited the home of the Montreal Canadiens hockey team, you would be going to a place with a rich legacy. You would visit one of the fabled sports dynasties of our time. What the New York Yankees once were in baseball, and what the Boston Celtics once were in basketball, the Montreal Canadiens once were in hockey. Over a forty-year period, from 1953-1993, the Canadiens dominated the league, winning twenty-four Stanley Cup championships.

If you visited their arena in Montreal, I understand you would see huge banners hanging from the ceiling, celebrating world championship after world championship. After seeing these banners, if you had the opportunity to visit the locker room, you would be surrounded by trophies, photographs, and other mementos of their sterling dynasty in the history of sports.

Every rookie who made the team would be surrounded by this rich legacy as he walked into the locker room. He would read these words emblazoned on the locker room wall: "Hold the Torch High." And those rookies would feel a charge, a mandate, and a responsibility to hold the torch high for the Montreal Canadiens hockey team.

That's our charge as disciples. Hold the torch high.

2 Timothy 3:16

All Scripture is breathed out by God and profitable
for teaching, for reproof, for correction, and for
training in righteousness.

Coming to the end of his life, Paul writes to his young disciple, Timothy, that all Scripture is breathed out by God. Let that sink in: the words of the Bible come from the very breath of God.

This is a book like no other book, and these are words like no other words. These words are full of life, power, and grace. These words can transform lives and change eternities. These words are God's own words.

There are so many words today: in e-mail, Twitter, Facebook, newspapers, magazines, books, radio, television, and junk mail. So many words, but they are all human words. The words of the Bible are God's words, breathed out by the Spirit of God.

We need to hear them, read them, and heed them.

I cannot convey how much this book has meant to me. Taking time to soak in these words day after day for more than forty years has meant the world to me. God has revealed himself to me. He has shown me who he is and who I am. He has shown me the nature of life, truth, and reality.

He has met me. He has encouraged me. He has guided me.

In the darkest times of my life, when I felt overwhelmed, undone, and not sure that I would make it, the Bible has been a rock to stand on, a sure foundation in the storms of life.

There is no replacement. There is no substitute for this book.

Abraham Lincoln once wrote, "I believe the Bible is the best gift that God has ever given to man. All the good from the Savior of the world is communicated to us through this book. I have been driven many times to my knees by the overwhelming conviction that I had nowhere else to go."

Every day, get alone with God and an open Bible, and breathe in these words. Words of truth, words of hope, words of life. Words breathed by God.

2 Timothy 4:7

I have fought the good fight, I have finished the race,
I have kept the faith.

In my twenties, as a professional distance runner, I ran marathons around the world. My concern for these 26.2-mile races was not to start well, but to finish well. In fact, I wanted to run the last half of the race faster than the first half.

The spiritual life is a marathon, not a sprint, and God wants us to finish strong. As Paul neared the finish line of his life, he could testify, "I have fought the good fight, I have finished the race, I have kept the faith." Three staccato statements that make the same point: I finished the course God gave me. I endured faithfully to the end.

Interestingly, Paul uses the perfect tense because the finish line was so close. It's a done deal.

The journey wasn't easy. There was pain and suffering, hard work and toil, difficulty and danger. In fact, our words *agony* and *agonize* come from the Greek words for *fight* and *fought*, as if Paul is saying, "I have agonized the good agony." It was tough, but he endured.

That's what God has called you to do: endure, faithful to the end, and finish strong.

William Wilberforce exemplified endurance and finishing well. After his conversion to Christianity as a young man, he began a tireless battle in British Parliament to pass legislation to end the slave trade. He proposed bills in 1789, 1791, 1792, 1794, 1796, 1798, and 1799. They all failed. But in 1806, nineteen years after he began his battle, a bill was passed in Parliament that prohibited British ships from being used in the slave trade.

For the rest of his life, he continued to fight for the complete abolition of slavery.

In 1831, near the end of his life, he wrote, "Our motto must continue to be perseverance. And ultimately I trust the Almighty will crown our efforts with success."

In 1833, both houses of Parliament passed the Abolition of Slavery bill. Three days later, William Wilberforce died. He was buried in Westminster Abbey in national recognition of his forty-five years of struggle on behalf of African slaves.

Here is a man who could say, as Paul said, "I have fought the good fight, I have finished the race, I have kept the faith."

Titus 3:5

*He saved us, not because of works done by us in
righteousness, but according to his own mercy, by the
washing of regeneration and renewal
of the Holy Spirit.*

The Bible is clear and emphatic: God saves us. We don't save ourselves, we don't earn our salvation. God saves us by his mercy, not because of our good works.

Yet, though the Bible is clear and emphatic, the human tendency is to not believe the gospel of grace and revert to the religion of works.

What's the difference between religion and the gospel? Religion is all about doing. The gospel is all about receiving.

Religion is my work for God. The gospel is God's work for me.

Religion is the performance plan. The gospel is the grace plan.

With religion, I obey to be accepted. With the gospel, I obey because I'm accepted.

Religion focuses on rule-keeping. The gospel focuses on the cross of Christ.

With religion, I serve God out of fear and insecurity. With the gospel, I serve God out of grateful love.

With religion, my identity is based on how I measure up. With the gospel, my identity is based on Christ's love and grace.

With religion, I feel pride when I measure up and guilt when I fail. With the gospel, I feel neither pride, because God did it all, nor guilt, because I'm completely forgiven.

With religion, I see God as harsh. With the gospel, I see God as gracious.

What do you have: religion or the gospel?

Hebrews 4:12

For the word of God is living and active, sharper
than any two-edged sword, piercing to the
division of soul and of spirit, of joints and of marrow,
and discerning the thoughts
and intentions of the heart.

The Bible is not a dry, dead, or dusty theological tome. Oh no! It is alive. It is the living, breathing Word of God. If you come to the Bible with an open and humble heart, ready to meet God and obey God, then God will meet you in the pages of Scripture and speak to you. Martin Luther once wrote, "The Bible is alive, it speaks to me; it has feet, it runs after me; it has hands, it lays hold on me."

Not only is the Bible alive, but it is active and powerful. The word translated as "active" is a Greek word behind our word *energy*. The term carries the idea of transforming or explosive power. The Bible is powerful enough to change lives. The Spirit uses the Word to transform the people of God.

The purpose of the Bible is not to satisfy our curiosity, but to change our lives. The goal is transformation, not information.

To be more specific, as you spend time in the Bible with a heart humble before God, over weeks and months and years, God will change you:

· You will worry less and trust God more.
· Your fears will diminish and your faith will grow.
· You will become less self-centered and self-absorbed, and more other-centered and unselfish.
· You will understand more of God's heart for you, and you will rest in his love.
· Your outbursts of anger and sullen resentment will vanish. A heart of forgiveness and grace will grow.
· The power of money and greed will subside.
· The strangleholds of addiction will be broken.

These changes and others may not happen overnight, but over time, you will become a different person. God will change you from the inside out.

Not only is the Bible alive and powerful, it is also piercing and penetrating. It pierces to the core of our being, to the essence of who we are.

The Bible is like a surgeon's scalpel. God is the surgeon who wields his scalpel to help us, not hurt us.

When the Bible talks about soul and spirit, joints and marrow, the point is not to give lessons in psychology or anatomy, but to say that no part of us is immune from this scalpel. The Bible penetrates the impenetrable and extricates the inextricable.

All about us there is a flood of words, and most of these words are shallow words, surface words, superficial words–but not God's words. These words are the most penetrating words in the universe. The Bible exposes who we really are. The Bible reveals our blind spots, which are blind to us, but usually not to others. The Bible even uncovers our secret motives. It pierces.

In a passage from James Bryan Smith and Brennan Manning's biography of Rich Mullins, the singer reflects on the Bible:

> The Bible is not a book for the faint of heart—it is a book full of all the greed and glory and violence and tenderness and sex and betrayal that befits mankind. It is not the collection of pretty little anecdotes mouthed by pious church mice—it does not so much nibble at our shoe leather as it cuts to the heart and splits the marrow from the bone. It does not give us answers fitted to our small-minded questions, but truth that goes beyond what we even know to ask.

What an amazing book the Bible is. Alive, powerful, piercing. There is no book like this book.

Hebrews 9:27

And just as it is appointed for men to die once, and after that comes judgment.

The Moken, often called "sea gypsies," are a small nomadic tribe of 181 fishermen that spend most of the year on their boats fishing in the Andaman Sea, from India to Indonesia and back to Thailand. However, they spend their Decembers living in shelters on the beaches of Thailand. In December 2004, in the hours before the infamous tsunami crashed ashore, the Moken were living on those beaches. They were in harm's way and would have likely all perished had they not listened to their elders.

In a 2004 article, "How Sea Gypsies Survived the Tsunami," Roger Thomas explained how for generations, the elders of the tribe had passed along one piece of wisdom. According to the tribe's sixty-five-year-old village chief, Sarmao Kathalay, that wisdom was this: "The elders told us that if the water recedes fast, it will reappear in the same quantity in which it disappeared."

And that is exactly what happened. The sea drained quickly from the beach, leaving stranded fish flopping on the shore. How easy it would have been for those who live near the sea to run down and fill every basket available with fish. Some people did just that in other areas of southern Thailand, but not the Moken. When the water receded from the beach, the tribal chief ordered each one of the 181 tribal members to run to a temple in the mountains of South Surin Island. When the waters crashed ashore, the 181 sea gypsies were safe on high ground.

The Moken had been warned, and they heeded the warning to their great benefit.

God has also warned us of a coming tsunami: a tsunami of judgment. In passages like Hebrews 9:27, there is the clear warning that judgment follows death. There is no biblical evidence for another opportunity after death to trust Christ as Savior.

We have been warned of coming judgment. But there is grace available now, found in Jesus, free for the taking.

Hebrews 11:1

Now faith is the assurance of things hoped for,
the conviction of things not seen.

Peter Kuzmic, a theologian from Croatia, once wrote, "Hope is the ability to hear the music of the future; faith is the courage to dance to it today."

Faith and hope go together, don't they?

The first verse of Hebrews 11, often called the "Hall of Faith" chapter, describes faith. The point is not that faith is absolute certainty with no doubts whatsoever. The rest of the chapter makes it clear that the emphases of this verse are the phrases "things hoped for" and "things not seen."

Faith inevitably involves the future, the hoped for, the things not yet seen. Faith involves the unknown, the unseen, and the unsettled.

For example, say you are unemployed and desperately need a job. This is a faith opportunity, an opportunity to trust God. It involves the unknown, the unseen, and the unsettled. It involves things hoped for, things not yet seen.

You do not know exactly what will happen—the what, when, where, and how. So you trust God. You are not in control. In fact, faith means giving up control—something that's hard for most of us humans.

This is the nature of faith. Faith trusts God in the midst of uncertainty. Faith trusts God to come through for us, in his timing and in his way.

So when it comes to faith, the point is not that I have absolute certainty. In fact, I do not focus at all on how much faith I have. I do not focus on my faith at all. Rather, I focus on the object of my faith. I focus on God.

The issue is not the size of my faith, but the size of my God. Is God bigger than my problem? Is God bigger than my need?

Focus on your God, not on your faith.

Lord, help me to see you for the great God you are. Help me to put my trust in you for an unknown future. Amen.

Hebrews 11:6

And without faith it is impossible to please him, for whoever would draw near to God must believe that he exists and that he rewards those who seek him.

Hebrews 11 is one of the greatest chapters on faith in the Bible, and verse 6 is the pivotal verse in the chapter. This verse is a ringing clarion call to the absolute importance of faith: "And without faith it is impossible to please him."

Unless we trust in God and not ourselves, we cannot please God. Unless we believe that God will take care of us, we cannot please God. Unless we rely on God's power and not our own resources, we cannot please God.

At the end of your life, will it be said that you were a man or woman who lived by faith? Did you trust in God to come through for you? Did you have a faith that delighted the heart of God? Or by contrast, did you tend to rely upon your own resources as you went through life?

The Bible tells us, unequivocally, that it is impossible to please God unless we live by faith. I wonder: Why does faith matter so much to God? Why does it please the infinite God so much when we trust him?

Two things come to mind. First, it matters to God how we view him. Yes, God is the infinite God, but he is also the personal God. God has feelings too. If I see God as a stern taskmaster who is hard to please and hard to live with, this grieves his heart. But if I see God as bursting with tender love and relentless compassion, as a God who is patient, kind, and easy to live with, our God loves it.

My second thought: trusting God goes with loving God. Do you love a God that you don't trust with your heart? Do you trust a God that you don't feel a tender love and affection for? No, you don't. Trust in God and love for God are inextricably bound together, and God longs for us to love him back.

There are probably many reasons why your faith matters so much to God, but here are the two big reasons:

1. Your faith reflects the way you see God.
2. Your faith is directly tied to your love for God.

No wonder God tells us, "And without faith it is impossible to please him."

Hebrews 11:7

*By faith Noah, being warned by God concerning
events as yet unseen, in reverent fear constructed an
ark for the saving of his household. By this he condemned the world and became an heir of the
righteousness that comes by faith.*

Faith always involves the unseen. In 2 Corinthians 5:7, Paul declares, "We walk by faith, not by sight."

Faith involves the unseen God. Faith trusts in the yet unseen actions of God to deliver us, rescue us, and protect us. We trust God for that which is not yet visible to us.

Noah is a prime example. When God called Noah to build an enormous ark, there was no flood in sight. There was no rain. There was no storm. There was not even a decent beach.

And yet, God said to build it. So Noah, by faith, started building.

So often in our lives we want clarity. We want to see what God is doing, how God will deliver us, and exactly what will happen. But God is more concerned that we trust him on what is yet unclear and still unseen.

In *Ruthless Trust*, Brennan Manning tells a marvelous story about Mother Teresa:

> When the brilliant ethicist John Kavanaugh went to work for three months at "the house of the dying" in Calcutta, he was seeking a clear answer as to how best to spend the rest of his life. On the first morning there he met Mother Teresa. She asked, "And what can I do for you?
>
> Kavanaugh asked her to pray for him. "What do you want me to pray for?" she asked.
>
> He voiced the request that he had borne thousands of miles from the United States: "Pray that I have clarity."
>
> She said firmly, "No, I will not do that."
>
> When he asked her why, she said, "Clarity is the last thing you are clinging to and must let go of."
>
> When Kavanaugh commented that she always seemed to have the clarity he longed for, she laughed and said, "I have never had clarity; what I have always had is trust. So I will pray that you trust God."

God will give us clarity when we need it. Meanwhile, he wants us to trust him for the unseen, for the uncertain, for the unclear.

Hebrews 11:8

By faith Abraham obeyed when he was called to go
out to a place that he was to receive as an inheritance.
And he went out, not knowing
where he was going.

A braham does the impossible. He leaves his ancestral home, his people, his city, and all that he knows, and strikes out on a long and dangerous journey, not knowing where he will end up or if he will even arrive. In the ancient world, people did not do this sort of thing.

Abraham did it for one simple reason: faith. He trusted God enough to obey. He believed that God was God, and that if God told him to leave, then leaving was the best thing to do.

What will the life of faith look like for us? This is what we see in Abraham's life:

1. People of faith don't play it safe. Faith invariably involves risk, the unseen, and the unknown. If we go through life playing it safe, being comfortable and cozy, never on the edge, then we are not living by faith. For example, giving 10 percent of your income is an act of faith. *Will I have enough if I do that? It seems crazy,* you might think. People of faith don't play it safe. They live an adventure, trusting God to protect them and guide them.

2. People of faith obey God no matter what. We may not understand why we should obey. Abraham didn't understand why he needed to leave, what God would do, or how God would take care of him, but he obeyed. Understanding can wait, but not obedience. Faith obeys God no matter what. Is there something in your life right now where you need to obey, even if you don't understand everything?

3. People of faith are not immune from problems. God promised to make Abraham a great nation and as many descendants as the stars in the sky. But how long did Abraham wait for a son? Twenty-five years. Twenty-five interminable years. I hope you do not have to wait twenty-five years for whatever you're

waiting for, but we all wait at times. Living by faith does not mean exemption from problems; it simply means that we have the greatest problem solver already inside of us.

4. People of faith trust God for the impossible. It is impossible for a couple to have a child when a woman is ninety years old. But God loves to put us into impossible situations so that we have no other option except to trust him, because if there's any other option, we are inclined to take it. What is the biggest need in your life right now? Does it seem impossible to you? If so, remember God's words to Sarah: "Is anything too hard for the Lord?" (Gen. 18:14)

Hebrews 11:17-18

*By faith Abraham, when he was tested, offered up
Isaac, and he who had received the promises was in
the act of offering up his only son, of whom it was
said, "Through Isaac shall your offspring be named."*

Abraham and Sarah had waited twenty-five years for this boy.
He was the miracle baby born when they were way too old.

In *The Life You've Always Wanted*, John Ortberg describes
this baby in their old age:

> Take this child born in the geriatric ward, for which
> Medicare picked up the tab, this child named Isaac—
> which means "laughter." Abraham and Sarah laughed
> at first because they didn't believe; they laughed at the
> sheer impossibility of it. They laughed because they
> were told they would have a son when they reached an
> age when they didn't even dare to buy green bananas.
> And after the child was born, they laughed because
> they did believe. They laughed that when Sarah
> went to Wal-Mart, she was the only shopper to buy
> both Pampers and Depends. They laughed that both
> parents and the baby had to eat the same strained
> vegetables because nobody in the whole family had
> a single tooth.

Yet God was now calling Abraham to sacrifice this boy. It
seemed crazy.

But Abraham had walked with God a long time. He knew that
God was God, and that he, Abraham, was not. He knew that God
could be trusted, even in impossible situations.

Abraham obeyed God. He prepared to do the unthinkable.
But at the very last moment, God stopped him.

Abraham discovered again that God could be trusted.

Do you know that God is God and you are not? Do you know
that God can be trusted? Even when what he is asking you to do
seems outrageous?

In a ChristianityToday.com entry, the writer Brennan
Manning wrote of how much God loves it when we trust him:

The splendor of a human heart that trusts and is loved unconditionally gives God more pleasure than Westminster Cathedral, the Sistine Chapel, Beethoven's Ninth Symphony, Van Gogh's Sunflowers, the sight of 10,000 butterflies in flight, or the scent of a million orchids in bloom. Trust is our gift back to God, and he finds it so enchanting that Jesus died for love of it.

Father, may we be a people who delight your heart because we trust you.

Hebrews 11:28

By faith he kept the Passover and sprinkled the blood,
so that the Destroyer of the firstborn might
not touch them.

The tenth plague was the death of every firstborn male in Egypt. To prevent the plague from striking the Jewish firstborns, God told the Jews to do a most unusual thing.

Each family was to kill a lamb and then smear its blood around the front door of their home. What a messy, bloody activity. Why did God want such a bloody act?

Because God was teaching his people about sin, sacrifice, and substitution. He was teaching his people that sin is serious to a holy God, and that "without the shedding of blood there is no forgiveness of sins" (Heb. 9:22).

God was teaching his people about sacrifice. The penalty for sin was death (in the Bible, bloodshed symbolizes death). If sin was to be forgiven or atoned for, then a sacrifice must be paid. There had to be death.

Finally, God was teaching his people the spiritual truth of substitution. Because of our sin, we deserve to die, but God, in his mercy, allows a substitute, a lamb, to die in our place.

But the sacrifice of a mere animal could never really atone for human sin, so the sacrifice of countless animals in the Old Testament was just to foreshadow a substitute who would come one day and really pay for sin. This substitute was God himself, God in the flesh. Every lamb sacrificed in Egypt, along with every animal sacrificed in the Old Testament, alluded to the substitute. No wonder that when Jesus begins his ministry, his anointed prophet John calls out, "Behold, the Lamb of God, who takes away the sin of the world" (John 1:29). Jesus, our substitute, dies in our place so that we won't have to die for our sin.

All of this truth, about sin and sacrifice and substitution, was apparent in the bloody doorframes back in Egypt.

That blood on the doorframes was the only hope for those Jewish families. The blood of Jesus, the blood on the cross, is the only hope for you and me. Precious blood indeed.

Hebrews 11:31

*By faith Rahab the prostitute did not perish with
those who were disobedient, because she had
given a friendly welcome to the spies.*

Do you think God was a bit embarrassed to have a prostitute
listed in his Hall of Faith?

Not at all. God uses flawed people: people who have failed,
people with a past, people with messy lives. People like us.

Indeed, the very next verse names more flawed people. Gideon, Barak, Samson, Jephthah, and David, the first five listed, all
had significant failures.

Gideon did not believe God's Word, and he needed God to
prove his promise with a fleece. Twice.

When God called Barak to lead the army into battle, he was
so timid that he told Deborah he would go "only if you go with
me" (Jud. 4:8).

Samson had all kinds of trouble with women, and he ended
up blind and a slave.

Jephthah made a foolish vow that caused the death of his
daughter.

David was guilty of adultery and murder, and most of his kids
were a mess.

And yet all five are heroes in God's Hall of Faith. Moreover,
they follow Rahab on the list. Do you think God might be trying
to tell us something? God uses flawed people who dare to trust in
him. You don't have to be perfect to be used by God.

In fact, there is one big advantage to having some failures
and weaknesses: You are less likely to be filled with pride and
self-righteousness, and you are more likely to be dependent and
desperate.

Never listen to the enemy when he says that God has written
you off and will never use you again.

Hebrews 11:32

And what more shall I say? For time would fail me to tell of Gideon, Barak, Samson, Jephthah, of David and Samuel and the prophets...

In the next few verses, we see example after example of miracles and triumphs: "...who through faith conquered kingdoms, enforced justice, obtained promises, stopped the mouths of lions, quenched the power of fire, escaped the edge of the sword, were made strong out of weakness, became mighty in war, put foreign armies to flight. Women received back their dead by resurrection" (Heb. 11:33-35a).

Sometimes, the life of faith is a life of incredible triumphs.

At other times, there is tragedy and suffering. The very next verses list example after example of heartache and pain:

> Some were tortured, refusing to accept release, so that they might rise again to a better life. Others suffered mocking and flogging, and even chains and imprisonment. They were stoned, they were sawn in two, they were killed with the sword. They went about in skins of sheep and goats, destitute, afflicted, mistreated—of whom the world was not worthy—wandering about in deserts and mountains, and in dens and caves of the earth. (Heb. 11:35b–38)

That's the life of faith: sometimes there is triumph and victory, but at other times, there is heartbreak and tragedy. Through it all, people of faith trust their God.

If we are going to walk by faith and not by sight, then we will trust God in the good times and the bad times. We will not compare our experience with that of others. We will know that God is God and we are not. We will know that we humans cannot possibly understand all that an infinite God does.

And we will trust him, no matter what.

Hebrews 12:1-2a

*Therefore, since we are surrounded by so great a
cloud of witnesses, let us also lay aside every weight,
and sin which clings so closely, and let us run with
endurance the race that is set before us, looking to
Jesus, the founder and perfecter of our faith.*

Ray Kroc, the legendary CEO of McDonald's, kept an elaborately framed statement by Calvin Coolidge on his office wall. It was Kroc's favorite inspirational quote:

- Nothing in the world can take the place of persistence.
- Talent will not; nothing is more common than unsuccessful men with great talent.
- Genius will not; unrewarded genius is almost a proverb.
- Education will not; the world is full of educated derelicts.
- Persistence, determination alone are omnipotent.

In fact, when Kroc was CEO of McDonald's, every executive's office had this statement framed on the wall.

I can understand why. I love this quote too. Endurance is simply one of the most vital traits that anyone can have. If you have endurance, it will make up for a lot of other limitations.

Certainly, we need endurance in the spiritual life. For all of us, there are times when we grow weary and lose heart. We struggle with sin and addictions. People let us down. Churches are full of imperfect people. Prayers go unanswered, or rather, we don't get the answer we want when we want it. Marriage can be hard. Parenting can be overwhelming. We battle physical pain or mental illness.

Life is hard. This is not heaven.

So we need endurance. "Let us run with endurance the race that is set before us."

In order to endure, God gives us three vital principles: take encouragement from others who endured, get rid of anything that holds you back, and especially, fix your eyes on Jesus.

Jesus endured tough times, and if we fix our gaze on Jesus, we too can endure.

Three practical suggestions to help you stay focused on Jesus:

1. Take unhurried time to meet with Jesus every day. Let other things go, but don't neglect time with Jesus. It is your greatest privilege.
2. Practice the presence of God throughout the day. He is right there with you all the time. Live in his presence. Talk with him. Draw close.
3. Sing to him. Worship music is powerful and soul transforming. It helps you stay focused on Christ.

James 1:2

Count it all joy, my brothers, when you meet trials of various kinds.

God is telling you that when you experience setbacks, disappointments, and heartbreak, count it all joy. When you have car trouble, when the refrigerator breaks down, rejoice. When you have chronic back pain, when you lose your job, when you hear the diagnosis of cancer, give thanks. "In all those times of pain and suffering, count it all joy. Be glad, give thanks, rejoice, and bring praise to me." Don't complain, whine, grumble, groan, or grow bitter. Instead, count it all joy.

Let me ask you: Do you do this? Are you doing it right now with whatever challenge or setback you are facing?

This response to suffering is exceedingly rare. It sounds ludicrous. But this is God's clear command, both in this passage and in other passages, such as Romans 5:3, Philippians 4:4, and 1 Thessalonians 5:16-18.

Why does God command us to count every trial as a joy? Because God is God, and he will redeem every trial to bring good out of it for his people. James 1:3 goes on to say, "For you know that the testing of your faith produces steadfastness." Romans 8:28 gives us the sure promise that "And we know that for those who love God all things work together for good." God uses suffering to produce endurance, to build faith, to shape our souls, to grow our hearts.

In a DesiringGod.org blog post, John Piper once wrote, "This is not a little piece of advice about the power of positive thinking. This is an utterly radical, abnormal, supernatural way to respond to suffering. It is not in our power. It is not for the sake of our honor. It is the way spiritual aliens and exiles live on the earth for the glory of the great King."

David McCullough has written a classic biography of John Adams, our second president, in which he records this experience: "John Adams said he has 'an immense load of errors, weaknesses, follies and sins to mourn over and repent of.' These were 'the only affliction' of his present life. But St. Paul taught him to rejoice ever more and be content. 'This phrase "rejoice ever more" shall never be out of my heart, memory or mouth again as long as I live.'"

This is God's will for us: that in every trial, we count it all joy. Because we know God is at work, redeeming our suffering for our sakes. This phrase should dwell in our heart, memory, and mouth for as long as we live.

James 1:5

*If any of you lacks wisdom, let him ask God, who
gives generously to all without reproach,
and it will be given him.*

This is a promise to claim and act upon, a practical, much-needed promise for a thousand situations of life, both big and little.

If you need wisdom, just ask God. God is a generous God, and he will give you wisdom. What a promise.

You run into a stumbling block in your marriage because you and your wife see things so differently. Ask God for wisdom.

Your sixth-grader is struggling with a difficult teacher who doesn't seem to treat your child fairly. What should you do? Ask God for wisdom.

You have a problem with one of your employees. He has a great heart and everyone likes him, but he just doesn't do a good job with his work. How can you help him improve? Are you hurting the company? Ask God for wisdom.

You have a splendid ministry opportunity at church. It fits your passions and gifts so well, but you have been overscheduled lately. Do you accept the ministry position? Ask God for wisdom.

In all of these situations and so many more, claim this promise, and come to God for wisdom. Come to him for little and big things. Come repeatedly and come joyfully, come expectantly and come tirelessly, for God has promised to give you wisdom.

James 1:19

*Know this, my beloved brothers: let every person be
quick to hear, slow to speak, slow to anger.*

One short verse, three power-packed principles. These three axioms are so simple that most people miss them and do the opposite: they are slow to listen, quick to speak, and quick to get angry. But not the wise man or woman. Wise people are quick to hear, slow to speak, slow to anger. Just like Christ was.

First, be quick to hear. The first responsibility of love is listening. People starve to be heard and understood. If we listen to people, really listen to people with our full attention, those people will feel so loved by us. So simple, yet so powerful.

Paul Tournier wrote in his book, *Escape From Loneliness*:

> It is impossible to overemphasize the immense need humans have to be really listened to, to be taken seriously, to be understood. No one can develop freely in this world and find the full life without feeling understood by at least one person.
>
> Listen to all the conversations of our world, between nations as well as those between couples. They are for the most part dialogues of the deaf.

Second, be slow to speak. If we are always talking, then we won't be listening, and that's what people need from us, not our words but our ears. Besides, if we are hasty in our words, it is likely that we will say things we regret.

In *The Friendship Factor*, Alan Loy McGinnis relates an anecdote on the difference between a talker and a listener:

> A young woman was taken to dinner one night by William E. Gladstone, the distinguished British statesman, and the following night by Benjamin Disraeli, his equally distinguished opponent. Asked later what impression these two celebrated men had made on her, she replied thoughtfully: "When I left the dining room after sitting next to Mr. Gladstone, I thought he was the cleverest man in England. But after sitting next to Mr. Disraeli, I thought I was the cleverest woman in England."

Finally, be slow to anger. Decide that you will not erupt with anger but will give people the benefit of the doubt. You ask questions to clarify what people mean. You have a long fuse.

This is wisdom: quick to hear, slow to speak, slow to anger.

James 5:14

*Is anyone among you sick? Let him call for the elders
of the church, and let them pray over him, anointing
him with oil in the name of the Lord.*

There are plenty of candidates in the Bible for the "most disobeyed verse." In the book of James, I think of James 1:2:
"Count it all joy, my brothers, when you meet trials of various
kinds." Or there's James 1:19: "Know this, my beloved brothers:
let every person be quick to hear, slow to speak, slow to anger."
And there are plenty of others.

But at the top of the list, I would put James 5:14: "Is anyone
among you sick? Let him call for the elders of the church, and let
them pray over him, anointing him with oil in the name of the
Lord." Many churches don't do this. Most Christians don't obey
this.

Why not? Is it a hassle to call for the elders? Is it a bit awkward to smear oil on someone's forehead? Do we not still believe
that God heals people? Or do we not really believe in the power
of prayer?

Perhaps all of these are involved, but God's command stands
clear: do it. If there is sickness, then call for the elders, who are
God's representatives, to shepherd the body. Let them pray over
you, anointing you with oil as a symbol of the Holy Spirit.

Who knows what God might do when we obey him no matter
what?

James 5:17-18

Elijah was a man with a nature like ours, and he prayed fervently that it might not rain, and for three years and six months it did not rain on the earth. Then he prayed again, and heaven gave rain, and the earth bore its fruit.

Wow! It didn't rain for three-and-a-half years. Then Elijah prays for rain, and the heavens open up.

What a prayer. What clout with God. What power.

And I'm thinking, *Well, that's because it's Elijah.* Elijah was special. Elijah was different. Elijah was one of the most powerful prophets in the Bible. Why, Elijah didn't even die, he just ascended right up to God.

So my prayers could never have the effect that Elijah's prayers had, right?

Maybe you think that too. But is that why God inspires James to give the example of Elijah's prayer? So we would recognize that our prayers could never do that?

I doubt it. I don't think that is God's heart at all; in fact, I know it's not. God, knowing that we would think Elijah was exceptional and special, begins the example with these weighty words,

"Elijah was a man with a nature like ours."

What is God saying to us here? Could God be telling us that our prayers can do the impossible, the unheard of, the miraculous? Do I need to view the power of prayer in a whole different way? Do I need to pray with a boldness and expectancy I've never had before?

1 Peter 1:18-19

Knowing that you were ransomed from the futile ways inherited from your forefathers, not with perishable things such as silver or gold, but with the precious blood of Christ, like that of a lamb without blemish or spot.

In his book, *A Cup of Coffee at the Soul Café*, Leonard Sweet tells the story of a film made by two Londoners. In 1971, they began to film the homeless. The film captured their daily rituals, their trials, and their joys. Some were alcoholics, others mentally disturbed. Some were articulate and others unintelligible. One of England's leading composers, Gavin Bryars, agreed to help with the audio aspects of the film. During his work, he became aware of a constant undercurrent of sound that appeared whenever one certain homeless man was filmed. At first, the sound seemed like muttered gibberish. But after removing the background noise, Bryars discovered the old man was singing.

Bryars learned that this homeless man did not drink or socialize with others. The old man was alone and filthy, but he also had a sunny demeanor. What distinguished him from the others was his quiet singing. For hours, he would sing the same thing over and over. The man's weak voice was untrained, but it never wavered from pitch. He repeated the simple phrases of the song again and again.

One day at the office, the composer looped together the first thirteen bars of the homeless man's song, preparing to add orchestration to the piece. He left the loop running while he went downstairs for a cup of coffee. When he returned, he found his fellow workers listening in subdued silence, and a few were even weeping. The old man's quiet, trembling voice had leaked from the recording room and transformed the office floor. Here is what he sang:

> Jesus's blood never failed me yet
> Never failed me yet
> Jesus's blood never failed me yet
> There's one thing I know
> For he loves me so

433

Though not a Christian, Bryars created and produced an accompaniment to this homeless person's song of trust in Jesus. The result was a CD titled *Jesus's Blood Never Failed Me Yet*. The old man died before he heard it.

The old man got it: "Jesus's blood never failed me yet." It will be the story of every person who puts his or her trust in Jesus.

1 Peter 2:9-10

But you are a chosen race, a royal priesthood, a holy nation, a people for his own possession, that you may proclaim the excellencies of him who called you out of darkness into his marvelous light. Once you were not a people, but now you are God's people; once you had not received mercy, but now you have received mercy.

Two things are essential to a healthy, thriving, and joy-filled spiritual life. First, knowing who God is. Second, knowing who you are. The second depends on the first. Define yourself by who you are in God.

1 Peter 2:9-10 is one of the clearest passages on who we are in God. This is who we are:

"A chosen race." God has chosen you. He has set his love on you and adopted you. You did not choose him, but he chose you, or perhaps you chose him because he chose you. Either way, you are loved, chosen, adopted.

"A royal priesthood." Every believer is considered a priest, bringing people to the grace of God and praying for them. That's who you are: one of God's priests. Moreover, you are a royal priest. You are royal because you belong to the family of the King.

"A holy nation." Holy. You are holy and blameless in God's eyes because the blood of Christ has washed all your sins away. You are just as holy as Jesus Christ because God sees you in Christ and through his blood.

"A people for his own possession." You belong to God. You are known, you are loved, you are adopted. Indeed, who you are is based on whose you are, and you are God's.

"God's people." Again, you belong to God. You are one of his people.

"Recipients of God's mercy." You are not just the object of God's choice. You are the object of God's mercy. God has poured mercy, grace, and love into you and over you. You are much loved, completely forgiven, blood-bought.

There are condemning voices out there saying that you're bad, that you're such a failure, that God can never use you and is angry at you.

Don't listen to those voices. Shut your ears to every voice except God's voice. Read again what God says about you.

Take this attitude: God said it and I believe it, so that settles it.

1 Peter 3:18

For Christ also suffered once for sins, the righteous for the unrighteous, that he might bring us to God, being put to death in the flesh but made alive in the spirit.

This is a clear, concise statement on the substitutive atonement of Jesus. When Jesus died on the cross, he died in our place. He died in my place and in your place.

He died as our substitute. The righteous died for the unrighteous so that we might become right with God.

In his superb book, *Center Church*, Tim Keller writes about the various images of atonement in the Bible and how substitution is the key idea behind all of them:

> But perhaps the single most consoling and appealing theme is what theologian Roger Nicole has called the one, irreducible theme that runs through every single one of these models—the idea of substitution. Dr. Nicole taught that, regardless of the grammar being used, the essence of the atonement is always Jesus acting as our substitute. Jesus fights the powers, pays the price, bears the exile, makes the sacrifice, and bears the punishment for us, in our place, on our behalf. In every grammar, Jesus does for us what we cannot do for ourselves. He accomplishes salvation; we do nothing at all. And therefore the substitutionary sacrifice of Jesus is at the heart of everything.

1 Peter 5:6-7

Humble yourselves, therefore, under the mighty hand
of God so that at the proper time he may exalt you,
casting all your anxieties on him,
because he cares for you.

God tells us to humble ourselves, and there are many ways we do
that. One of those ways is to pray. We humble ourselves when
we come to God in prayer and cast all our anxieties upon him.

The proud person does not pray. He will not pray. He cannot
pray.

The proud person feels, deep inside, *I can do this myself. I've
got this.* Oh, he usually doesn't say that, but his actions do. By his
actions, he declares, "I can handle this myself." His actions give
him away.

By contrast, the humble person thinks, *I cannot handle this
on my own. Lord, I need you. In fact, if you don't come through for
me, I'm sunk. Lord, please rescue me. Lord, please take care of this
problem. Lord, help!*

We humble ourselves when we call out to God and tell him of
all our anxieties. We humble ourselves and exalt the Lord because
we implicitly declare, "Lord, you can take care of this problem.
Lord, you are able, you are mighty, you are God. You are my
strong deliverer and you care about me. You are good. I can trust
you with this problem because you are a trustworthy God."

We exalt God when we cry out to him, and we humble
ourselves.

And the result? We receive God's peace. We give God our
anxiety, and God gives us his peace.

Humility always brings peace. Pride always brings anxiety.

1 Peter 5:8

Be sober-minded; be watchful. Your adversary the
devil prowls around like a roaring lion,
seeking someone to devour.

We have an enemy. An unseen, evil enemy with lots of assistants.

This enemy, the devil, is like a roaring lion. This image tells us he is fierce, dangerous, hungry, and ever ready to inflict harm.

The devil is not just a roaring lion, but a roaring lion seeking someone to devour, and that someone includes you. He and his minions want to devour you, hurt you, destroy you. They want to distance you from God in any way possible, through deception, accusation, condemnation, and temptation. They want to convince you that God isn't good, that God cannot be trusted, that God is mad at you, that God is disappointed in you, that God doesn't really love you, that God is a cosmic killjoy.

Satan wants to destroy your marriage and convince you that some other spouse would be much better for you. He tries to persuade you that you should get a divorce because God wants you to be happy. He seeks to bring anger, pride, debt, fear, a lack of forgiveness, and guilt into your marriage.

In all kinds of ways, Satan is out to devour your soul, ruin your family, and damage your spiritual life.

What do we do? Wake up and fight the battle. Be vigilant. Be alert. Be aware that there is a battle, that there is an opponent, and that he is real.

If you were on a cruise ship, you could drift off to sleep and take a nap. But you are on a battleship, so you should be fully alert, scanning the horizon for signs of the enemy.

If you don't often pray that God will protect you and your family from the enemy, then you are not alert and vigilant. If you are not aware that the voices in your head that condemn you, accuse you, tempt you, and lie to you are the voices of the enemy, then you are not alert and vigilant. If you are not aware that conflicts and misunderstandings are at times caused or exacerbated by the enemy, then you are not vigilant.

We don't focus on the enemy, but we are aware of the enemy and his schemes. Be alert and vigilant.

1 John 1:9

If we confess our sins, he is faithful and just to forgive
us our sins and to cleanse us from
all unrighteousness.

King Frederick II, an eighteenth-century king of Prussia, was visiting a prison in Berlin. Lloyd H. Steffen in *The Christian Century* recounts this story. Each of the inmates tried to explain how they were innocent and had been unjustly imprisoned, all except one. This one sat quietly in a corner while the rest protested their innocence. Seeing him sitting there oblivious to the commotion, the king asked him what he was there for.

"Armed robbery, Your Honor."

The king asked, "Were you guilty?"

"Yes, sir," he answered. "I entirely deserve my punishment."

The king then gave an order to the guard. "Release this guilty man. I don't want him corrupting all these innocent people."

It is always best to confess our sins, honestly and forthrightly.

There is power in confession. To confess our sins to God is to pull a drain plug on guilt. All our sin and guilt swooshes down the drain, vanishing forever in God's grace.

When we confess our sins, we simply agree with God about our sins.

"Lord, I was dishonest with Bob."

"Father, forgive me for losing my temper with Tommy."

"Oh God, forgive my pride. I didn't need to brag about my job with those people."

In *Wishful Thinking: A Theological ABC*, Frederick Buechner puts the matter poignantly: "To confess your sins to God is not to tell him anything he doesn't already know. Until you confess them, however, they are the abyss between you. When you confess them, they become the bridge."

I find the same thing happens in my marriage. If I am unkind or insensitive with Gayle, we may still be married, but there is now a barrier between us. We are connected in a legal and judicial sense, but we are not connected in a relational and fellowship sense. But when I apologize to her, everything changes. Our closeness and oneness is restored. There is power in confession.

God gives us a wonderful promise in 1 John 1:9: "If we confess our sins, he is faithful and just to forgive us our sins and to cleanse us from all unrighteousness."

This is the Christian bar of soap. When we confess our sin, he will restore us to full, untarnished fellowship with him.

Confession is part of prayer. We don't need to be overly introspective, but neither should we be insensitive to the Spirit's gentle work. When God graciously (it is an act of grace) reminds us of our sin, then we should immediately and sincerely confess it to God to experience the fresh joy of his cleansing grace.

In one sense, a legal and judicial sense, all our sin has already been forgiven. In Romans 8:1, we learn that all our sin was nailed to the cross, and we are under no condemnation.

But in another sense, a relational and fellowship sense, our relationship with God is hindered by our sin. There is a barrier between us until we confess our sin to God. This is the point of 1 John 1:9.

1 John 4:8

Anyone who does not love does not know God,
because God is love.

God's essential nature is to love. He doesn't have to try to love. This is just the way he is in everything, in every way, and at all times. God cannot help but be loving because God is love. This is his essential nature.

This does not mean that love defines God, but that God defines love. Moreover, that God is love is not the only thing about God, but it is the main thing about God. More than we can possibly imagine, God is a loving God.

It has been pointed out that there is nothing you could do to make God love you more, and there is nothing you can do to make God love you less. On the one hand, God's love is perfect and infinite, so he could not possibly love you more. On the other hand, God's love for you is relentless and unconditional, and he could not possibly love you less.

Moreover, God's love for you is intensely personal and emotional. It is not generic. It is not just that God loves people in general. No, God loves you personally. He loves you as though you were the only person in the world to love. He has even numbered the hairs on your head.

The renowned theologian, Karl Barth, wrote volumes of dense theology. In fact, some would consider him the greatest theologian in four hundred years, since the time of John Calvin. He was once asked to sum up, in one sentence, the thousands of pages of theology he had written. He paused and then replied, "Jesus loves me, this I know, for the Bible tells me so."

Indeed, God is love.

1 John 4:10

In this is love, not that we have loved God but that he loved us and sent his Son to be the propitiation for our sins.

The love of God is the foundation of the entire spiritual life. Not our love for God, although that is very important, since to love God is the greatest commandment. But underneath our love for God is God's love for us, which is more foundational than our love for him. Our love for God is simply a response to God's love for us.

We will not go higher, deeper, or further than our experience of God's love for us.

Moreover, when it comes to God's love, the greatest example of that love is found in the cross of Christ. That God would send his own Son to the planet to become a man and then die on a cross, bearing our sin, is the greatest proof that God cares about us. God cares about us more than we could possibly fathom.

John White, a psychiatrist and writer, penned passionate words about the cross and God's love in his book *The Fight*:

> He welcomes you because his Son died for you. His breast has always yearned for you and his arms yearned to enfold you. Christ's death has now made it possible for the Father to do what he wanted to do all along. So come boldly—sprinkled by blood. Let him enfold you to the warmth of his bosom while his hot tears wash over your body.
>
> Hot tears? Does the expression sound irreverent or sentimental? I have no words that do justice to the love that led to the death of God's Son. The universe ought to have stopped in its tracks, and I, for one, am sorry it didn't. No more heinous crime was ever committed against God nor greater act of love consummated on behalf of the criminal. Are you blasphemous enough to suppose that your dead works, your feeble efforts can add to the finished work of a dying Savior? "It is finished!" he cried. Completed. Done. Forever ended. He crashed through the gates of hell, set prisoners free, abolished death and burst in new life from the tomb. All to set you free from sin and open the way for you to run into the loving arms of God.

1 John 5:13

I write these things to you who believe in the name of
the Son of God that you may know
that you have eternal life.

John boils down the purpose for the entire letter of 1 John in this verse: "This is why I'm writing. This is my burden. I want you to know that you have eternal life."

Not hope you have eternal life, not think you have eternal life, but know you have eternal life. Like any loving father, our Father in heaven wants us to be secure in our relationship. He wants us to know who we are, whose we are, and what he's given us. He wants us to have assurance about our eternal destiny.

And to whom is John writing? Who gets this assurance of eternal life? Who needs this message? All those who believe in the name of the Son of God, who are trusting Christ as Savior.

This is a promise to claim and stand upon. If you believe in Christ as your Savior, if you trust in Christ and not your own goodness or works, then you can rest on the authority of God's Word: you have eternal life.

Revelation 1:1a

The revelation of Jesus Christ, which God gave him to show to his servants the things that must soon take place.

In 1941, Winston Churchill wrote of his emotions about the attacks on Pearl Harbor. As recounted by Robert Bartley in *The Wall Street Journal*:

> Now at this very moment I knew the United States was in the war, up to the neck and in to the death. So we had won after all! Silly people—and there were many, not only in enemy countries—might discount the force of the United States. Some said they were soft, others that they would never be united. They would fool around at a distance. They would never come to grips. They would never stand blood-letting.
>
> But I had studied the American Civil War, fought out to the last desperate inch. American blood flowed in my veins. Being saturated and satiated with emotion and sensation, I went to bed and slept the sleep of the saved and thankful...
>
> [With America in the war] Hitler's fate was sealed. Mussolini's fate was sealed. As for the Japanese, they would be ground to powder.

Churchill's message, "We're going to win," is the same message of the book of Revelation.

The book of Revelation (singular, not plural—the revelation of Jesus Christ) was written in AD 95, when the cruel Roman emperor Domitian ruled. During Domitian's reign, Christians throughout the Empire were persecuted severely, and many were executed. Revelation was written to encourage believers in the Roman province of Asia Minor (today western Turkey) to be loyal to Christ, not Caesar, despite the ongoing persecution.

The book contains many theological controversies and conundrums, but if you encapsulate the message of the book in a few words, here it is: Jesus Christ wins. Or, to elaborate a bit: Jesus Christ is the Sovereign Ruler and Judge, and he is coming again to rule in triumph and glory.

In fact, there is no other book of the Bible that places more focus on the greatness, glory, grandeur, sovereignty, and majesty of Jesus Christ than the triumphant book of Revelation.

Revelation 1:5b-6

To him who loves us and has freed us from our sins
by his blood and made us a kingdom, priests to
his God and Father, to him be glory and
dominion forever and ever. Amen.

In his greeting to the seven churches, John bursts forth in excited praise of Jesus. He exalts Jesus specifically for three things:

"To him who loves us." The book of Revelation is known as a book that focuses on the sovereignty, majesty, holiness, and judgment of Jesus Christ, and all of that is true. Yet the book does not go five verses before Jesus is praised as the one "who loves us."

We must never lose sight of the gracious compassion, outrageous love, and relentless tenderness of Jesus for us. Until you know and feel Jesus's love for you, you do not fully know Jesus's heart. Let Jesus love you.

"To him who has freed us from our sins by his blood." Invariably, when the New Testament mentions the love of God, it also mentions the cross of Jesus, for the cross is the final proof of God's love for us. Because Jesus loves us, he died for us on the cross, and has freed us from our sins by shedding that blood.

Note the past tense: "has freed us." You are forgiven and free if you have trusted Christ as your Savior.

Do you feel free from your sin? If not, whose voice are you listening to: that of the great liberator, or that of the evil accuser?

"To him who has made us a kingdom, priests to his God and Father." We are the kingdom of Jesus. The kingdom of Jesus is not land or geography; it's people. Our mission is to advance that kingdom through the lives of more and more people.

We are also priests to serve our God. We are priests because we have access to God, because we bring intercession to God, and because we serve God. In the New Testament, priests are not the professionals who wear collars and robes like our pastors and missionaries. Every believer is a priest. You are a priest to serve your God and spread his kingdom.

Revelation 2:4

*But I have this against you, that you have abandoned
the love you had at first.*

Antoine de Saint-Exupery said, "If you want to build a ship,
don't drum up people together to collect wood and don't assign them tasks and work, but rather teach them to long for the
sea." I believe his insight applies to the Kingdom of God. If you
want to build a church that pleases God, don't recruit people for
tasks, projects, and ministries. Teach them to long for Jesus.

Above all else, a church must be a place where people long for
Jesus, where people are pursuing Jesus, where people are falling
in love with Jesus.

There was a great church in Ephesus founded by the Apostle
Paul. They were tremendous lovers of God. However, thirty years
later, Jesus sends them the sobering message, "But I have this
against you, that you have abandoned the love you had at first."

The church was full of people who worked hard for God, but
they had left their first love. They were workers, but not worshippers. They had religious duty, but they did not have a love affair
with Jesus.

Fortunately, Jesus tells them what to do to recapture that first
love: "Remember therefore from where you have fallen; repent,
and do the works you did at first" (Rev. 2:5). Three things: remember, repent, repeat.

First, "Remember therefore from where you have fallen." If
you can, deliberately think back about your feelings, thoughts,
and actions during your first weeks and months as a follower of
Jesus Christ. Remember.

Second, repent. Jesus gives the Ephesian church a simple one-
word command: repent. Come to God in brokenness and repentance, in confession and surrender. Ask God to change you. Turn
from yourself to your God.

Third, repeat. That is, repeat the things you did in your early
Christian life. "Repent, and do the works you did at first." Did
you pray fervently? Sing from your heart? Gather with Christian
friends? Eagerly read the Bible as a love letter? Give generously?
Share your faith freely? Repeat all those things.

Ken Gire, in his book *The Divine Embrace*, relays the story
of a teenage girl in the atheistic Soviet Union who knew nothing

of the Bible, nothing of the doctrines of the church, nothing of the differences between denominations. She also knew nothing of Jesus until the day she chanced upon a copy of Luke's Gospel. When she finished reading it, her immediate reaction was, "I fell in love with him."

Jesus is looking for people who will love him back. Jesus is looking for worshippers. Jesus is looking for people who have an incurable disease: the disease of being smitten with Jesus.

Are you smitten with Jesus? Do you have a love affair with Jesus? Did you start out with a white-hot passion for Jesus, but now the fire has grown cold?

Above all else, God wants to be loved. He wants to be wanted.

How is your heart for God these days?

Revelation 3:15-16

I know your works: you are neither cold nor hot.
Would that you were either cold or hot! So, because
you are lukewarm, and neither hot nor cold,
I will spit you out of my mouth.

In the Book of Revelation, we learn that Laodicea had a lukewarm water supply. The nearby city of Hierapolis had hot springs that were great for bathing. The nearby city of Colossae had pure cold water that was great for drinking. But not Laodicea. They only had lukewarm water, which was not great for anything.

Jesus is saying to the church at Laodicea, and no doubt to lots of churches today: You are lukewarm as a church. You are neither hot nor cold. You are just lukewarm. Yuck! It makes me want to spit you out of my mouth.

Those are strong and sobering words.

A church is lukewarm when it is proud and self-reliant, as the church in Laodicea was. They were wealthy, and this led them to self-sufficiency. "For you say, I am rich, I have prospered, and I need nothing, not realizing that you are wretched, pitiable, poor, blind, and naked" (Rev. 3:17).

This is a sober warning to every church in the United States, for we live in an affluent culture, and we must be wary, extremely wary, of pride and self-sufficiency.

How do we know if we have pride and self-sufficiency like the church in Laodicea?

The best indicator, the sure indicator, is prayerlessness. If there is little prayer in the church, if prayer is seen as a preliminary courtesy before you get to the real work of planning and talking, if prayer is not seen as the lifeblood of the church, then you can bet that church has a spirit of self-sufficiency rather than a spirit of desperateness and dependence.

Jackson Senyonga, a leading pastor in Uganda, has remarked, "In America, the cry of sin is louder than the cry of intercession."

George Verwer, founder of Operation Mobilization, commented, "The lack of prayer is the greatest scandal in the church today. It is a greater scandal than the disunity, the immorality, the lack of love."

Our lack of prayer indicates our pride, our self-righteousness, our self-sufficiency.

Revelation 3:20

Behold, I stand at the door and knock. If anyone
hears my voice and opens the door, I will come in to
him and eat with him, and he with me.

This is an amazing thing. Jesus had just rebuked the Laodicean church with blistering language. They were a proud, self-reliant church, and Jesus let them have it.

But he loved them.

He did not write them off and forget them, by no means. In fact, he gives them a vivid picture: "I stand at the door of your church. I'm knocking. I want to come in and have fellowship with you, dine with you, be with you. I long to be close to you. But I won't knock the door down. You open it. Open it with a heart of brokenness, a heart of repentance, a heart of humble dependence."

Jesus longs for us too. Even when we mess up, he yearns for us. He doesn't cast us away. He longs to be close with us again, if only we will respond with brokenness and repentance.

The ball is in your court. Jesus is right there. He died for you and rose from the dead. He longs to save you. He is your only hope. Will you respond with repentance and trust? Will you say yes to Jesus?

Perhaps you hear the knocking even now.

Revelation 5:9

*And they sang a new song, saying, "Worthy are you
to take the scroll and to open its seals, for you were
slain, and by your blood you ransomed
people for God from every tribe and
language and people and nation."*

I once worshipped at a church in the Middle East. It was filled with people from all over the world. I was fascinated as people walked into the room from India and Pakistan, from Kenya and Nigeria, from Australia and New Zealand, from Germany and Britain. The church included people from dozens of countries, and I found the environment exhilarating. I thought to myself, *This is a microcosm of heaven, where there will be people from every tribe and language and people and nation.*

Though there are only 195 countries in the world, there are about 16,472 distinct groups of people with their own way of thinking and living. It is these groups, not political countries, that are God's focus in the Bible. For example, when Jesus commissioned his followers, "Go therefore and make disciples of all nations" (Matt. 28:19), he is referring to groups of people, not to nation states. He uses a form of the Greek word *ethnos* from which we get "ethnic" or "ethnicity." Jesus commissioned us to go and make disciples of all the groups in the world, all 16,000 or so.

Every one of these groups of people matters to God. Every one of these groups needs to hear that there is a God in heaven who loves them, and every one needs to see the glory of Christ proclaimed. Every one of these groups will be represented before God's throne in eternity, and every one is on God's heart.

Because all of these people matter to God, they must matter to us as well.

Every single one.

Revelation 5:11-12

Then I looked, and I heard around the throne and the living creatures and the elders, the voice of many angels, numbering myriads of myriads and thousands of thousands, saying with a loud voice, "Worthy is the Lamb who was slain, To receive power and wealth and wisdom and might And honor and glory and blessing!"

Revelation 5 is perhaps the most stunning example of worship in the entire Bible.

Can you imagine this scene? It opens with God on his throne holding a scroll. No one is found who is worthy to open the scroll, which contains the judgments poured out on earth during the end times. John is weeping because no one is found.

Then there is a voice proclaiming that the Lion of Judah will open it. John looks for the Lion, but instead he sees a Lamb. A Lamb that was slain, but is now standing.

And then, four amazing creatures and twenty-four elders fall down before the Lamb in fervent, wholehearted worship. They begin singing a song of praise to the Lamb.

And then, a vast array of innumerable angels appears around the throne, singing praise to the Lamb who was slain.

At the next moment, the sky is filled with every creature in all creation, singing together a song of praise to the Father and the Son.

Can you imagine such a crescendo of worship and praise? It will be the emotional equivalent of ten thousand Super Bowls and ten thousand World Series, and in each one your team wins at the last moment. The glory of God will be suffocating.

At this point, the four amazing creatures will proclaim: "Amen! So be it! Yes!" And the elders, absolutely overwhelmed and undone by it all, can only fall down on their faces to worship.

What an amazing event this will be.

One day, this will all happen, and we will be there.

Can you imagine?

Revelation 12:7

*Now war arose in heaven, Michael and his angels
fighting against the dragon.
And the dragon and his angels fought back.*

We live in a world of unseen spiritual reality. Ninety-eight percent of matter is invisible, so perhaps it is no surprise that there is an invisible world of spiritual reality. Shakespeare wrote in *Hamlet*, "There are more things in heaven and earth, Horatio, than are dreamt of in your philosophy."

From Genesis to Revelation, we are told of an unseen spiritual world, a world of angels and demons, a world of epic spiritual battle. In Revelation 12, the curtain is pulled back on the spiritual realm, and we see the fierce battle raging across the cosmos:

> Now war arose in heaven, Michael and his angels fighting against the dragon. And the dragon and his angels fought back, but he was defeated, and there was no longer any place for them in heaven. And the great dragon was thrown down, that ancient serpent, who is called the devil and Satan, the deceiver of the whole world—he was thrown down to earth, and his angels were thrown down with him." (Rev. 12:7-9)

We may not be certain what all the symbols of Revelation refer to, but there is no mistaking the reality of the battle. What does the Bible teach us about this battle?

1. You are a target in the battle. Yes, you. Satan and his demons will try to devour your soul and ruin your life. They use deception, condemnation, accusation, temptation, and intimidation. Be alert.
2. Fight this battle in Christ's strength. Put on the full armor of God and be strong in the Lord, not in yourself.
3. Fight the battle with your sword. Just like Jesus in Matthew 4, wield your sword, the Word of God, to defeat the enemy. We ignore God's Word at our spiritual peril.

4. Worship is a powerful weapon in the war. The root issue of the war is worship: Satan wants the worship that rightfully belongs to God. When we worship God, we declare our love and loyalty to God and draw near to him. God pours out his Spirit upon us and demons flee. Worship is warfare.
5. Prayer is a wartime walkie-talkie.

John Piper puts it best in *Let the Nations Be Glad*:

We cannot know what prayer is for until we know that life is war. Life is war. That's not all it is. But it is always that. Our weakness in prayer is owed largely to our neglect of this truth. Prayer is primarily a wartime walkie-talkie for the mission of the church as it advances against the powers of darkness and unbelief. It is not surprising that prayer malfunctions when we try to make it a domestic intercom to call upstairs for more comforts in the den. God has given us prayer as a wartime walkie-talkie so that we can call headquarters for everything we need as the kingdom of Christ advances in the world.

Revelation 12:10

And I heard a loud voice in heaven, saying, "Now the salvation and the power and the kingdom of our God and the authority of his Christ have come, for the accuser of our brothers has been thrown down, who accuses them day and night before our God."

In *Mere Christianity*, C.S. Lewis clarifies the spiritual reality:

> One of the things that surprised me when I first read the New Testament seriously was that it talked so much about a Dark Power in the universe—a mighty evil spirit who was held to be the Power behind death, disease, and sin. The difference is that Christianity thinks this Dark Power was created by God, and was good when he was created, and went wrong. Christianity agrees…this is a universe at war.

The writer Frederick Buechner has a similar warning in *A Sacred Journey: A Memoir of Early Days*:

> Reality can be harsh and you shut your eyes to it only at your peril because if you do not face up to the enemy in all his dark power, then the enemy will come up from behind some dark day and destroy you while you are facing the other way.

Most succinctly, John Eldredge warns in *Waking the Dead*: "To live in ignorance of spiritual warfare is the most naïve and dangerous thing we can do."

One of Satan's strategies is accusation. In fact, in Revelation 12:10, he is called "the accuser of our brothers." Satan's characteristic activity is to accuse and condemn us. How many Christians have been totally defeated and discouraged because they listened to Satan's accusations rather than listening to the voice of God? God says to us, "There is therefore now no condemnation for those who are in Christ Jesus" (Rom. 8:1), and "As far as the east is from the west, so far does he remove our transgressions from us!" (Ps. 103:12). How many Christians have cowered back in fear and guilt because they listened to Satan's nefarious lies?

Don't do it. Stand firm against the enemy. Stand firm in Christ's strength, and claim the promises of God's Word. Rest in the grace of Christ Jesus, grace that is greater than all your sin.

Revelation 19:11a

Then I saw heaven opened, and behold, a white horse!
The one sitting on it is called Faithful and True.

Seven long centuries before the first coming of Christ, the Jewish prophet Isaiah was moved to call out in prayer, "Oh that you would rend the heavens and come down, That the mountains might quake at your presence—As when fire kindles brushwood. And the fire causes water to boil—To make your name known to your adversaries, and that the nations might tremble at your presence!" (Is. 64:1-2).

This passionate prayer, for God to open the heavens and come to earth in triumph and glory, will be answered in Revelation 19. "Then I saw heaven opened, and behold, a white horse! The one sitting on it is called Faithful and True" (Rev. 19:11a).

This event is the second coming of Christ, not just the climactic event of the book of Revelation, but the climactic event of the entire Bible and all of human history.

When the prophet Isaiah prayed for this event, he prayed that Christ would rend the heavens and come down, and that he would make his name known.

That is exactly what will happen. Jesus Christ will tear the heavens open and come to this planet, revealing his name and glory to all the earth. This four-fold name reveals the glory of Jesus:

1. Faithful and True: Jesus is faithful to all of his promises. He is true in all he says. His name is a name we can trust.
2. An Unknown Name: This is a name of mystery, which reflects the fact that we cannot fully understand our great God. He is so far above us, so far beyond us.
3. The Word of God: This is a name of power, for God's Word is powerful. He created the galaxies with his mere word. Jesus Christ has the power to create life and to execute judgment.
4. King of kings and Lord of lords: This is a name of majesty. Jesus is none other than God, the sovereign and majestic God. All greatness, power, authority, and glory belong to Jesus Christ.

When Jesus returns, he will reveal his name, and every knee will bow.

Come, Lord Jesus.

Revelation 20:1-2

*Then I saw an angel coming down from heaven,
holding in his hand the key to the bottomless pit and
a great chain. And he seized the dragon, that ancient
serpent, who is the devil and Satan, and bound him
for a thousand years.*

In *The Sacred Romance,* Brent Curtis and John Eldredge comment on the ongoing spiritual war:

> What is clear is that Satan has lost the battle. Twice.
> The first time he was hurled in disgrace from the halls
> of heaven by Christ and his angels. The second time,
> he was unable to hold the crucified Christ within the
> gates of hell and was forced to hand over to him the
> keys to death and Hades. But for a time he is placed
> on what feels like a very long leash to do what he can
> among us with his roaring.

The war is raging around us all the time, but it will not last forever, and there is no doubt in the outcome. Jesus Christ will defeat Satan and his demons, and Satan will be banished forever.

Satan was defeated at Christ's first coming, when Christ died on the cross to pay for sin and then triumphed over death with his resurrection. However, the sentencing of Satan will not be executed until Revelation 20, at the time of Christ's second coming.

At that time, an angel, probably Michael the archangel, will seize Satan and throw him into the bottomless pit. It is only fitting that an angel be the one to execute judgment on Satan because Satan is a demon or evil angel, and his counterpart is a good angel. Never think that Satan's counterpart is God. God has no counterpart, for is so far above everything and everyone else. He is the incomparable God.

No, Satan's counterpart is the archangel Michael, according to Revelation 12:7. And it is likely that Michael is the angel who will execute judgment on Satan. Satan will be bound in the bottomless pit for a thousand years.

For now, Satan is under impending judgment, but he is still at large. However, that does not scare us, for Christ is in us, and we need not be intimidated or deceived by Satan. Alert to the spiritual war and the satanic attack on our souls, we resist the devil and stand strong in Christ's strength.

Revelation 21:1

Then I saw a new heaven and a new earth, for the
first heaven and the first earth had passed away,
and the sea was no more.

Heaven will be better than we can imagine. Far better. What we find in the Bible is not so much a description of heaven as a hint of it, a hint of heaven's beauty, glory, and wonder. Heaven will exceed our wildest dreams.

Think about all the best things in life and magnify them a million times. For me, that includes things like:

- A sense of closeness to Jesus
- Loving and being loved
- Close friends laughing and talking together
- Satisfying work that makes a difference in people's lives
- Using your God-given abilities and gifts
- Traveling to exciting and beautiful places around the world
- Running on a soft forest trail through the Redwoods
- Hiking in Yosemite
- Eating Blue Bell mint chocolate chip ice cream
- Watching exciting basketball games (or better yet, playing in those games)

Think of the best things in life and magnify them a million times. Then take out all of the world's suffering: all the pain, fear, guilt, and death, all the divorce, abuse, disease, and struggle. Put it all in the most incredible South Pacific paradise setting, and you begin to get the idea of heaven's glory.

Best of all is the immediate and tangible presence of the God who loves you.

If you spent five minutes in heaven, there's no way you would want to go back to earth.

We use the expression, "I thought I'd died and gone to heaven" to express abundant happiness, for heaven is a place like no other.

And it's your home for all eternity. Glory!